THE BEST BUDDHIST WRITING 2005

THE BEST
BUDDHIST
WRITING
2·0·0·5

Edited by Melvin McLeod
and the Editors of the *Shambhala Sun*

SHAMBHALA
Boston & London · 2005

Shambhala Publications, Inc.
Horticultural Hall
300 Massachusetts Avenue
Boston, Massachusetts 02115
www.shambhala.com

9 8 7 6 5 4 3 2 1

First Edition
Printed in the United States of America

⊗ This edition is printed on acid-free paper that meets the
American National Standards Institute z39.48 Standard.
Distributed in the United States by Random House, Inc.,
and in Canada by Random House of Canada Ltd

Library of Congress Cataloging-in-Publication Data
The best Buddhist writing 2005 / edited by Melvin McLeod
and the editors of the Shambhala Sun.
p. cm.
ISBN 1-59030-275-3 (pbk.: alk. paper)
1. Buddhism. I. McLeod, Melvin.
BQ4055.B47 2005
294.3—dc22
2005007767

Contents

Introduction

It's always fascinating—and sometimes an honor—to watch a movement in its pioneering phase. Buddhism in America is in its early days, and if we look at the selections in this book as a record of how it's doing, I think we can feel optimistic.

Of course, it could be argued that Buddhism has already been in America for a long time. Its formal introduction is usually dated at 1893, when the Zen teacher Soyen Shaku addressed the World's Parliament of Religions in Chicago. So that was more than a hundred years ago. And more than fifty years ago, Buddhism began making serious inroads into American culture through a small, brilliant, Buddhist-inspired group of rebels who came to be known as the Beats. By the early 1970s, outstanding Asian Buddhist teachers had taken up residence in the United States and were training Americans in Buddhist practice, while other young Westerners headed off to the East to study Buddhism there. Finally, immigrants from Buddhist countries, as distinct from American "convert" Buddhists, brought with them Buddhism as it was traditionally practiced in their respective homelands.

So can decades, or even a century, be called "early days"? Yes, they can, in the case of Buddhism. The essence of Buddhism lies beyond the conventional marks of development, such as monasteries, translations, and centers of learning (and even these are in their infancy in the West). More than that, there is an ineffable, mysterious, nonconceptual spirit to genuine Buddhism—a whole different way of thinking and being, hard to put your finger on and very different from the rationalist and theistic traditions we've been brought up in. While the outer forms of Buddhism—the philosophy, meditation practice, and institutions—have come quickly to America, that subtle spirit will take much longer to develop, perhaps hundreds of years, as it has in other cultures that Buddhism has entered.

Yet I see real signs of the genuine Buddhist spirit in this collection of writings. For twelve years now, as editor in chief of the *Shambhala Sun*, I have watched the development of Buddhism in America. I see in the teachings and stories in this volume a growing depth and subtlety—a sense of that mysterious spirit—in how Americans are teaching and writing about dharma. Less and less are they relying on what they've been told by others. More and more, they are speaking from a real understanding of their own. Of course this is just a beginning, but these pioneering days are exciting and inspiring.

Fortunately, as American practitioners, we are not completely on our own. Outstanding Asian masters continue to teach in the West, and some of the best are represented in this book: His Holiness the Dalai Lama, Thich Nhat Hanh, Gehlek Rimpoche, and The Dzogchen Ponlop Rinpoche. They provide a beacon and an anchor to Buddhism in America, a living connection to the wealth and insight of thousands of years of Buddhist tradition. Yet even these traditionally trained Buddhist masters are part of this pioneering era, for they have had to learn how to present the Buddhist dharma in a new language, in a modern culture, and to people who begin with different philosophical premises and personal concerns than Asian Buddhists do.

I think you will find writings and teachings of great meaning in this collection. They have meant a lot to me. The two themes that predominate are wisdom and compassion, and indeed, these are the two great principles of Buddhism, traditionally compared to the wings of a bird. Wisdom and compassion flow back and forth throughout this book. Sometimes the emphasis is on what Buddhism teaches about the true nature of the mind, the self, and the world. This is the wisdom. In other places, the heart predominates:

we learn how everything changes when we put others before ourselves, and we learn something about how to do it. This is compassion. It is to ego the most unnatural thing in the world, and to our true nature, the most natural.

The personal stories in this collection are stories of struggle, but they are also hopeful. The Buddhist path is not easy or painless. We read stories here of practitioners coming to grips with their own obsessions, problems, and foibles, coming face to face with their own mind. It's not always a pretty sight to look at ourselves honestly in the mirror of meditation, but the openness and insight that come are always refreshing. And it's okay to laugh, too.

Finally, there are excellent discussions here of how Buddhist principles, practice, and insight can be applied to the modern world. Buddhism cannot remain simply a vehicle for personal spiritual development. So much of our pain—and our joy—is wrapped up in our relationships with others and with the world around us. Buddhism has already had a profound impact on how Americans think about politics, the environment, health care, and the arts. I think you'll find essays here that say important things about changing not only ourselves but the way we relate to the world around us.

Far from being the final word on anything, this collection is just a snapshot, a look at what Buddhism in America offered in the year 2004. Yet underlying these essays, memoirs, and teachings—many of them so well written and moving—are Buddhism's ancient truths. Some say these truths were discovered by one man twenty-five hundred years ago, the man we came to call the Buddha, the Awakened One. Others say these truths have been discovered and rediscovered since beginningless time, and will continue to be discovered forever into the future. It will be to the benefit of all beings if genuine dharma in America—reflected here at one moment in its early history—becomes a genuine and brilliant manifestation of the Buddha's awakening.

In selecting the best Buddhist writings for this book, I have looked at English-language books, magazines, journals, and Web sites published and generally available in North America during the calendar year 2004. Some of the selections here were previously published abroad or in different forms, but were published in North America in their current form in 2004. As editor-in-chief of the *Shambhala Sun* and of *Buddhadharma: The Practitioner's Quarterly*, I continually survey the field of Buddhist writing. I apologize if I have missed worthy material for this anthology. Publishers and writers may contact me at editor@shambhalasun.com about books or articles that they would like considered for next year's anthology.

The collection here is a reflection of the insight and skill of the outstanding editorial staff of the *Shambhala Sun* and *Buddhadharma*. They are Barry Boyce, Andrea McQuillin, Tynette Deveaux, Molly De Shong, and Jeff Pardy. Thanks also go to James Gimian, the publisher of the *Shambhala Sun* and *Buddhadharma*. Our ongoing discussions about the future of Buddhism in America and what defines genuine dharma are very important to me.

At Shambhala Publications, I would like to thank editor Kendra Crossen Burroughs for her impeccable professionalism, and my good friend Peter Turner, president of Shambhala, for asking me to edit the *Best Buddhist Writing* series.

Saying "thanks" is ridiculously inadequate when someone has had a profound impact on Buddhism in the West, and even worldwide. But I would like to express my gratitude to Eido Shimano Roshi, who has helped me take a long view of Buddhism in the West, and to my own Buddhist teachers, the late Chögyam Trungpa Rinpoche, the Padmasambhava of this era, and Khenpo Tsultrim Gyamtso Rinpoche, a joyous and profound yogi. May their blessings continue in ways we cannot fathom.

MELVIN MCLEOD
Editor-in-chief
Shambhala Sun
Buddhadharma: The Practitioner's Quarterly

THE BEST BUDDHIST WRITING 2005

The Great Way Is Not Difficult

John Tarrant

Buddhism is a religion like no other (in fact, it has been questioned whether it should be classified as a religion at all). Buddhism is not about a deity, for it has none. It is not about received scriptures or commandments. It is not even about virtue or good conduct, although those are obviously important things. Buddhism is first of all about an experience of mind, and therefore, about the way we experience ourselves and our world. What is the particular experience of mind that Buddhism points to, and how does it differ from the way we usually live? Here is Zen teacher John Tarrant on a famed koan that is one of Buddhism's pithiest statements on this question.

The goal of the Zen koan is enlightenment, which is a profound change of heart. This change of heart makes the world seem like a different place; with it comes a freedom of mind and an awareness of the joy and kindness underlying daily life.

Koans are not intended to prescribe a particular kind of happiness or right way to live. They don't teach you to assemble or make something that didn't exist before. Many psychological and spiritual approaches rely on an engineering metaphor and hope to make your mind more predictable and controllable. Koans go the other way. They encourage you to make an ally of the unpredictability of the mind and to approach your life more as a work of art. The surprise they offer is the one that art offers: inside unpredictability you will find not chaos, but beauty. Koans light up a life that may have been dormant in you; they hold out the possibility of transformation even if you are trying to address unclear or apparently insoluble problems.

A koan shows you two conditions for your mind: a *with* and a *without* condition. This is a natural way to understand things—life as a Botox advertisement in which you are shown a haggard, careworn face, *with* wrinkles, and then the improved version, smooth as a baby's backside, *without* wrinkles. A koan uses this natural eagerness to compare things in an interesting way: when you work with the koan, what you are either *with* or *without* is your map, your cherished beliefs, your story about how your life should be at the moment in which you find yourself.

The *with* condition is what, in an unexamined way, you believe to be true. Beliefs have consequences; they build their own fictional world. When you believe something, you usually want the world to agree with you, to back up your story. Of course it rarely does, so your story will come with conflict built into its plotline. In the *without* condition, you see the world without wanting it to be different from the way it is. The *without* condition is an act of imagination. You ask yourself, "What might the world look like if I loved it as it is, just as it is?"

Here is a koan that shows the power of imagining life when you are not depending on the stories you usually tell yourself. It also can show you what life is like in the *with* condition, when your maps of the world vary from the actual territory of the world.

The Koan

Zhaozhou often quoted this saying by Sengcan:
The great way is not difficult
if you just don't pick and choose.

Everyone knows that some events are just bad and make you sad or angry, and some are good and make you glad. Yet what everyone knows might not be true. For example, there might be a certain coercion to the attitude that weddings must be happy and funerals have to be sad. It could prevent you from meeting the moment you are in. What if events don't have to be anything other than what they are? Children laugh at funerals; some tears shed by brides are from disappointment rather than joy. Being fired or losing someone dearly beloved could open an unexpectedly beautiful new life. You might be armored against an unpleasant event that turns out not to be. Instead of wrestling toward what you are convinced ought to be going on, it might be refreshing to approach events without armor, meeting their nakedness with your own nakedness. That might also be a kind approach, since it sets up no conflict in your own heart.

There is a legend in which the Buddha comes upon the mind of not picking and choosing. On the edge of his own profound change of heart, the Buddha meditates all night under a fig tree, and an image comes to mind. He remembers that, as a child, while his father plowed a field in an annual ceremony, he was left in the shade of a rose apple tree. At this moment the boy has no minders around to distract him; he is under no one's gaze. His father is absorbed in plowing. The air is pleasant, the leaf light green, the shade cool. With nothing on his mind, the child does not want or fear anything. The sun seems to stand still. It is delicious to be alive. He feels a happiness not born of desire. The boy moves his eyes over the whole field. He can find no resistance, no tension, no inner conflict; everything is sufficient. There is nothing to add, nothing to subtract. And it occurred to him that exploring this approach, which he discovered in childhood, might be the direction in which enlightenment lies.

Here, not picking and choosing is something a boy wanders into; it is the natural state of an undisturbed mind. Then the boy notices that thoughts and feelings are always rising and that they are not themselves disturbing: thoughts and feelings are things in the world as much as flowers and parasols, and he doesn't have to either agree with them or quarrel with them. It's easy not to pick and choose about his own reactions, about his picking and choosing.

Everyone knows that Buddhism is about nonattachment, and people might think that not picking and choosing is about having no preferences. Yet nonattachment might lead to warfare with the part of you that enjoys the world. In this case nonattachment would be just another tyrannical belief and itself a source of unhappiness. Not picking and choosing could be the opposite of nonattachment, something more unsettling and demanding. If someone asks you, "Vanilla or chocolate?" and you notice that today you would like vanilla, and say so, that might be not picking and choosing. If you say, "I don't mind, what are you having?" then that could well be picking and choosing. You might be trying to guess what your host wants. You might want vanilla but be unwilling to reveal yourself by saying so.

I discovered something about this koan when my sister called from Australia and told me my mother was dying. I got off the plane in August in Launceston, Tasmania, to gusts of wind and cold rain. Water lay in sheets on the paddocks; the luggage on the carts was glistening. The hills were as green as in dreams; merino sheep had green seeds sprouting in their wool.

My sister took me straight from the airport to my mother's bedside in the hospice. My mother, the doctor thought, was waiting for my arrival and might not last the night. "Dying of what?" I asked him. "Nothing, everything." He was a doctor who considered life and imagined that you might join him in considering it, too. He reflected for a moment. "There isn't a reason. She's just worn out."

My mother was extremely wasted; her hair was baby fine, bone white, and drifted above her skull. Her skin had an uncanny translucence relieved by large dark blotches where nurses had tried to find a vein and she had bled under the surface.

I held her hand and sat with her. The next morning she was still alive, so I did the same thing. My sister was negotiating with the nurses about the oxygen levels. This was an intense activity. My father was trying to encourage Mum to stay in this world, to eat—for him, for life. "May I tempt you with just a spoonful of this custard, Alison? You might get a taste for it."

She was heedless, impatient, rude: "You don't know what you are talking about. Oh, you don't care, you have never listened to me, never!"

"Oh, Alison," he said disconsolately.

Everyone had something to do but me. I began to consider love. Immediately I noticed that whenever I wanted anyone to be different, the room filled with sorrow and pain. Under that condition, I began to struggle and feel terrible grief. There was nothing wrong with this really. It was intense and interesting, but my mother didn't seem to need it of me. My father or sister didn't need it either. It also wasn't something I needed. Then for whom did I struggle and feel grief?

I noticed that it was easy to think that my father should accept that my mother was dying and let her go. Acceptance, the last stage, and all that. And it was easy to think that my mother should bless Dad on her way out—why not? Or I could think that I should be able to help, sand off the edges of the conversation, oil the wheels.

With any of these thoughts the room became small and fearful. There was a sense of strain, of needing to change others, of the hopelessness of that task, of picking and choosing. Wanting to change myself also led to this strain. This was the *with* condition—*with* wrinkles, *with* delusions of control. But when I wanted no one to be different, the room was large and at peace. It was obvious in the "Why didn't I think of this before?" way that important things can be. Obvious seemed good. I didn't think my mother should live longer or that it might be better if she died more quickly or more painlessly. What she was doing was good enough. I wanted my mother to have the death that was hers and saw that only she could know what that was. And how my father kept her company was up to him. I could trust him to know what he must do.

In the *without* condition, it seemed likely that my father spoke out of love, and that my mother pushed him away out of love. In a long marriage, the codes spoken by the couple might make no sense to outsiders, including their own children. My mother's apparent attack on my father could have meant: "I've always felt oppressed and this is my final verdict on marriage." Yet she could just as easily have meant, "I'm so sorry to be leaving you. I'm doing my best, but I think I can't stay. I don't want to give you false hope." And my father's cajoling might also have been saying, "I'll keep you company as long as I can, so that you don't need to be lonely."

In that room, I did whatever came to me without thinking much about it. Mainly, I read aloud the slightly bleak, old-fashioned poets she liked—Matthew Arnold, Thomas Hardy, some Robert Frost. I read from an old grade 10 reader, *A Galaxy of Poems Old and New*. My name was written inside it in a child's script, and also the name of the boy who had owned it before me. Sometimes, as I read, I held her hand. It was the fag end of winter. Gales set in, and winds off the great Southern Ocean beat against the windows, offering a kind of companionship mixed with awe that seafaring people become familiar with. I was comforted by the wind roaring in the dark and confident that, as I walked, a path would appear. Everyone seemed to be free then, and the hospice room was large and kind, a peaceful place to spend a late winter afternoon, watching gaps of light appear, robins hop with twigs in their beaks, and then the rain bash against the windows again, the season beginning to turn.

Something else about the hospice. The story in our family was that Mum was often difficult. I had evidence, memories; psychotherapists had agreed with these memories. But after sitting in that room, not wanting anyone to be different, I didn't want anything about my life to have been different either. My sister and I started to tell each other Mum's Famous Outrages—the "Can you believe she did that?" stories—but our hearts weren't in it. I noticed that, while I remembered the stories, my body didn't. I could no longer be sure what was intended in my mother's actions or my father's, or my own. It was easy to think that what had once been received as harshness could have been a step along one of affection's twisting paths.

In the end, my mother defeated the expectations of the hospice and everyone else's expectations too. She came home and lived to see another Christmas. It turned out to have been an opera singer's farewell concert; a rehearsal for another farewell, at a future, unspecified time.

The night my mother died she was back in the hospice and I called her from California. I had no particular urgency and no sense that this phone call was more at an edge than any other. I heard her say, "Hello?" very sweetly and then ask herself impatiently which end she should talk into. She sounded like the colonel in an English mystery—someone intolerant of innovations such as shirts with collars attached and telephones that didn't need to be wound up. She knew that I was on the other end, but she couldn't converse and manage the phone at the same time. This might just have been the effect of a stroke she had had many years before. Her intelligence was frustrated when her body did not understand what was being asked of it, had no grasp of basic Tasmanian.

It seemed that she was speaking into the ear end of the phone and listening to the speaking end. That is a likely explanation for the gurgles and thumps I was hearing in California. Like many human problems, it was absurd; the problem prevented me from explaining the problem to her. "Oh hell," she said, "bloody thing! I never liked it." By the clatter, it was clear that she had either dropped the handset or hurled it away.

I called back several times, thinking that she might by chance pick the receiver up right way around. But since she hadn't hung up the phone, the line was engaged. The nurse's station didn't answer. Before dawn the next morning I heard my father's voice come through the answering machine. "Mum died, John. That's all I have to say. Bye." I felt a love for him and also felt that my mother had indeed said farewell in a completely satisfactory way.

So those are my examples of the *with* and *without* conditions. With and without a belief about how it should be. There is nothing wrong with believing people should die a certain way and, for that matter, feeling the thrill of certainty that comes with any strong emotion, including grief. This too is life. If you don't dislike your own dislike, not picking and choosing is just present. It's not a discipline or a good thing that must be achieved. On the other hand, freedom is always interesting. When I was without what I should do and might do and could do, I just did what was obvious and was given to me. I experienced that as one of the shapes of love.

John Cage has a famous piece of music called *4'33"* in which all of the notes are silent. While it has often been performed at the piano, the score calls for any number of people playing any number of instruments. Everything else that happens ends up being the piece. The cough, the siren coming up the avenue, your wondering if anything is going to happen, the air conditioner, your memory of church in childhood, your sense of waiting for something. What is really happening is always happening now. It's always now. What happens when you think something else is happening is what is happening.

My mother's funeral had another fine John Cage moment. My sister and I found that my parents' sound system was very old, and the funeral chapel system needed tapes or CDs, not vinyl. We searched through rarely opened drawers, finding cassettes of Highland flings and odd arias until we settled on a tape of a Vivaldi piece. I gave this to the funeral director, a pleasant man who had known my mother through other occasions. The idea was that, as we pushed the button to send Mum into the fire, he would start the tape and Vivaldi would fill the chapel. So we stumbled through our loving, difficult readings and tiny speeches; then the button was pushed, and as the coffin advanced solemnly into the furnace, dysfunctional squawks came like a shower of arrows out of the sound system. The tape kept trying to play and its clicks and grindings were amplified very efficiently into the overhead speakers. The coffin was gone. We could hardly back up and try again. So that was her music. No picking and choosing. The director confessed that he had inserted the tape wrongly. I shook his hand and told him that the ceremony was perfect. Everyone has their own death, and realizing this seems to allow everyone to have their own life as well.

After my mother died, I dreamed that she was walking slowly and with some effort along a path in the country. It seemed that she could feel my gaze. Yet, as if she knew that this matter was for her alone, she did not turn to speak, or ask anything. She met what rose up before her as a task, and now it was her task to go on foot into death. I watched her walk along that trail until she passed out of my sight. She seemed to know what she was doing. There wasn't any picking or choosing involved for either of us.

Recognizing Our Natural State ꥼ

Chokyi Nyima Rinpoche
with David R. Shlim, M.D.

We think we have to work in order for the mind of enlightenment to arise.
Actually it's there all the time, and shows itself to us frequently. But caught
up in our dramas, we don't notice it. So Buddhism isn't about creating
anything; it's about clearing away obscurations so that we can notice our
natural state of mind. That's called meditation, and there are many
different kinds. One of the most profound is the Tibetan system known
as Dzogchen, with its emphasis on openness, simplicity, and ease. Chokyi
Nyima Rinpoche, one of the greatest living Dzogchen teachers, joins
with David R. Shlim, M.D., to offer us a meditation teaching that is
both practical in its advice and profound in its view.

When we train in meditation, the first step is to allow our attention
to be calm. Why? Because it is in the atmosphere of calm that intelligence and compassion naturally blossom. As water clears when
undisturbed, mind clears when undisturbed. During a human life,
there is so much hope and fear, so much worry and anxiety, even
in a single day. We experience all kinds of negative emotions—

endlessly. We cannot always fulfill our expectations and ambitions. Just having unfulfilled desire in itself is painful. One way to pursue spiritual practice is to check which of our desires are realistic. How many of our ambitions can we honestly hope to achieve? It's good to have some pragmatic limits.

We may need permission, from time to time, to allow ourselves to relax, to not be so hard on ourselves—to simply be at ease and happy. We need to learn to be kind to ourselves. The more we let ourselves feel free and easy, the happier we are. The more stress we put on ourselves and constrict our way of being, the more uncomfortable we are. This is an obvious fact, one we are familiar with from our own experience.

If we want to be happy, we should learn what it takes to be happy. Feeling content is not primarily dependent upon external things. External things form the setting, but only the setting. The main thing is your mind. If you know how to allow your mind to be free and easy, then wherever you go, you'll be comfortable. Whomever you are with, it will be okay. On the other hand, if you are feeling frustrated, stressed, unhappy, or unfulfilled, wherever you go and whomever you are with, you'll still be uncomfortable.

For each and every one of us, the most important thing is our state of mind. That which feels joy or sorrow, pleasure or pain, is just our mind. But our mind doesn't have to simply react to things around us. It can be steered in different directions. You can direct yourself toward what is good, and by doing so, you get accustomed to positive thoughts. If you direct yourself toward being negative, that also can become a habit. If you allow yourself to become apathetic and not care much, you become insensitive and dull. The word *spiritual* refers to directing or steering our mind toward something good, something noble. Simply that. One of the most important factors in accomplishing that goal is to know how to let ourselves be completely at ease.

Many people try very hard to be physically healthy by engaging in various exercises and diets. A lot of energy is put into being physically well. Shouldn't we also be doing something to let our mind be healthy as well? Mind is more important than the body—the body is simply the mind's tool for doing things. When the mind thinks, "Get up and walk," the body gets up and walks. If the mind thinks, "Sit down," the body sits down.

Most of us lead very busy lives. The tasks that we are so busy carrying out usually have a purpose. Generally, we could say that this purpose is to ensure that what comes afterward is comfortable. In other words, our whole life is actually spent preparing for what comes next. This process carries some built-in anxiety because we are attached to a particular outcome. Wanting to make sure things go a certain way intrinsically creates hope and fear. Even a tiny worry about whether the future is going to be okay is always a little bit painful. If the aim of all our activity is to create well-being in our life, but the preparation consists of being ill at ease, when exactly do we accomplish our aim?

It is not necessary to be constantly worried about being well or happy. It's okay to relax. Of course we need to be attentive to how things are going. We can't completely ignore our responsibilities, but we don't have to be obsessively concerned either. We can take it easy some of the time. If it were necessary to worry and be anxious unremittingly in order to achieve our goals, then that would be fine. If it were useful to accomplish our aim, then we should do that. But actually we are just giving ourselves a hard time. I'm not saying you should be unconcerned with how your life is unfolding. There's just no need to be overly anxious.

If you want compassion and wisdom that is natural and uncontrived, it does not happen unless it arises from a calm state of mind. Training in being calm can be called meditation. You can also call it any other name you want. To be completely relaxed, you need to rest in a way that is beyond thinking, beyond concepts—and yet aware. This type of awareness can be termed unconditioned suchness. Resting in that state is the true relaxation. However, just relaxing and being calm is not the same as resting in unconditioned suchness. When we consciously try to relax and be calm, there is still the self-conscious sense of dwelling in a calm state. Notions are still present: "I am calm. I'm resting. I must be calm. Calm, calm, calm. Now I'm not calm anymore. I got up."

Suchness means our basic nature, something unconditioned that is present within each of us. When our attention is occupied with dualistic thinking, our basic nature is obscured, and the resultant state of mind is called obscured suchness. But the instant that this preoccupation with clinging to duality is allowed to subside and vanish, then that state of mind is called unobscured suchness.

Unconditioned suchness is already present as the nature of every sentient being, all of the time. All the trouble arises from simply not knowing that this is the case. It is quite likely that from time to time we have a moment when we are just present in our basic nature, but this experience is probably quite short. Since we aren't accustomed to recognizing this nature, we can't acknowledge it for what it is.

Recognizing our basic nature has nothing to do with being religious or spiritual, or calling ourselves Buddhist. Since we are not in the habit of recognizing our basic nature, we simply can't nurture and extend these brief glimpses. As a result, we fail to prioritize what is really important. We just ignore our basic state and carry on with whatever we are doing. What is of truly vital importance is not recognized as such, and what is actually inconsequential we treat as being very important.

Our basic nature—whatever it truly is—becomes obvious to us the instant the state of mind that obscures our basic nature is allowed to vanish. That direct experience of our basic nature, even if it lasts only a moment, is called recognizing our natural state. This is true for any of us, no matter who we are. The terms *karma, obscurations,* and *disturbing emotions* describe states of mind in which our attention is clinging to duality. They all disappear the instant we recognize our unobscured suchness. What remains is profound compassion and wisdom.

There are many ways to relax and be calm. One could achieve a stupid, half-asleep state, like a bear in hibernation. Bears stay calm for many months in hibernation, but there is no awareness in that state. The best way is to be calm in a very present, lucid way. The calm feeling should be associated with an awake presence. That is the basis for the terms *thought-free wakefulness* and *self-existing awareness*, which refer to a lucid state untainted by clinging. These terms come directly from a tradition within Tibetan Buddhism known as *Dzogchen*, which is a particular form of practice that is an ultimate, direct way of training the mind in recognizing one's natural state.

Compassion and loving-kindness are the basic factors that create harmony and well-being for ourselves and others. Compassion is such a compelling quality that whenever a feeling of strong compassion comes into your mind, it clears away whatever negative emotions are present. They just fall away. At the same time compassion is of great benefit to those around you. When you experience pure and sincere compassion with an open and expansive frame of mind, at that very moment there is no longer any place for rivalry or anger. They have vanished. You may have experienced this yourself.

Let's say that your goal is to promote peace in the world. What is required is that everyone develop loving-kindness and compassion. There's no other way. We can't induce every other person in the world to immediately become more compassionate, so your primary responsibility is to make your own loving-kindness and compassion more open, more impartial. The purity of your compassion depends on your will, your motivation. One of the important points to keep in mind while striving to be kind is to expect less in return, to not hope for positive feedback or a reward. You need to avoid thinking, "I did a good deed, so they ought to treat me nicely in return. But they are not, so therefore I'm justified in feeling angry. I will certainly not bother to be kind to them next time." You want to avoid thinking like that.

There are various levels of practice that we refer to with the word *meditation*. The first levels of meditation require some effort. Something is held in mind, and we apply some effort to keep something—a kind of focus—in our mind. This type of meditation has the effect of calming our mental processes, making our nature more gentle. The highest, most eminent form of practice is called the great meditation of nonmeditation. This practice is not a religion or a philosophy. It is not something new that was created by the Buddha. It is the original state—how our nature is already from the beginning. Nonmeditation refers to resting in unconditioned suchness. It is the quintessence of a calm mental state.

Touching
the Earth

Thich Nhat Hanh

*Buddhism speaks of two truths. The ultimate truth is beyond any
possible form or concept. It is the true nature of mind and is the province
of wisdom. Relative truth is the insubstantial world of beings, perceptions,
feelings, and things. This is the realm of the heart, of compassion for all
suffering beings. Wisdom and compassion are brought together in this
extraordinary series of meditations by Thich Nhat Hanh. Even he, one of
the great Buddhist teachers of our age, must strive constantly to fulfill his
vows, acknowledge that he often falls short, and start afresh. At any time,
we too can renew our commitments—whatever they may be—and make
a fresh start.*

At the foot of the mountain
there is a stream.
Take the water from the stream and wash yourself,
and you will be cured.

These words are taken from a well-known Beginning Anew ceremony traditionally used in Vietnam. "Beginning Anew" comes
from the Chinese words *chan hui*. It means expressing our regret for

mistakes we have made in the past, coupled with a deep and transforming energy to act differently from now on. Because we know
that we can act differently, we do not need to feel guilt.

The principal meaning of the practice of Beginning Anew is
to bathe in the water of compassion. Compassion gives us a chance
to return to the joy of being alive. Once the mind is concentrated on
loving-kindness and compassion, their energy is produced and
strengthened. When the nectar of compassion flows in your heart,
you can see clearly how to put an end to all your afflictions.

The Beginning Anew practice is based on the compassion of
the Earth. When we touch the Earth, we take refuge in it. We receive
its solid and inclusive energy. The Earth embraces us and helps
us transform our ignorance, suffering, and despair. Wherever we
are, we can be in touch with the Earth. Wherever we are, we can
bow down to receive its energy of stability and fearlessness. As
we touch the Earth, we can follow our breathing. We release all our
instability, fear, anxiety, disease, and anger. We know the Earth
can absorb our negativity without reacting to us or judging us.
In this way, we are able to transform what is painful and difficult
to accept within us. We are able to strengthen our capacity to look,
speak, and act with understanding and compassion towards ourselves, our loved ones, and all members of our society. Touching
the Earth communicates our gratitude, joy, and acceptance to our
Mother Earth. With this practice, we cultivate a relationship with
the Earth and, in doing so, we restore our balance, our wholeness,
and our peace.

The preface to the *Kshitigarbha Sutra* says: "Earth means that
which is stable, thick, and has a great capacity for embracing." The
energy of mindfulness and concentration produced by Touching
the Earth has the capacity to awaken us to the nature of reality, to
transform us, to purify us, and to restore joy and vitality in our life.
As soon as we begin to practice, we can taste the benefits. And
the feeling of being at peace, refreshed, and revitalized by the Earth
will continue long after our sessions of practice.

TRUE HAPPINESS

Lord Buddha, you and your Sangha [the community of Buddhist practitioners] are my teachers who have given me birth in the spiritual life and continue to nourish me every day. I am your disciple, your younger brother or sister, your son or daughter. I aspire to be your worthy continuation. You did not look for happiness in fame, wealth, sex, power, and luxurious food and possessions. Your great freedom, love, and understanding brought you happiness.

Thanks to your great understanding, you were not obstructed by your own mind or your surroundings and you were not caught in wrong thinking. You did not think, speak, or do things which would bring about suffering for yourself or others. Lord Buddha, thanks to this great understanding, you had limitless love for all species. This love comforted, liberated, and brought peace and joy to countless beings. Your great understanding and compassion gave you great freedom and happiness. My deepest desire is to follow in your footsteps. I vow that I shall not seek happiness in the five sense pleasures. I shall not think that wealth, fame, sex, power, and luxurious food and material objects can bring me true happiness. I know that if I run after these objects of craving, I shall incur great suffering and make myself a slave to these things. I vow not to run after a position, a diploma, power, money, or sex. I vow that every day I shall practice to give rise to understanding, love, and freedom. These elements have the capacity to bring true happiness for me and for the Sangha body now and in the future.

Touching the Earth

With body, speech, and mind in oneness, I touch the Earth three times to experience and to solidify my deep aspiration. *[Ring bell]*

LIVING IN THE PRESENT

Lord Buddha, I recognize my deep habit energy of forgetfulness. I often allow my mind to think about the past, so that I drown in sorrow and regret. This has caused me to lose so many opportunities to be in touch with the wonderful things of life present only in this moment. I know there are many of us whose past has become our prison. Our time is spent complaining or regretting what we have lost. This robs us of the opportunity to be in touch with the refreshing, beautiful, and wonderful things that could nourish and transform us in the present moment. We are not able to be in touch with the blue sky, the white clouds, the green willow, the yellow flowers, the sound of the wind in the pine trees, the sound of the running brook, the sound of the singing birds, and the sound of the laughing children in the early morning sunlight. We are also not able to be in touch with the wonderful things in our own selves.

We are unable to see that our two eyes are two precious jewels. When we open our eyes, we can be in touch with the world of ten thousand different colors and forms. We do not recognize that our two ears are two wonderful sense organs. If we were to listen attentively with these two ears, we would hear the soft rustling of the wind in the branches of the pine, the twittering of the golden oriole, or the sound of the rising tide as it plays its compelling music on the seashore in the early morning. Our hearts, lungs, brains, as well as guided meditations for touching the earth, our capacity to feel, to think and observe, are also wonders of life. The glass of clear water or golden orange juice in our hands is also a wonder of life. In spite of this I am often unable to be in touch with the way life is manifesting in the present moment, because I do not practice mindful breathing and mindful walking to return to the present moment.

Lord Buddha, please be my witness. I promise I shall practice to realize the teachings you have given us. I know that the Pure Land is not an illusory promise for the future. The Pure Land is available to me now, wonderful in all aspects. The path of red earth with its border of green grass is the Pure Land. The small golden and violet flowers are also the Pure Land. The babbling brook with small, shiny rocks lying in its bed is also the Pure Land. Our Pure Land is not only the fragrant lotuses and bunches of chrysanthemums, but is also the mud which nourishes the roots of the lotus and the manure which nourishes the chrysanthemums.

The Pure Land has the outer appearance of birth and death, but looking deeply, I see that birth and death are interdependent. One is not possible without the other. If I look even more deeply, I will see that there is no birth and no death; there is only manifestation. I do not have to wait for this body to disintegrate in order to step into the Pure Land of the Buddha. By the way I look, walk, and breathe, I can produce the energies of mindfulness and concentration, allowing me to enter the Pure Land and to experience all the miracles of life found right in the here and now.

Touching the Earth

Lord Buddha, I touch the Earth twice to be deeply in touch with you and with the Pure Land of the present moment. *[Bell]*

LIVING DEEPLY

Lord Buddha, by nourishing the awakened understanding of impermanence in me, I have understood clearly the Five Remembrances that you have taught us to meditate on every day.

1. I am of the nature to grow old; there is no way I can escape growing old.
2. I am of the nature to have ill health; there is no way I can escape having ill health.
3. I am of the nature to die; there is no way I can escape death.
4. Everything that I cherish and value today I shall in the future have to be separated from.
5. My only true inheritance is the consequences of my actions of body, speech, and mind. My actions are the ground on which I stand.

Thanks to nourishing the awareness of impermanence, I am able to cherish each day. World Honored One, you knew how to use your time, health, and youth to lead a career of liberation and awakening. I am determined to follow your example, not running after power, position, fame, and profit. I no longer want to waste my time.

I vow to use my time and energy to practice transforming my afflictions, giving rise to understanding and love. Lord Buddha, as your descendant and your continuation, I vow to practice so that your career of understanding and love can continue to live in all future generations of practitioners.

By nourishing the awareness of impermanence, I see the precious presence of the people I love: my parents, teachers, friends, and fellow practitioners. I know that my loved ones are as impermanent as I am. There are times when I am forgetful, and I imagine that my loved ones will be alongside me forever, or for as long as my life lasts. I think that they will never grow old, they will never be sick, and they will never be absent from me. I do not value their presence. I do not find joy and happiness in being with them. Instead I speak and behave unkindly. At times, I even have a secret wish that my loved ones would go far away from me when I feel irritated with them. I have made them suffer; I have made them sad and angry, because I have not known how to value them. I am aware that at times I may have treated my father, mother, brother, sister, teacher, Dharma brothers and sisters, or partner in these thoughtless, cold, and ungrateful ways.

Lord Buddha, with all my heart I express regret for these faults. I shall learn how to say things like: "Father, you are still alive with me and it makes me so happy." "Brother or sister, you are a solid presence alongside me. To have you in my life gives me much joy." "Mother, I am a very lucky person to have you in my life." "Sister or brother, you refresh me and make my life more beautiful." I vow to practice using loving speech, first of all towards those I love closely and after that towards everyone.

Touching the Earth

Lord Buddha, the teacher of gods and humans, please be my witness. *[Bell]* Respected teacher of filial piety, Mahamaudgalyayana, please be my witness. *[Bell]* Respected teacher who humbly hid his deep understanding, Rahula, please be my witness. *[Bell]*

RECOGNIZING FEELINGS AND EMOTIONS

Lord Buddha, thanks to practicing mindful breathing and walking, I am aware of what is happening around me. I can recognize different mental formations as they arise. I know that the wounds of my ancestors and my parents, as well as wounds from my childhood until now, still lie deep in my consciousness. Sometimes painful feelings associated with sadness rise up in me, and if I do not know how to recognize, embrace, and help them to calm down, I can say things and do things that cause division or a split in my family or my community. When I cause division around me, I also feel divided in myself. Lord Buddha, I am determined to remember your teachings, to practice mindful breathing and walking and produce more positive energy in my daily life. I can use this energy to recognize the painful feelings in me and help them to calm down. I know that suppressing these feelings and emotions when they come up will only make the situation more difficult.

Lord Buddha, thanks to your teachings, I know that these feelings and emotions for the most part arise from narrow perceptions and incomplete understanding. I have wrong ideas about myself and other people. I have ideas about happiness and suffering that I cannot let go of. I have already made myself suffer a great deal because of my ideas. For example, I have the idea that happiness and suffering come from outside myself and are not due to my own mind. My way of looking, listening, understanding, and judging has made me suffer and has made my loved ones suffer. I know that by letting go of these ideas I will be happier and more peaceful in my body and mind. When I let go go of my narrow ideas and wrong perceptions, my painful feelings and emotions will no longer have a basis from which to arise.

Lord Buddha, I know that I still have so many wrong perceptions that prevent me from seeing things as they really are. I promise that from now on I shall practice looking deeply to see that the majority of my suffering arises from my ideas and perceptions. I shall not blame others when I suffer, but shall return to myself and recognize the source of my suffering in my misperceptions and my lack of deep understanding. I shall practice looking deeply, letting go of wrong perceptions and helping other people let go of their wrong perceptions so that they can also overcome their suffering.

Touching the Earth

Homage to the Bodhisattva of Great Understanding, Manjushri. *[Bell]*
Homage to the elder of Great Understanding, Shariputra. *[Bell]*
Homage to the elder who recorded the teachings, Ananda. *[Bell]*

LISTENING DEEPLY

Lord Buddha, I know that I still need time to learn the practice of deep listening of bodhisattva Avalokiteshvara. Although my intention to listen deeply is strong, if, while I am listening, the seed of self-criticism is watered in me, it becomes difficult. Perhaps the other person does not yet know how to practice loving speech. The words of the other person may contain blame, judgment, and accusation. This waters the seeds of anger, hurt, and self-criticism in me. When these seeds manifest in my mind consciousness, I lose my capacity to listen deeply and I close myself off from the other person. Although I may not say anything, the other person has the feeling that they are talking to a wall.

Lord Buddha, you have shared with me that whenever the mental formations of irritation and anger arise, I can return to my mindful breathing. I breathe lightly and embrace these mental formations. I remind myself that I am here listening to this person so that he can have an opportunity to speak about his suffering. I can help relieve her suffering through the compassionate practice of listening deeply. Without compassion in my heart, I am not truly practicing deep listening.

If I am not successful at listening deeply, I shall apologize to the person who is speaking. I can say: "I am sorry, Brother. I am sorry, Sister. I am sorry, Mother or Father. Today I do not have enough peace of mind to listen to you deeply. May I ask to be able to continue listening to you tomorrow?" I promise that I will not allow myself to fall into the trap of practicing only with the outer form without any substance.

Touching the Earth

Lord Buddha, with body, speech, and mind in perfect oneness, I touch the Earth three times to remember carefully my vow to practice deep listening. *[Bell]*

Lord Buddha, I express my regret to you, the Tathagata, for the times I have failed in my practice of listening deeply. I vow to practice better when I next have the occasion to listen deeply. *[Bell]*

ONENESS WITH THE EARTH

Lord Buddha, looking deeply at the Earth I see the light and warmth of the sun that allows everything to be born and grow. I also see the streams of fresh water that flow on this planet and bring life to the Earth. I also sense the presence of the atmosphere and all the elements in space, like oxygen, carbon dioxide, hydrogen, and nitrogen. Without the atmosphere, the water, and the sun there could not be the beautiful adornments of the Earth, the green willow, the purple bamboo, and the yellow flowers. I see everywhere the four elements of earth, water, fire, and air, how they interrelate with everything and inter-are in me. I shall touch the Earth and remain close to the Earth to see that I am one with Mother Earth; I am one with the sunlight, the rivers, the lakes, the ocean, and the clouds in the sky. The four elements in my body and the four elements in the body of the cosmos are not separate. I vow to return and take refuge in Mother Earth to see her solid and resilient nature within myself.

Touching the Earth

I touch the Earth before the bodhisattva Dharanimdhara, Earth Holder, and the bodhisattva Kshitigarbha, Earth Store. *[Bell]*

ONENESS WITH ALL BEINGS

Lord Buddha, I see that I am part of the wonderful pattern of life that stretches out in all directions. I see my close relationship with every person and every species. The happiness and suffering of all humans and all other species are my own happiness and suffering. I am one with someone who has been born disabled, or someone who is disabled because of war, accident, or sickness. I am one with people who are caught in situations of war, oppression, and exploitation. I am one with people who have never found happiness in their family and society. They do not have roots; they do not have peace of mind; they are hungry for understanding and love. They are looking for something beautiful, true, and wholesome to hold on to and to believe in. I am one with people at their last breath who are afraid because they do not know where they are going. I am the child living in miserable poverty and disease, whose legs and arms are as thin as sticks, without any future. I am also the person who is producing armaments to sell to poor countries.

I am the frog swimming in the lake, but I am also the water snake who needs to nourish its body with the body of the frog. I am the caterpillar and the ant, but I am also the bird who is looking for the caterpillar and the ant to eat. I am the forest that is being cut down, the water and the air that are being polluted. I am also the one who cuts down the forest and pollutes the water and the air. I see myself in all species and all species in myself.

I am one with the great beings who have witnessed the truth of no birth and no death, who are able to look at the appearances of birth, death, happiness, and suffering with calm eyes. I am one with the wise and good people who are present a little bit everywhere in this world. I am one with those who are in touch with what is wonderful, and can nourish and heal life. I am one with those who are able to embrace the whole of this world with their heart of love and their two arms of caring action. I am a person who has enough peace, joy, and freedom to be able to offer fearlessness and the joy of life to living beings around me. I see that I am not alone. The love

and the joy of great beings who are present in this world is support-
ing me and not allowing me to drown in despair. They help me
to live my life peacefully and joyfully, fully and meaningfully. I see
myself in all the great beings and all the great beings in myself.

Touching the Earth

Lord Buddha, I shall touch the Earth three times to recognize that I
am one with all the great bodhisattvas who are presently on this
Earth and to receive their tremendous energy. I also touch the Earth
to be in touch with the suffering of all species so that the energy of
compassion can arise and grow in me. *[Bell]*

The Flame at the Tip of the Candle ⟩⟩

Claude Anshin Thomas

Here is how Thich Nhat Hanh and his community changed one person's life. Claude Anshin Thomas was a traumatized Vietnam veteran, trying to turn his life around but still deeply scarred by the violence he had experienced—and committed—in Vietnam. To his great surprise, he was healed by the love and compassion of the very people he considered the enemy.

Picture a candle burning. The flame at the tip is hot and bright, sending light into the darkness. This image supported me as I walked through the darkness of my life, the necessary path to waking up, to turning things around.

By 1990 I had abstained from drugs and alcohol for seven years. Now there were fewer places to hide from the reality of Vietnam. All my feelings about the war had been tightly repressed until then, and now they were coming to the surface. I couldn't push them away any longer.

At this time I was living in Concord, Massachusetts, and I was in counseling with a social worker, a wonderful, generous woman. When I got to the point where I felt totally overwhelmed by my emotions and wanted to die, she supported me, and in a spiritual way, she held me. I was trapped in the prison of self, confined by guilt, remorse, anxiety, and fear. I became so tormented that I was unable to leave my house. Physically and emotionally, I was under siege, bunkered in. My counselor continued to phone me and gently yet persistently invite me to come to her office. She continued to support the reality that I had *not* gone completely mad and helped me to understand that what was happening to me was the result of getting in touch with my feelings about the war, perhaps for the first time.

At a certain point she told me about a Buddhist monk who had worked with Vietnam veterans and had some success in helping them become more at peace with themselves. She suggested I read some of his books. It was only later that she told me he was Vietnamese. Because I had committed myself to healing, I said: "Sure, okay, I'll read the books," but I wasn't able to, because they were written by a Vietnamese man—the enemy. Every time I would envision reading them, I would think about the time a group of monks opened fire on us.

Six months later someone else, a woman in a therapy group I had joined, gave me a catalog from the Omega Institute, a holistic education center in Rhinebeck, New York. One of the pages of this catalog was bookmarked for me. When I opened it I saw a photo of that very same Vietnamese Buddhist monk, Thich Nhat Hanh, and an announcement that he was leading a meditation retreat for Vietnam veterans. Up to that point I had an excellent excuse for not going to see him: He lived in France and I didn't have the money to travel because I was unable to work; I was unemployable. There was a note in the catalog, highlighted for me in yellow, saying that scholarships were available for those in need. I couldn't use the excuse of not having any money. I had made the commitment that I was willing to go to any length to heal, so I had to take this step.

I called to make arrangements to go to the retreat. I explained to the person on the phone that I had a very difficult time being around people. I became anxious and uncomfortable in ordinary social circumstances and needed to be by myself. I also informed her that I had a very hard time sleeping at night, a polite way of indicating my intensely disturbed sleep pattern. The people at the Omega Institute were nervous about having me, one of those so-called unstable Vietnam vets, attend this retreat, so they called the organizers and asked if it was all right for me to participate. The sponsors said, "We don't turn anyone away." This was the response of the Vietnamese—my enemy. *They* said: "We don't turn anybody away." My countrymen, the people I fought for, wanted to reject me, yet again.

I drove to the retreat on my motorcycle. At that time I was riding a black Harley Davidson. I was dressed in a typical fashion for me: black leather jacket, black boots, black helmet, gold mirror glasses, and a red bandanna tied around my neck. My style of dress was not exactly warm and welcoming. The way I presented myself was intended to keep people away, because I was scared, really scared.

I arrived at the retreat early so I could check the place out. Before I could think about anything, I walked the perimeter of the whole place: Where are the boundaries? Where are the dangerous places where I'm vulnerable to attack? Coming here thrust me into the unknown, and for me the unknown meant war. And to be with so many people I didn't know was terrifying to me, and the feeling of terror also meant war.

After my recon I went down to the registration desk and asked where the camping area was, because I didn't want to camp where anyone else was camping. I was much too frightened to be near so many strangers. This time each day, sunset, was filled with fear—fear of ambush, fear of attack, fear of war exploding at any moment. Rationally I knew that these things wouldn't happen, but these fears, like the reality of war, are not rational.

I put my tent in the woods, away from everybody else, and I sat there asking myself, "What am I doing here? Why am I at a Buddhist retreat with a Vietnamese monk? I have to be out of my mind, absolutely crazy."

The first night of the retreat, Thich Nhat Hanh talked to us. The moment he walked into the room and I looked into his face, I began to cry. I realized for the first time that I didn't know the Vietnamese in any other way than as my enemy, and this man wasn't my enemy. It wasn't a conscious thought; it was an awareness happening from somewhere deep inside me.

As I sat there looking at this Vietnamese man, memories of the war started flooding over me. Things that I hadn't remembered before, events I had totally forgotten. One of the memories that came back that evening helped me to understand why I had not been able to tolerate the crying of my baby son years earlier.

At some point, maybe six months into my service in Vietnam, we landed outside a village and shut down the engines of our helicopters. Often when we shut down near a village the children would rush up and flock around the helicopter, begging for food, trying to sell us bananas or pineapples or Coca-Cola, or attempting to prostitute their mothers or sisters. On this particular day there was a large group of children, maybe twenty-five. They were mostly gathered around the helicopter. As the number of children grew, the situation became less and less safe because often the Vietcong would use children as weapons against us. So someone chased them off by firing a burst from an M60 machine gun over their heads. As they ran away, a baby was left lying on the ground, crying, maybe two feet from the helicopter in the middle of the group. I started to approach the baby along with three or four other soldiers. That is what my nonwar conditioning told me to do. But in this instance, for some reason, something felt wrong to me. And just as the thought began to rise in my head to yell at the others to stop, just before that thought could be passed by synapse to speech, one of them reached out and picked up the baby, and it blew up. Perhaps the baby had been a booby-trap, a bomb. Perhaps there had been a grenade attack or a mortar attack at just this moment. Whatever the cause, there was an explosion that killed three soldiers and knocked me down, covering me with blood and body parts.

This incident had been so overwhelming that my conscious mind could not hold it. And so this memory had remained inaccessible to me until that evening in 1990. As I sat there looking at this monk, Vietnam just came rushing back to me. All the unaddressed, repressed thoughts, feelings, and perceptions. I understood for the first time how the war had taken away my ability to have relationships. How the effects of war had prevented me, like my father before me, from having an intimate relationship with my son, or with anyone. I had left my three-year-old son and his mother not because I couldn't stand to be with them, which is what my suffering was telling me, but because I couldn't stand to be in my own skin.

Being in the presence of this monk and his assistant, a nun who was also Vietnamese, memories of the war continued to rush through me, and I was terrified all over again. In one instance, people from the retreat were standing in a circle, doing some exercises. I wouldn't join the circle because it didn't feel safe. When Sister Chan Khong began to walk away from the circle, I started to panic because I didn't have a gun. I was confronted by the memory of walking into that "pacified" village and the monks opening fire on us with their automatic weapons. And now here I was observing a Vietnamese nun leaving a group of American veterans who were unarmed and vulnerable. I was so frightened I thought that I might explode. Who could be trusted? Who?

At the retreat, Thich Nhat Hanh said to us, "You veterans are the light at the tip of the candle. You burn hot and bright. You understand deeply the nature of suffering." He told us that the only way to heal, to transform suffering, is to stand face-to-face with suffering, to realize the intimate details of suffering and how our life in the present is affected by it. He encouraged us to talk about our experiences and told us that we deserved to be listened to, deserved to be understood. He said we represented a powerful force for healing in the world.

He also told us that the nonveterans were more responsible for the war than the veterans. That because of the interconnectedness of all things, there is no escape from responsibility. That those who think they aren't responsible are the most responsible. The very lifestyle of the nonveterans supports the institutions of war. The nonveterans, he said, needed to sit down with the veterans and listen, really listen to our experience. They needed to embrace whatever feelings arose in them when engaging with us—not to hide from their experience in our presence, not to try to control it, but just to be present with us.

I spent six days at the retreat. Being with the Vietnamese people gave me the opportunity to step into the emotional chaos that was my experience of Vietnam. And I came to realize that this experience was—and continues to be—a very useful and powerful gift. Without specific awareness of the intimate nature of our suffering, whatever that suffering may be, healing and transformation simply are not possible and we will continue to re-create that suffering and infect others with it.

Toward the end of the retreat I went to Sister Chan Khong to apologize, to try to make amends in some way for all the destruction, the killing I'd taken part in. I didn't know how to apologize directly; perhaps I didn't have the courage. All I could manage to say was: "I want to go to Vietnam." During the retreat they had said, if we who had fought wanted to go to Vietnam to help rebuild the country, they would help arrange it. And so I asked to go to Vietnam; it was all I could say through my tears.

Sister Chan Khong looked at me as I was crying and said: "Before you go to Vietnam, perhaps it would be a good idea to come to Plum Village," which is Thich Nhat Hanh's monastery and retreat center in France. She said, "If you come in the summer, many Vietnamese people are there—refugees, boat people—and you can learn to know the Vietnamese in another way. Come to Plum Village; we can help you; let us help you!" I was overwhelmed by this offer of help. No one in my own country had made such an offer to me, an offer of support and help to live differently, to find peace.

At a very deep and profound level I understood the truth and sincerity of the offer. But the fact that it was being made by my enemy was both profound and confusing. In war it is impossible to distinguish safe from unsafe, good from bad. It is quite like the confusion of an abused child: All adults become potential abusers, even those who sincerely want to help. Violence and war contaminate daily life and personal interactions, permeating them with fear and distrust.

I replied to Sister Chan Khong's offer with deep gratitude and with hesitation. I said, "I'd like very much to come, but I can't. I don't have the money." And she answered, "Don't worry about the money." My travel expenses ended up being paid for with donations from the people who attended the retreat, and my stay in the monastery was supported by the Vietnamese community at Plum Village. My enemy embraced me and helped me in ways that my own country never did.

As soon as I agreed to go to the monastery in France, I felt a sense of lightness. A great weight lifted. I was excited and deeply touched by the act of caring and support offered to me by the Vietnamese. A couple of days later, however, I was again overcome by fear. In this country no one had ever reached out, offered help, without wanting to use me in some way. Why should I believe that my enemy, of all people, would help me, would embrace me like this? My fear said, "The only reason they are inviting me is that they want to put me on trial and then put me in jail or execute me for war crimes." My rational mind said, "I don't think this is the truth." But the fear was too deep to resist.

I knew that what I needed to do was to embrace my fear, look deeply into the nature of it, and go to France anyway. I promised myself I would go. "If they are going to kill me," I thought, "if that's what's going to happen, maybe at last I will have some peace."

That first summer at the monastery I stayed for six weeks. The community at Plum Village included about four hundred Vietnamese people. Everywhere I turned brought up another memory for me, brought me more and more in touch with the reality of the war—with the suffering I had witnessed, the despair I had felt, the trauma all of us on both sides had experienced. Everyplace, it was everyplace.

In Plum Village there are two separate living areas: a lower hamlet and an upper hamlet. The upper hamlet is where the Western people live; the lower hamlet is almost all Vietnamese people.

When I arrived, there was a discussion about where I would stay. I thought I would probably live with the Westerners, but Sister Chan Khong said, "No, you will live with the Vietnamese." I wasn't able to do that exactly, to live within and among the Vietnamese. So I went to a place in the woods, maybe a quarter of a mile away from the community, and put up a tent. I set a perimeter around my tent of about twenty to thirty meters, and I put up booby traps—not to hurt anyone seriously, more to let me know that someone was there and to frighten them away.

Ten days before I left Plum Village, I took the booby traps down. I went to talk to Sister Chan Khong, and I told her about the booby traps. I explained that I hadn't wanted to hurt anyone; I just wanted to protect myself. She said to me, "It's good that you can take them down, but if you need to put them back up, put them back up." This was a kind of unconditional acceptance that I had never experienced.

What the Vietnamese community did was love me. They didn't put me on trial. They offered me an opportunity to look deeply into the nature of my self, to walk with them in mindfulness and begin the process of healing and transformation. It wasn't anything in particular that they said to me; it was simply being in community with Vietnamese people. Each face I saw brought another memory. The smell of food cooking brought memories; watching the celebrations brought memories. I saw the young women in their beautiful clothes, their *ao dais*, and I could hear the sound of war—automatic weapons fire, rockets, explosions, screaming—and smell gunpowder, blood, and death, and I remembered all the attacks on the villages that I had witnessed and participated in.

I couldn't talk. I couldn't say what I was feeling; I couldn't talk about my experiences because I believed that if I did, the Vietnamese people would surely hate me—if they knew who I was, that I had been a soldier in Vietnam. What I didn't know but found out later was that in community meetings the abbot and his assistant had told the Vietnamese residents and retreatants just who I was and why I was there, and knowing this information, the Vietnamese community seemed to love me more.

During my stay at Plum Village I was overwhelmed with feelings of guilt, and whenever I tried to talk about them with the monks and nuns, they would say, "The past is in the past. There is only the present moment and it's beautiful." One day a Mirage jet from the French air force flew at a very low level directly over the hamlets of Plum Village. The jet appeared with the unmistakable and deafening roar of a military fighter, swift and sudden, and I dove to the ground in panic. As I looked around for the carnage, the aftermath of such a swift, brutal attack, I realized that I was war reacting. I pulled myself up off the ground, shaking and in tears. The monk I was working with asked me if I was all right. I began to talk with this monk about my feelings in the moment, and he began with the "the past is in the past, there is only the present moment and it's beautiful" mantra. I responded angrily to this monk, in fact I was so angry that I almost hit him with a shovel. Instead of hitting him, I yelled: "The past is not always in the past, sometimes it's in the present moment and it's not beautiful and I hate it!" I talked about this incident with the abbot's assistant, and she explained that while it is true that the past is in the past, and there is only the present moment, if you are living intensely in the present moment, the past and the future are also here. "One just needs to learn how to live with this experience like still water." Her words, this image, helped me.

After that first visit in 1990, I returned to the monastery often. In 1992 Thich Nhat Hanh invited me to wear the robes of a monk. Having no intention of becoming a monk and feeling very uneasy with his gesture, I said to him: "I can't wear the clothes that monks wear; I'm not interested in being a Buddhist monk." He looked at me and smiled, put his hand on my shoulder, and said: "You are more of a monk than a monk." And he announced to all the people sitting there that I was a "Tao master." Everybody had a good laugh, probably because we all sensed that the abbot had just made a very profound statement; at that moment we simply could not understand the full meaning of it, and so we laughed nervously.

Although it seemed to me that this was my first contact with Buddhism, in fact I had indirectly begun the study of Zen when I was fourteen years old. At that time I studied karate, a Korean style called Hap Ki Do. At the age of sixteen I was invited to live for nine months as a monk with my teacher, and although this introduced me to Zen practice, it was a practice without the Buddha's teaching. Zen without the Buddha's teaching is dangerous. You develop a very deep sense of concentration, tap into the power concentration without the guidance of the Buddha's transformative insights into the nature of our suffering—and the ever-present dangers of selfish desire, craving, and ignorance. I went on to study in yet another martial tradition, Chinese in origin, and by 1989 I was very involved not only in the study of these ancient arts but also in teaching them.

By the time I went to Plum Village, I had been studying and teaching karate for twenty-seven years. I had taught at five different schools and had instructed many students. There were, of course, lapses in my practice of the martial arts. There were several years after returning from Vietnam when I was lost in my suffering and trapped in my dependence on drugs and alcohol. But when I cleaned up, I returned to the martial arts, and then one day in 1989, while teaching a class of advanced students, I realized that what I was actually doing was watering the seeds of violence, that I was teaching people how to fight and to kill, and I understood that I could not continue to do this; so I stopped.

By my stopping and calming, the violence of the martial arts had the opportunity to be transformed. The robes of a martial artist became the robes of a monk. I didn't realize this transition immediately; it was only after Thich Nhat Hanh invited me to give a talk for the first time. He asked me to speak at a retreat being held at Plum Village for helping professionals. It was the very first time that I spoke publicly about Vietnam, my actions during the war, and the resulting effects. It was also the first time that I had spoken in front of a group of nonveterans.

From that first talk came the invitation to speak more, then invitations to facilitate mindfulness meditation retreats. I found that this expanded my own path of healing. It was through one of these invitations to speak that I connected with the Zen Community of

New York, which led me to a meeting with its abbot, Bernie Glassman (Baisen Tetsugen Roshi). He invited me to become ordained as a novitiate in the Japanese Soto Zen Buddhist tradition, which was the beginning of my path to taking monk's vows in that tradition. So the karate *ghi*, the robes of fighting, were transformed through the practice of meditation—stopping and becoming calm—into the robes of peace.

Since my ordination as a Zen novitiate and subsequently as a monk, my efforts have been directed toward actualizing the image of the light at the tip of the candle. I participate in and facilitate mindfulness meditation retreats, retreats in which I live as a homeless person, and mindfulness meditation retreats in which writing has a key role (a practice I was introduced to by writer and activist Maxine Hong Kingston). I've also taken up the practice of pilgrimage. In the tradition of the ancient Zen monks of China and Japan, I take a begging bowl and only the most minimum of possessions, and I walk from one place to another. My intention is to meet whatever life puts in front of me, to experience life directly. I have walked in this way from Auschwitz, Poland, to Vietnam and from New York to California.

After taking novitiate vows, I also began to teach meditation practice to veterans and prisoners. The tools of meditation serve as a bridge for those who are interested in and committed to moving from a place of violence to a place of nonviolence. I also go into active war zones and work with soldiers, noncombatants, and refugees using the tools of meditation, of living more consciously, as a bridge from violence to nonviolence.

What I have discovered through meditation practice is that I have long wanted to work with all who are affected by violence, by the many expressions of war. Although I strongly felt this call to service, I wasn't entirely sure of how to do this. I just knew that this was somehow very important and that I had to do something. I saw that most nonveterans did not understand veterans. I knew that most nonveterans around the world do not realize their responsibility in war or how deeply they are affected by it. I also felt a deep need to bring attention to the transgenerational effects of war and the inheritance of suffering. It is important to realize that veterans are not the only ones who bear responsibility for the atrocities of war. Nonveterans sanction war, support the waging of war, supported troops being sent to Vietnam—and it is nonveterans who so often turn their backs on the returning soldiers in an effort to avoid their own complicity in the war.

When I came back from Vietnam, it was to a society and culture that attempted to wash its hands of its responsibility in that war by marginalizing those who had served. This clearly communicated that those who served were the ones who were responsible and that those who did not serve were somehow absolved of responsibility. But if we look deeply into this matter, we can know that those who don't fight are not separate from those who fight; we are all responsible for war. War is not something that happens external to us; it is an extension of us, its roots being within our very nature. It happens within all of us.

When I talk with other veterans of the Vietnam War or the Persian Gulf War, or with Russian veterans of their war in Afghanistan, Cambodian veterans of their civil war, Bosnian soldiers, Croatian soldiers, Serbian soldiers, Kosovo Liberation Army soldiers, soldiers from any war, I hear the same story. They say that they are not understood and that nonveterans avoid contact with them, resisting all but the most superficial connection. I believe that nonveterans don't make the effort to understand us because to touch the reality of our experience would mean that they would have to touch the same sort of pain and suffering inside themselves, and consequently recognize their responsibility.

The fact that war puts soldiers in a position to kill people, to act violently, doesn't mean that noncombatants don't have the same potential. We can pretend that we're not violent. Whenever we are confronted with violence, we as individuals and as a society can attempt to hide from it, we can attempt to ignore it, we can attempt to push it away. But if we don't touch this part of ourselves, if we don't own our complicity in the many wars that are being fought around the world and at home, if we don't become aware of our own potential for violence, then we're not whole, we're not balanced.

What does it say about our culture that we seem to thrive on violence, both real and staged, that violence has become a media staple? When violence strikes close to home, such as at the shootings at Columbine High School, we look for an excuse—the psychopathology of the adolescents, their dysfunctional families—rather than recognizing that the actions of these young men are one reflection of the ethos of the larger society.

The Anthropology of Myself ∂⟩

Faith Adiele

*Faith Adiele was a young African-American woman having a rough
time in her second year at Harvard. She signed up for a research project
investigating the lives of Thai Buddhist nuns, and decided to try the
experience firsthand. She got far more than she bargained for—a rainy
season retreat of intense introspection in a nunnery of the famed Forest
Tradition. With great courage and fortitude, guided by a wise abbess,
she undertook the journey that all serious meditators do—the pains,
joys, and hard work of a long time alone with your own mind.*

Despite the name Faith, I'm an unlikely candidate for spiritual aspirations. Strangers are surprised to learn that I spent a Lenten season as a Buddhist nun in the Thai forest. Their eyes widen, taking in
all of me, as mine drop, seeking the floor lights marking the exit. I
dread the questions, but even more I dread my stock answers,
chanted like an unholy mantra. Yup, I'm not Asian. Nope, I'm not
some New Ager on a holy trek to the food co-op. Nah, I don't particularly believe in religion. I don't even believe in camping. To compli-
cate matters further—their eyes narrow, homing in on me—I am
black. Physically soft. Pierced! And what they may not know—

addicted to African dance grooves, snacks involving processed flour *and* sugar, good jewelry, and bad television.

Friends, too, are surprised to learn the details. It's no secret Faith lacks discipline. She can't even make it to the gym—forget about enlightenment! Anyone who knows me knows that I couldn't have risen at three-thirty each morning and spent nineteen hours a day in meditative practice. Aren't I the one always saying that seven-thirty comes but once: dinnertime? I certainly didn't go from sitting fifteen minutes in meditation to seventy-two hours at a stretch. How many hours? Nope, not Faith! The only thing to suggest that other-worldliness might be possible is a quaint refusal to smash bugs and an inability to keep shoes on my ringed, painted feet. But that's not enough, is it?

Understandably, friends and strangers ask questions, the answers they expect embedded in the queries themselves: *Wasn't it hot? Weren't you lonely? Weren't you scared?* The answers are all invariably yes. Yes to hot, lonely, scared. Yes also to missing physical intimacy and movies and Pop-Tarts. And yes to my fear of everything the phrase "tropical forest" conjures—giant spiders and hissing cobras and forest fires and prehistoric monitor lizards. Yes to my fear of everything Buddhist asceticism suggests—a single meal a day, sleeping on wooden floors, meditating on decomposing corpses. Yes, yes, yes, there were times I shuddered and sobbed in a Southeast Asian night so dark I couldn't tell if my eyes were open or shut. Times I detested the Buddha and Asia and so-called personal growth. Times when nothing was more terrifying than the prospect of sitting with the contents of my own mind for nineteen hours a day.

For many years I didn't talk about being a Buddhist nun. The reasons varied. For one, the subject presented two Great American Conversational No-nos: Religion and Race. I'd been taught that religion was a private, touchy subject. My parents split over their differences, and our town condemned my family's liberal spiritual beliefs. Added to that, I'd been raised Unitarian, a vague, good-natured philosophy that required little of adherents save rejection of a Trinity—the very thing Buddhism espoused in the form of Buddha, dharma, and sangha. In truth, Buddhism seemed fertile with shame. It wasn't a black religion, after all. God knew my connection to black America was tenuous enough, given my mixed, African parentage, Scandinavian immigrant upbringing, and privileged college life. Spending a year developing an interior life seemed like a luxury reserved for students with trust funds and time to burn. How would indulgent endeavors uplift the race? There was also the shame of having fled America. It confirmed that, like the Tragic Mulatta of literature, I was (alas! hand to cheek) weak, tainted. Frankly, I didn't need the strange looks and demands to account for myself.

Even today, with Eastern philosophies in the mainstream, ordination is an unlikely, discomfiting topic. Now the problem, in this age of Extreme Sports, Adventure Travel, and Radical Makeovers, is that I haven't changed in the way that people expect. Where I should be *über*-nun, I'm not even what is perceived as a practicing Buddhist. I don't meditate regularly; I nurse anger; I despise tofu. Dammit, I don't appear to have *learned* anything! So how can anyone learn from me?

How do I begin to explain that, though I lived the role more seriously than anything in my life, being a Buddhist nun actually had little to do with being a Buddhist or with being a nun? It was about hacking a difficult path through the jungle, clawing my way from one paradigm to another. The change was the journey itself, and anyone can get there, down any trail. This is specifically the story of a silent girl who threw off an overcoat and stripped away everything underneath. A new kind of traveler—the Hungry American who set out in search of faith without a map. The Sarcastic American who used a journal to write her way through the trees to a new self. It has taken me all this time—more than a decade—to understand the strange decision made one afternoon in the dreaming shade of a Thai temple, as pale butterflies knocked against my warming flesh. Despite arising from failure, my decision was an act of resistance, of downright defiance. I chose life. And in telling the tale, I choose it still.

THE EDGE OF THE FOREST

Wat Thamtong is just as beautiful as I remembered from my first and only visit. Inwardly I rejoice; so I am not completely insane! The green-and-gold landscape, echoing the colors of the traditional Siamese roof, is one solace. Maechi Roongdüan, the head nun of the temple, is another. During my registration she stands round-faced and smiling, as she has on our previous two meetings, emanating that stolid dignity like a shade I want to rest beneath.

Once Maechi Roongdüan sees my friends off, she asks me to join her on the path overlooking the stream. Lowering herself onto a stone bench, straight-backed as always, robes pooling around her, she pats the seat next to her and smiles.

Trying to mimic her slow grace, I feel myself plop into place.

After searching my face, she raises her brows and gives me a look as if to say, *So here we are! Now what?*

I grin.

She announces in English: "Wat Thamtong is not a *wat.*"

Somehow I have the sense not to show how much this rattles me. What does she mean, "not a *wat*"? I'm here to study *wat*! Perhaps she means it's not like Wat Phra Singh, a fancy royal temple and tourist destination. That's fine. I want a working congregation precisely in order to observe the famed reciprocal relationship between temple and community. Since Thamtong *maechi* [Thai Buddhist nuns] are so well known, I hope to see how much of the standard ceremonial, counseling, and educational functions they provide to laypeople in exchange for donations of food and money.

"This is a retreat center for intensive meditation practice," Maechi Roongdüan elaborates. My brain clicks. This is what she was trying to explain the day Ajarn Boon and I visited, only I wasn't listening.

"Intensive meditation?" I ask tentatively. Inside I'm screaming. I've never meditated in my life!

She nods, a gentle, fluid bending forward, exposing a crop of dark stubble against an ivory neck. "We practice the Forest Tradition." I nearly bolt from my seat and dart down the path. Maybe I can still catch the minivans as they tear up the trail! A Forest Temple!

The rigorous Forest Tradition, a return to the Buddha's ascetic practice, is the stuff of legend, the obsession of bony hermits in the drought-ridden northeast—not the territory of beaming robust women in Chiang Mai Province.

In all the *wat* I visited in the months preceding my ordination, monks lived relatively comfortable, albeit disciplined, lives. They consumed two moderate meals a day. They divided their time between religious study, temple chores, and ministry. They came and went freely, accompanied by young novices or laymen who handled their money for them; the streets and roads teemed with saffron robes.

Of course I don't expect to live this exact life. I know that *maechi* are often relegated to the wat ghetto, cooking and cleaning and serving monks to earn their keep. Religious study is generally not open to them, certainly not at the two Dhamma universities in Bangkok, and travel is restricted. However, as Thamtong is known for its equitable and enlightened treatment of *maechi*, I expect to experience as full a monastic life as is possible for women.

"This is one of the few places that allows women to practice the Forest Tradition," Maechi Roongdüan says, nodding firmly, a move I recognize from childhood, my mother announcing a new family policy of great morality and equal inconvenience. "Monks and *maechi* come from all over the country for temporary residence."

And of course this news-bite does it, as she might—and my mother certainly would—have guessed! Always the cultural ambassador, I plump in the wake of her words. I've stumbled (albeit through no skill of my own) into the situation of the century—a Forest Temple for women. Even better, I am the sole Westerner and first black resident!

"The day," she explains, "is devoted to intensive meditation practice and mindful chores." Fair enough. She continues, "We rise at three-thirty in the morning and do not sleep before eleven at night."

My eyelashes flutter like the butterflies darting around us. "Pardon?" Three-thirty! And I was worried about getting up at four-thirty or five, standard *wat* rising time. My inability to function before 8:00 A.M. is legendary. And furthermore, how is it possible not to sleep before eleven? Are we really expected to function on four and a half hours of sleep? To devote nineteen hours to meditation and mindfulness? Surely there must be a siesta!

"There is no lying down permitted during waking hours," Maechi Roongdüan volunteers smoothly, as if she can read my little mind's feverish calculations. "We eat a single meal, and only liquids are allowed after noon."

I feel like I've jumped off the triple-tiered roof and landed on my back, the wind knocked out of me. For weeks everyone has worried about my ability to subsist on two meals a day. I'm not sure whether this concern is an extension of the Thai preoccupation with foreigners' eating habits or a veiled reference to my weight. Whatever the motivation, it's moot now. I have bigger problems.

I'm digesting this new situation when Maechi Roongdüan hits me again: "Most communication is forbidden. That means no speaking, reading, or writing except when absolutely necessary. Our mail is censored and our contact with lay society limited. Ajahn Boon and I agreed that yours would be nonexistent."

My eyes threaten to flood. I've never heard of contemporary monastics taking vows of silence. This is the stuff of myth. I understand the decision to restrict my visitors and letters, given the relative brevity of my ordination, but how can I be me and do what I will do if I can't read or write? My *purpose* is research. Besides, a major portion of ordained life is Dhamma study, so how can reading and writing be forbidden?

Again, Maechi Roongdüan anticipates my objections in the approximate time it takes me to formulate them. "This will be hard for you," she allows. "So perhaps you should keep a journal. I only ask you to restrict the time you spend writing in it. I also ask you to focus on the practice as if you were any other *maechi*. Then, at the end of your stay, you can interview any woman who agrees to participate in your study."

She widens her eyes, indentations like thumbs in clay where the eyebrows should be. "Is that fair?"

How can I argue with her logic? I did, after all, indicate a desire to replicate the *maechi* experience for myself, and she opened her *wat* to me, accepting me without question. The least I can do is abide by her schedule.

I nod, and she continues her description of life at Thamtong, most likely a repeat of what she told us the day I turned off my ears and brain and decided with some unfamiliar part of me that I needed to ordain.

Scheduled daily activities consist of three things only: communal prayer and Dhamma study from 4:00 to 5:00 A.M., sweeping the temple grounds from 7:00 to 8:00 A.M., and mealtime at 8:30 A.M.

She points to the caves like dark eyes watching us from above.

"You may remain in your room during Dhamma study."

I stiffen my features to remain impassive. Unsure of how I feel, knowing how closely Thai women study foreigners, a giggle at the ready; nonetheless, Dhamma study seems like one of the few opportunities for communal interaction. Do I really want to forgo it?

"I will come to teach you privately each evening at six o'clock."

It is settled. I cannot refuse such an honor. My presence obviously complicates her life, adding another duty to her personal schedule. She appears not to mind, however.

Before leaving, Maechi Roongdüan gives me a brief lesson in the simplest levels of walking and seated meditation. I try my best to focus. For seated meditation, I'm supposed to clear my mind and concentrate only on my breath, inwardly noting the rising and falling of my diaphragm. Distractions—internal or external—are to be noted as they arise. For walking meditation, I should break down each step in walking and make internal "note" of it before proceeding. Every desire, such as wanting to stop, should be noted prior to taking action.

"Eventually you will progress to higher levels," she assures me. I must look skeptical. She explains that for seated meditation, it means focusing on an increasing number of key points on the body. For walking meditation, it entails noting each tiny movement involved in walking, such as raising the heel, lifting the arch, swinging the foot, touching the ground.

"Do walking meditation for twenty to thirty minutes at a time. And sitting for fifteen to twenty. I'll return in a few hours."

Back in my room, I stare at the walls, shoulders shaking with the effort to keep from screaming. As a child, no matter how hard life became, I always had books. And even in college, where I seemed to have lost everything else, I had the distractions of television and sleep. These very things are now forbidden. All I have are the contents of my own mind.

My body and mind feel thick, as cottony as my stubborn robes. I've been dazed, perhaps even concussive, for hours, Maechi Roongdüan's terrifying announcements just one more in a series of strange occurrences beginning the instant I stumbled out of the darkened sanctum of Wat Phra Singh and slipped on new shoes.

When she returns in the afternoon, Maechi Roongdüan stands on the path outside my room and calls: "Maechi Faith!"

"Yes?" I come to the doorway. I feel like a silly Thai girl, perpetually teetering on a giggle. How is that I, who have been *maechi* for all of one afternoon, am called by the same title as she?

I stand aside for her to enter, but she says, "Come," and turns toward the path. Perhaps there is a rule of deportment banning us from entering each other's sleeping quarters.

We walk to the *sala*, an open-air pavilion, to practice sitting and walking postures. Maechi Roongdüan says, "At first you will be bored. Everyone in their rooms. No one to talk to. All day and nothing to do. You'll have to 'note': to focus on all that you do and all that you intend to do. And when you become bored, note it. You will see that it rises and falls, comes into being and fades—just like everything else. You have to live in the present, be aware only of the present. If you see this, you see the Dhamma."

She cautions me to work gently into "mindful life," sleeping and eating little. I should be aware in all four postures: standing, walking, sitting, and even sleeping. Kneeling down, touching the mat, spreading out the body. The rise and fall of the abdomen as I wait for sleep. Upon waking, I should take a deep breath and note, *knowing, knowing, knowing,* thereby becoming aware of my body and myself at the instant of awakening.

"Meditation is simply training the mind to become alert and aware," she explains. "At first it seems difficult and picayune." (She actually uses the English word "picayune"!) "Soon it will become automatic. Until then, note everything, gently. You do not need to try to think of 'truth.' Truth comes on its own once the mind is cleared."

Despite my first experience with meditation not an hour ago, this discourages me. How I can spend hours each day just blanking out my mind? When can I rest? And what's the point? How much calm does one person possibly need? How will all this time pass if I'm always slow, precise, aware? Going to the bathroom is an ideological act! I long for sleep, some mental respite.

With a smile, Maechi Roongdüan hands me two books, written in English and gathers her robes in a dimpled hand. "If I tell you the truth," she said, "you will forget it. But if you experience it, touch it for yourself, you will never forget." She stands, and I see the doors to my old life slamming shut. "You are here to prove the truth of the Buddha's Dhamma yourself."

I stare at her back, erect and graceful as it recedes. Somewhere in the deepest recesses of my mind, I've been clinging to the idea that this is only research, that despite shaving my head and eyebrows, despite taking the precepts, despite leaving friends and family behind to move into the forest, I didn't really have to change my life. Now I see it—I'm not here to observe women's monastic lives; rather, she intends to make a nun out of me!

The Anthropology of Myself

My first few days here in the *wat*, I copy out translations of prayers in three languages—Pali transcription, English, Thai. Now both the sacred and the profane grace the pages. I even call upon my meager math skills to construct graphs and charts of the time spent mindfully or in meditation.

And finally it registers. Not only am I collecting data for an anthropological thesis to be delivered in some future dream sequence (hazy save for the applause echoing through Harvard's marble halls), but I approach life the same way, through detachment and observation, experience reduced to bite-sized intellectual morsels to aid their digestion. Denied an external anthropological subject by Maechi Roongdüan, I've created one for myself *out* of myself! And hasn't she pointed the way, with her declaration that I am here to prove the truth of the Dhamma for myself? With the story of her own ordination being an experiment against Buddhism.

Somehow I've managed to compartmentalize my mind into both participant and observer, turning one unblinking eye on this bumbling, determined foreign *maechi*. Anthropologist and detective, I search daily for "the material and mental processes" the Buddhists claim make up the individual. In the absence of a science of the Other, I've become enamored of the anthropology of myself.

And so, in preparation for the inevitable encounter, I burn through Buddhist texts in Thai and English at a rate of a hundred pages a night. Every evening I crawl beneath my gauzy mosquito netting, wedge the lavender blanket under my aching legs, and hunch over my kerosene lantern. Some books Maechi Roongdüan finds for me, ending our nightly teaching with a flourish as she produces yet another book with the pale orange paper cover of Buddhist publications from the folds of her robes, a magician unleashing a string of monochromatic scarves. Others I brought with me, figuring boredom would force me finally to study them.

My research until now has focused on the sociological relationship between Theravada Buddhism and gender. Strange as it sounds,

I've read very little about the Buddhist tenets themselves and even less on meditation.

How to identify the catalyst for my growing obsession with practice? Part is certainly a Western drive to succeed, a subconscious plan to achieve through practice the only avenue of achievement open to me. Part grows undeniably from the power of what I'm experiencing during meditation: odd visions and sensations I keep to myself, recording them somewhat guiltily in my journal as if evidence of an unbalanced mind. And part is no doubt the ever-dutiful student in me responding to any teacher's instruction.

During the second week, Maechi Roongdüan tells me to increase the number of times I sit in meditation each day. We're sitting on the circular stone bench beneath my shade tree, the giant finger of dusk pressing itself into the narrow gully behind us as into a seam. The sunset air stains everything rosy, including the two of us, and for the first time all day, bugs stop gnawing at me.

"Pardon?"

Maechi Roongdüan smiles at my weak protest, her silent eyes saying, *You think yesterday's task was impossible? Try this one!* She is careful to parcel out challenges in manageable swallows. Even if she weren't my sole source of social interaction, I might follow. She is a natural leader, a no-nonsense preacher with a glittering, critical mind and a poet's furled tongue. What I hope to become. In the meantime, she has decided to ratchet up the experiment.

She nods, fluttering her eyelashes in imitation of me. "Yes, you heard me—increase the number of sittings."

I laugh. "It's like the Elvis song—*all I want is all you've got.*"

Now it's her turn. "Pardon?"

Today we attack *dukkha,* suffering, the first of the Four Noble Truths. The inherent dissatisfactory nature of life is the basic premise of Buddhist belief. "Meditation sets up situations where we can see—through our bodies—that life is *dukkha,*" she explains, placing the splayed fingers of her right hand on her breastbone. "This is why you should be meditating more frequently in each twenty-four-hour cycle." More tests for the lab!

And though I'm not convinced I have what it takes to comply with her request, I agree. I'm beginning to see that meditation's focus on the self, which may appear narcissistic or egocentric at first glance, is in fact the exact opposite. It is through the medium of ourselves that we realize the truth about everyone and everything else. All human reactions and worldly occurrences.

During meditation, I witness my body functioning like a miniature cosmos. The *dukkha* arises as pain in my back; the *anicca*, or impermanence of all things, presents itself as the pain fades. So too the cycle of life. Whatever knowledge and experience I acquire relates itself to the crises of humankind, the very flux of the universe.

Before, like many Westerners, I thought that Buddhism encouraged us to ignore worldly problems. I imagined the goal of meditation was to blank our emotions or refuse to acknowledge them, perhaps depositing them in the subconscious to fester. Now I see I was wrong. Buddhism tells us we must deal with the pains of the world in order to conquer them, a lesson I long embraced in political work. I've known since childhood that ignoring the bad only prolongs its reign. And now spirituality, my would-be escape from both society's and my own ills, teaches the same lesson. (Oh, how I should have known!)

As our rosy faces darken and still with the coming of tropical night, Maechi Roongdüan extracts an orange pamphlet from her sleeve entitled *The Foundations of Mindfulness* and talks about the importance of notation. "Awareness serves as a dam to desire," she explains. "By acknowledging our desires, we allow them to build and then fade. Saying, 'I don't want to think about that—it's not good,' allows it to fester. We then act explosively, without awareness-or control."

She begins to gather her robes, one hand twisting from inside, and elaborates. "For example, if a *maechi* develops the desire to go to the movies, she must note, *wanting to go to the movies*. Then she will know herself, her desire and the futility of it. The desire will increase, then eventually pass away." Her eyes twinkle, as if reading my entire history. "Notation gives us the time to establish volitional intention *before* action."

As she stands to leave, the sun drops behind her shoulder. Perhaps sensing my nightly panic as each time I'm left alone, my only human interaction concluded for yet another twenty-four-hour cycle, she smiles gently and tells me that I should be bored or I'm not doing it right (in that case, I must be doing one hell of a job). She departs, moving in that deliberate yet vigorous way of hers, leaving me alone beneath the tree.

In the dark I place my hand on the cement bench, feeling for her warm imprint.

Dignity and Restraint

Thanissaro Bhikkhu

One of the basic definitions of the Buddhist dharma is "passionlessness."
Of course, that doesn't mean a deadened state where you find no joy or
pleasure in life. What it means is that you are no longer the slave of every
passing attachment, temptation, or emotion. In this sense, to be passionless
is to be fully human—aware, joyous, sensitive, and free. Thanissaro
Bhikkhu, an American Theravadin abbot, laments two virtues that
are no longer fashionable in a society built on satisfying our cravings.

It's always interesting to notice how words disappear from common usage. We have them in our passive vocabulary, we know their meaning, but they tend to disappear from day-to-day conversation—which usually means that they've disappeared from the way we shape our lives. Several years back I gave a dhamma talk in which I happened to mention the word *dignity*. After the talk, a woman in the audience who had emigrated from Russia came up to me and said that she had never heard Americans use the word *dignity* before. She had learned it when she studied English in Russia, but she had never heard people use it here. And it's good to think about why. Where and why did it disappear?

I think the reason is related to another word that tends to disappear from common usage, and that's *restraint*: forgoing certain pleasures, not because we have to, but because they go against our principles. The opportunity to indulge in those pleasures may be there, but we learn how to say no. This of course is related to another word we tend not to use, and that's *temptation*. Even though we don't have to believe that there's someone out there actively tempting us, there are things all around us that do, that tempt us to give in to our desires. And an important part of our practice is that we exercise restraint. As the Buddha says, restraint over the eyes, ears, nose, tongue, and body is good, as is restraint in terms of our actions, our speech, and our thoughts.

What's good about it? Well, for one thing, if we don't have any restraint, we don't have any control over where our lives are going. Anything that comes our way immediately pulls us into its wake. We don't have any strong sense of priorities, of what's really worthwhile, of what's not worthwhile, of the pleasures we'd gain by saying no to other pleasures. How do we rank the pleasures in our lives, the happiness, the sense of well-being that we get in various ways? Actually, there's a sense of well-being that comes from being totally independent, from not needing other things. If that state of well-being doesn't have a chance to develop, if we're constantly giving in to our impulse to do this or take that, we'll never know what that well-being is.

At the same time, we'll never know our impulses. When you simply ride with your impulses, you don't understand their force. They're like the currents below the surface of a river: only if you try to build a dam across the river will you detect those currents and appreciate how strong they are. So we have to look at what's important in life, develop a strong sense of priorities, and be willing to say no to the currents that would lead to less worthwhile pleasures. As the Buddha said, if you see a greater pleasure that comes from forsaking a lesser pleasure, be willing to forsake that lesser pleasure for the greater one.

Sounds like a no-brainer, but if you look at the way most people live, they don't think in those terms. They want everything that comes their way. They want to have their cake and enlightenment, too; to win at chess without sacrificing a single pawn. Even when they meditate, their purpose in developing mindfulness is to gain an even more intense appreciation of the experience of every moment in life. That's something you never see in the Buddha's teachings. His theme is always that you have to let go of this in order to gain that, give this up in order to arrive at that. There's always a trade-off.

So we're not practicing for a more intense appreciation of sights, scents, sounds, tastes, smells, or tactile sensations. We're practicing to realize that the mind doesn't need to depend on those things, and that it's healthier without such dependencies. Even though the body requires a modicum of the requisites of food, clothing, shelter, and medicine, there's an awful lot that it doesn't need. And because our use of the requisites involves suffering, both for ourselves and for everyone else involved in their production, we owe it to ourselves and to others to keep pushing the envelope in the direction of restraint, to give up the things we don't need, so as to be as unburdensome as possible.

This is why so much of the training lies in learning to put this aside, put that aside, give this up, give that up. Developing this habit on the external level makes us reflect on the internal level: Which attachments in the mind would be good to give up? Could our mind survive perfectly well without the things we tend to crave? The Buddha's answer is yes. In fact, the mind is better off that way.

Still, a very strong part of our mind resists that teaching. We may give up things for a time, but our attitude is often, "I gave up this for a certain while, I gave up that for so long, now I can get back to it." On retreat people tend to make a lot of vows—"Well, I'll give up cigarettes for the retreat, I'll give up newspapers"—but as soon as the retreat is over they go back to their old ways. They've missed the whole point, which is that if you can survive for three months without those things, you can probably survive for the rest of the year without them as well. Hopefully, during those three months you've seen the advantages of giving them up. So you can decide, "Okay, I'm going to continue giving them up." Even though you may have the opportunity to say yes to your desires, you remind yourself to say no. This principle of restraint, of giving things up, applies to every step of the path. When you're practicing generosity, you have to give up things that you might enjoy. You realize the benefits that come from saying no to your greed and allowing other people to enjoy what you're giving away.

For example, when you're living in a group, there's food to be shared by all. If you give up some of your share so others can enjoy a bigger share, you're creating a better atmosphere in the group. So you have to ask yourself, "Is the gratification I get from taking this thing worth the trade?" And you begin to see the advantages of giving up on this level. This is where dignity begins to come back into our lives: We're not just digestive tracts. We're not slaves to our desires. We're their masters.

The same with the precepts: there may be things that you'd like to do or say, but you don't do them, you don't say them, because they're dishonest or hurtful. Even if you feel that you might get ahead or gain some advantage by saying them, you don't, because they go against your principles. You find that you don't stoop to the activities that you used to, and there's a sense of honor, a sense of dignity that comes with that: that you can't be bought off with those particular pleasures, with the temptation to take the easy way out. At the same time, you're showing respect for the dignity, the worth, of those around you. And again, this gives dignity to our lives.

When you're meditating, the same process holds. People sometimes wonder why they can't get their minds to concentrate. It's because they're not willing to give up other interests, even for the time being. A thought comes and you just go right after it without checking to see where it's going. An idea comes that sounds interesting, that looks intriguing, and you've got a whole hour to think about whatever you want. If that's your attitude toward the meditation period, nothing's going to get accomplished.

You have to realize that this is your opportunity to get the mind stable and still. In order to do that, you have to give up all kinds of other thoughts. Thoughts about the past, thoughts about the future, figuring this out, planning for that, whatever: you have to put them all aside. No matter how wonderful or sophisticated those thoughts are, you just say no to them.

Now, if you've been practicing generosity and have really been serious about practicing the precepts, you've developed the ability to say no skillfully, which is why generosity and the precepts are not optional parts of the practice. They're the foundation of meditation. When you've made a practice of generosity and virtue, the mind's ability to say no to its impulses has been strengthened and given finesse. You've seen the good results that come from being able to restrain yourself in terms of your words and deeds. You've seen that restraint means the opposite of deprivation. Now, as you meditate, you've got the opportunity to restrain your thoughts and see what good comes from that. If you really are able to say no to your vagrant ideas, you find that the mind can settle down with a much greater sense of satisfaction in its state of concentration than could possibly come with those ideas, no matter how fantastic they are.

You find that the satisfaction of giving in to those distractions just slips through your fingers as if it had never been there. It's like trying to grab a handful of water or a fistful of air. But the sense of well-being that comes with repeatedly being able to bring your mind to a state of stillness, even if you haven't gone all the way, begins to permeate everything else in your life. You find that the mind really is a more independent thing than you imagined it could be. It doesn't need to give in to those impulses. It can say no to itself.

The mind is even more independent when you develop the discernment that's able to dig out the source of those impulses and see where they come from, to the point where the whole issue of temptation is no longer an issue because there's nothing tempting. You look at the things that would pull the mind out of its stillness, out of its independence, and you realize they're just not worth it. In the past you were training the mind in a sense of hunger—that's what we do when we keep giving in to impulses: we're training ourselves in hunger. But now you train the mind in the direction of having enough, of being free, and you realize that the sense of hunger that you used to cultivate is really a major source of suffering. You're much better off without it.

It's important that we realize the role that restraint plays in overcoming the problem of suffering and finding true well-being for ourselves. You realize that you're not giving up anything you really need. You're a lot better off without it. There's a part of the mind that resists this truth, and our culture hasn't been very helpful at all because it encourages that resistance: "Give in to this impulse, give in to that impulse, obey your thirst. It's good for the economy, it's good for you spiritually. Watch out, if you repress your desires you're going to get tied up in psychological knots." The lessons our culture teaches us—to go out and buy, buy, buy; be greedy, be greedy; give in, give in—are all over the place. And what kind of dignity comes from following those messages? The dignity of a fish gobbling down bait. We've got to unlearn those habits, unlearn those messages, if we want to revive words like *dignity* and *restraint*, and to reap the rewards that the realities of dignity and restraint have to offer our minds.

The True Spirit
of the Grain

Edward Espe Brown

*Cooking and eating have long been recognized as important spiritual
practices—our state of mind is vividly displayed at the stove and the
table. The great Zen teacher Dogen said, "The kitchen is the heart of
the monastery," and for many of us, it is the center of our home. Edward
Espe Brown is a leading disciple of the great Zen teacher Shunryu Suzuki
Roshi, and he has learned a lot about eating sanely and cooking artfully.*

Suzuki Roshi once said to us, "I don't understand you Americans—
when you put so much milk and sugar on your cereal, how can you
taste the true spirit of the grain?" How, indeed? And who among us
had ever aspired to taste the true spirit of the grain, or even conceived that there was such a thing? Didn't we all just add condiments
to our liking?

In 1967, we were starting the first Zen meditation retreat community in the West—Tassajara Zen Mountain Center. Since I had
been meditating for two years and had worked as a cook for all of
two and a half months, I guess I was an obvious choice. Wouldn't I
like to be head cook at the new center? Not knowing I couldn't do it,
I said, "Sure."

Arriving at Tassajara in April, I became acquainted with the local customs, which included offering a wide variety of condiments for the morning oatmeal, cream of wheat or rice cream. White sugar was offered, and brown sugar certainly. And then—"Because some people don't want to eat sugar; you know, it's bad for you"—we also provided honey and molasses. Then there was milk.

Clearly this was an earlier era, before the intense fervor for soy milk, rice milk, 2 percent milk and nonfat milk. "Lactose intolerance" and "calorie consciousness" were not yet part of being spiritually advanced: "Drink thee a white liquid with little or no fat. Or better yet, exploit thee not the cow, but keep it white and light. Or, anyway, get some good karma points."

But I digress. Besides milk we put out cream or half-and-half. And for those who wanted it. . .canned milk! We might also have had small dishes of raisins and shakers of cinnamon. Hey, this is America—have it your way.

Roshi continued, "Do you think you can make every moment taste just the way you want it to? Add milk and honey to everything?" (Yes.) "How will you learn to appreciate the true spirit of the grain? How will you learn to experience things as-it-is?"

It's the first noble truth, I guess: Reality is fundamentally unfixable, and—the second noble truth—it doesn't taste the way you'd like it to. Yet when you let go of fixed ideas of what you want, and taste things with mindfulness and receptivity (truth number four), you can come to rest or settle in the "true spirit of the grain."

Life brings a variety of flavors. Wouldn't it be liberating simply to go ahead and taste the tart or bitter along with the sweet, the plain along with the superbly seasoned? Don't you get annoyed and fatigued when you feel you have to doctor everything? When welcomed, the oatmeal's plain, moist earthiness, hinting of sunlight, opens the heart. And tasting the heart of the oatmeal is tasting your own plain goodness. I know, an inner voice is saying you deserve the sugar, the whole-fat milk, the raisins, but do you want to slavishly chase after everything that voice hankers for?

For me, cooking was a sensual experience from the start. I looked, smelled, tasted, and touched. Is this so hard to comprehend?

I wonder, because again and again people want to get it "right," make it the way it "should" be (according to the recipe). I learned to cook using *The Zen Macrobiotic Cookbook*, but I wasn't following it exactly. It was a place to start. Of course, the whole tradition of cookbooks has a bit of pretense and high-status mongering: recipes from the famed restaurant, recipes to impress your family and friends (or really healthy dishes to nourish your loved ones). "Does what you cook measure up to what we cook? Better get our book!"

Yet most of what I was doing wasn't in the cookbook: I was marveling at the intricate cross section of a cabbage; cutting the celery stalks in commas, boomerangs and long strips; playing with colors. I would try putting the carrot pieces in the wooden bowl, the enamel-covered magenta bowl, the thrift-store emerald bowl, the silver bowl, only to shift later as the ingredients accumulated: Gosh, let's change that—green peppers in the candy-apple red bowl, red peppers in the lavender. No one else would see the magnificent display of colors arrayed before cooking. Subtle contrasts or stark? Should I have been a painter?

Cooking wasn't about getting something done. I was absorbed in a world of beauty, fragrance, and delight. And I wasn't alone any longer—I had all these companions. For dinner parties I bought my guests a large bottle of sake and busied myself serving food and refilling the little sake cups. I didn't need to be brilliantly social after all. I could provide the space. I could offer sustenance.

This is not so complicated, really, yet most of us need to be "taught": as Zen Master Tenkei said, "See with your eyes, smell with your nose, taste with your tongue, nothing in the universe is hidden. What else would you have me say?" Well, venerable Zen teacher, would you tell me how to get it right, so nobody complains? How do I make things taste the way I like? How about telling me that? And the venerable one answers, "There's not enough milk and honey in the entire universe." Or, "Upside-down idea. What are you thinking?"

Could you just have your own life? Come to your senses? Experience for yourself what's what? One day when I was tasting a soup—it could have been lentil or minestrone—I realized that it didn't taste the way I wanted it to taste. And how could I make it taste that way? More pepper, lemon, garlic, oil, butter? On the other hand, why not give it a rest—was there something sacred about the flavor I had in mind, that I had to make my soup taste that way? The problem with recipes is that they blind us to the reality that there are no recipes. Could we aim to bring out the best in one another?

I have hardly ever been able to follow food guidelines—"Eat this. Don't eat that." What do they—those who know—know? They are in their heads, speaking to other heads, about matters good and bad, about stuff right and wrong. I want life. I want to try things, taste things, savor things. I like being curious and seeing what I can discover and what pleases me deeply.

Years ago I came across a small article in *Prevention* magazine in which the author talked about a study that revealed how food prepared well in an aesthetically pleasing manner was more nourishing than the same ingredients prepared without care. I've always thought so. But to care about such matters is rare in our culture. Most of us give ourselves very little permission to have taste. It's a bad word. "Just eat it, honey, it's good for you," is one tendency. Another tendency is to eat junk food prepared with attractive flavor-buttons (that is, the appearance of taste): sweet, salt, grease, and perhaps a spot of salsa.

Permission to have taste is also permission to cultivate or develop taste: What do lentils taste like? How does salt change the flavor? Or pepper? Does garlic bring out the flavor of lentils or mask it? Which is which? Are we hiding the true spirit, or inviting it to come forward? You train your palate. And I believe this is a healthy way of living. It is intelligence at work, rather than blindly obeying the master (science, God, religion, nature, Zen, the Tao).

Colors, flavors, smells—wouldn't it be much more satisfying to live in this world, instead of the world of rules to be followed or disobeyed? That world of rules is where you perpetually wobble on the "goodness" scale, usually resting on "not quite good enough." Ah, to taste and enjoy, to play and discover—in that world, the true nature of things comes home to the heart.

Nothing Holy:
A Zen Primer ꩜

Norman Fischer

*Zen is the most enigmatic of Buddhist traditions, and intentionally so.
Its doctrine is not codified, its art is subtle, and its meditation techniques
are either formless or designed to be inaccessible to the conceptual mind.
Poet and Zen teacher Norman Fischer explains more about this "special
transmission outside the scriptures" and its influence and practice in
the West.*

A Zen Wave

Like ocean waters, intellectual currents are always in motion. They
churn up organic matter from below, creating and extending powerful nutritional mixtures. When groups of people at a particular historical moment begin to experience the world in a particular way,
naturally they meet and talk, ponder, read and write. They are open
to diverse influences. Eventually the energy of their discourse crests
and breaks like a sudden wave, and soon people around them find
themselves affected. So cultures mix, dissolve, and change.

In this way, a Zen wave broke on North American shores in the
middle of the twentieth century. It probably didn't begin as a Zen
wave at all, but rather as a reflex to the unprecedented violence the

first part of the century had seen. After two devastating world wars, small groups of people here and there in the West were beginning to realize, as if coming out of a daze, that the modernist culture they had depended on to humanize and liberalize the planet wasn't doing that at all. Instead it was bringing large-scale suffering and dehumanization. What was the alternative?

In the early 1950s, D. T. Suzuki, the great Japanese Zen scholar and practitioner, arrived at Columbia University in New York to teach some classes on Zen. Suzuki was a magnet for the yearning that was at that time still underground. The people who met him, attended his classes, or were otherwise influenced by his visit constitute a *Who's Who* of American cultural innovation at that time. Alan Watts, whose popular books on Zen were hugely influential, was there. So was John Cage, who from then on wrote music based on chance operations, on the theory that being open to the present moment, without conscious control, was the essence of Suzuki's—and Zen's—message. Cage influenced Merce Cunningham, the dancer-choreographer, who in turn influenced many others in the performance art field. For Allen Ginsberg, Jack Kerouac, Gary Snyder, Philip Whalen, and the other Beat generation poets, Zen was a primary source, a sharp tool for prying the lid off literary culture as they knew it.

Within ten years, lively Japanese Zen masters who, from their side of the Pacific, had also been dreaming a Zen wave, were coming to America to settle. With the 1960s and the coming of age of a new generation radicalized by the Vietnam War and psychotropic drugs, what had been churning underneath for decades broke out in a glorious and exhilarating spray. The first Zen centers in America were bursting with students willing to make serious commitments right away. It was an exciting and confusing time, perhaps unprecedented in the history of world religions.

I was part of this Zen wave. The cultural undercurrents I have been describing took place during my formative years. A student of literature and religion, I was sensitive enough to feel the brokenness that lay under the placid social veneer of the American culture I was raised in. So when I discovered Zen in the writings of D. T. Suzuki in the late 1960s, I was dumbstruck. Here was exactly what I needed, a completely new way of experiencing the world. The uncompromising, experiential, and immediate search for meaning that Zen proposed, without need of doctrine or belief, struck a chord in me. Like so many, I wasn't looking for a new religion: I wanted a way to blast through the options that seemed available to me. I wanted real freedom. Zen promised this.

So in 1970, I moved to California in search of Zen and an entirely new life. I learned how to meditate. I practiced alone in cabins in the redwood forest in Northern California for some years, until I saw that I needed to practice with others. I began my formal Zen training at the Berkeley Zen Center and, after five years there, enrolled in Tassajara, the first Zen monastery in the Western world. I have been practicing Zen full-time ever since.

ZEN ROOTS

What is Zen, and how does it differ from other schools of Buddhism?

Unlike Christianity, in which early, wild schisms led eventually to centralized control, Buddhism has always been open-ended and various. While a few key concepts (like the four noble truths, with their simultaneously gloomy and hopeful view of human nature) have always held firm, methods, philosophies, and interpretations have differed widely. India was the first Buddhist country. Through the centuries, it gradually spawned hundreds of sects and sub-sects, thousands of scriptures, and tens of thousands of commentaries on those scriptures. When Buddhism spread over Central Asian trade routes to China, all this material came at once. The Chinese were blasted with a cacophony of religious insight that was exotic, extravagant, and, most important, foreign. The Chinese had long cherished their own twin traditions of Confucianism and Taoism and were resistant to ideologies introduced by barbarians from beyond the borders of the "Middle Kingdom." There was also a severe linguistic challenge for the Chinese in digesting the Buddhist message from abroad. The Sanskrit language was so different from Chinese in sensibility and syntax that translation was almost impossible.

Gradually, Indian and Central Asian Buddhism began to be reshaped by its encounter with Chinese culture. This reshaping eventually led to the creation of Zen, an entirely new school of Buddhism. (The word *Zen* is the Japanese pronunciation of the Chinese *Ch'an*, which means "meditation." Here we use *Zen* because it is the word generally used in the West. Ch'an, though, did not come to Japan and become "Zen" until around the eighth century.)

Bodhidharma is the legendary founder of Zen in China. He is said to have arrived in China about 520 C.E. (Buddhism had by then been known in China for about four hundred years.) He was soon summoned to the emperor, who had questions for him. "According to the teachings, how do I understand the merit I have accrued in building temples and making donations to monks?" the emperor asked. Bodhidharma, usually depicted as a scowling, hooded, bearded figure, shot back, "There is no merit." "What then is the meaning of the Buddha's Holy Truths?" the emperor asked. "Empty, nothing holy," Bodhidharma replied. Shocked, the emperor imperiously asked, "Who addresses me thus?" "I don't know," Bodhidharma replied, turned on his heel, and left the court, to which he never returned.

He repaired to a distant monastery, where, it is said, he sat facing a wall for nine years, in constant meditation. A single disciple sought him out, and to test the disciple's sincerity, Bodhidharma refused to see him. The disciple stood outside in the snow all night long. In the morning he presented Bodhidharma with his severed arm as a token of his seriousness. The monk became Bodhidharma's heir, and thus began the Zen transmission in China. So, at least, the story goes.

This legend illustrates Zen's style and values. Zen is a pithy, stripped-down, determined, uncompromising, cut-to-the-chase, meditation-based Buddhism that takes no interest in doctrinal refinements. Not relying on scripture, doctrine, or ritual, Zen is verified by personal experience and is passed on from master to disciple, hand to hand, ineffably, through hard, intimate training.

Though Zen recognizes—at least loosely—the validity of normative Buddhist scriptures, it has created its own texts over the generations. Liberally flavored with doses of Taoism and Confucianism and Chinese poetry, and written in informal language studded with Chinese folk sayings and street slang, Zen literature is built on legendary anecdotes of the great masters. Buddha is barely mentioned, and when he is he is often playfully reviled. "Old man Shakyamuni," the saying goes, "is only halfway there." Like most Zen masters, Bodhidharma left little written material. But here are four Zen dicta ascribed to him, which are always quoted to illustrate the essential Zen spirit:

A special transmission outside the scriptures.
No dependency on words and letters.
Pointing directly to the human mind.
Seeing into one's nature and attaining Buddhahood.

This shoot-from-the-hip Zen spirit appeals to the American mind, which is as iconoclastic and anti-authoritarian as it is religious. In any case, it appealed to me and to the many others like me who were and are looking for a direct route to awakening. It has also appealed, over many generations, to millions of Buddhist practitioners in the Far East, who, conditioned by the Taoism and Confucianism that had been imported everywhere from China, could easily relate to the Zen message and style. Although the Zen school created controversy at first in all the countries it spread to, it eventually became by far the most successful school of Buddhism in China, Korea, Japan, and Vietnam. By the mid-1980s, the Zen traditions of all these countries had been transmitted to America.

Zen Methods

Although Zen eventually developed traditions of study and ritual, its emphasis on personal experience has always made it a practice-oriented tradition. The practice is meditation. "Sitting Zen" (Japanese: zazen) has, as Bodhidharma's legend shows, always been central in Zen training centers, where monks rise early each morning for meditation practice and do long retreats consisting of many, many silent, unmoving hours on the cushion. Zazen is an intensely simple practice. It is generally taught without steps, stages, or frills. "Just sit!" the master admonishes, by which he or she means, sit upright in good posture, paying careful attention to breathing in your belly until you are fully alert and present. This sense of being present, with illumination and intensity, is the essence of zazen, and although there are many approaches to Zen meditation, they all come back to this. Life's secret, life's essence, and the truth and power of Buddhist liberation all come down to this intense and illuminated presence which is beyond words and concepts. Though it cannot be explained, it can be experienced and expressed through the daily actions of a Zen life.

Because the practice of intensive zazen is so central, Zen practice is essentially monastic. That is to say, it depends on a life that allows for long periods of concentrated meditation. In the Zen monastery, life is entirely organized around sitting in the meditation hall. But zazen is also understood to be something more than this sitting. It is conceived of as a state of mind or being that extends into all activities. Work is zazen; eating is zazen; sleeping, walking, standing, going to the toilet—all are zazen practice. In Soto Zen, the Japanese school practiced extensively in the West, there is an especially strong emphasis on this "moving Zen." Soto monastic life tends to be highly ritualized, so as to promote concentration in all things. There is, for instance, a special elegant and mindful practice, called *oryoki,* for eating ritualized meals in the meditation hall.

Zen schools are more or less divisible into those that emphasize a curriculum of verbal meditation objects—like koans—and those that do not. Emphasizing daily life practice as zazen, Soto Zen centers generally do not work with a set koan curriculum and method, though koans are studied and contemplated. Because of this, Soto Zen has traditionally been criticized by the koan schools (the best-known koan school is the Rinzai school of Japan) as dull, overly precious, and quietistic, in contrast to the dynamic and lively engagement of the koan path. But the koan way also has its critics, who see the emphasis on words, meaning, and insight as working against real, nonconceptual Zen living. Koan training systems also have the disadvantage of fostering competition and obsession with advancement in the system.

In koan Zen, contemplation of a koan begins with zazen practice. The practitioner comes to intense presence with body and breath, and then brings up the koan almost as a physical object, repeating it over and over again with breathing, until words and meaning dissolve and the koan is "seen." This practice is done in the context of an intensive retreat led by a qualified, Zen koan teacher, whom the practitioner visits several times each day for an interview. In the interview, the student presents his or her understanding of the koan (however lame it may be) and receives a response from the teacher (however understated it may be) that reorients the search. Eventually, with luck, diligence, and a few judicious hints, the koan's essence is penetrated, and the practitioner enters the interview room with playful joy, capable of answering any sort of question about the koan, however nonconceptual or absurd the question may seem. The responses to koans are traditional stock answers, and although some real experience is generally necessary in order to "pass" a particular koan, it is clear that one can pass many koans without necessarily undergoing any significant spiritual transformation.

Like all systems, the koan system can degenerate into a self-protective and self-referential enclosure. It's the teacher's job to see that this doesn't happen, but sometimes it is not preventable. There are many different systems of koan study, but most of them emphasize humor, spontaneity, and openness. The koan method is, at its best, a unique and marvelous expression of human religious sensibility.

Zen Schools

Zen has had a long and varied history in several different Far Eastern cultures. Each culture has produced a tradition that is recognizable as Zen but differs slightly from all the others. Vietnamese Zen is the one most influenced by the Theravada tradition. It tends to be

gentle in expression and method, to emphasize purity and careful-
ness, and to combine Zen with some Theravadan teaching and
methodology. In China, Zen eventually became the only Buddhist
school, inclusive of all the others, so contemporary Ch'an includes
many faith-based Mahayana practices that existed initially in other
Buddhist schools, especially faith in and repetition of the name of
Amida Buddha, the savior Buddha who will ensure rebirth in an
auspicious heaven to those who venerate him. Korean Zen is the
most stylized and dramatic of the Zen schools, and also the most
austere. Korean Zen includes prostration practice (repeated, ener-
getic, full-to-the-floor bows of veneration) and intensive chanting
practice, and has a hermit tradition, something virtually unknown
in Japanese Zen.

Within each of the Asian Zen traditions there are several
schools, and within schools the styles of individual teachers often
differ greatly. Still, it is remarkable how essentially similar the various teachers within a particular Zen "dharma family" can be in personal style and mode of expression, even though, paradoxically, each
one is quite distinctive and individualistic. This uncanny fact—
radical individuality within the context of shared understanding—
seems to be an indelible feature of Zen.

LINEAGE AND TEACHER

A key Zen story, shared by all the schools: Once Buddha was giving a
talk on Vulture Peak. In the middle of the talk he paused and held up
a flower. Everyone was silent. Only Mahakasyapa broke into a smile.
Buddha then said, "I have the Treasury of the True Dharma Eye, the
ineffable mind of Nirvana, the real form of No Form, the flawless
gate of the Teaching. Not dependent on words, it is a special transmission outside tradition. I now entrust it to Mahakasyapa."

This story, however historically unverifiable, represents the beginning of the Zen transmission, said to start directly with the Buddha. The story tells us two things: First, although the Buddha taught
many true and useful teachings and techniques, the essence of what

he taught is simple and ineffable. Holding up a flower is one expression of this essence. Second, the very simplicity and ineffability of this essential teaching requires that it be handed on from master to disciple in mutual, wordless understanding. There can't be a Zen training program with exams and certifications, with objectives, goals, and demonstrable, measurable mastery.

While wordless understanding seems a bit mystical and precious, it may not be as strange as it seems. We are all familiar with the transformation that takes place in apprenticeship and mentorship relationships, processes that involve a wordless give and take between individuals, and in which something quite hard to define is passed on. My own teacher once made me a calligraphy that read, "I have nothing to give you but my Zen spirit." Although the "Zen spirit" may be hard to define, measure, and explicitly verify, it can be appreciated when you feel it.

I referred to "dharma families" in Zen. These are lineage families, and lineage is a key element in Zen training. While Zen practice can be done without benefit of a teacher, having a teacher is important and, in the end, crucial if one is to realize the depth of Zen practice and make it completely one's own. Although the Zen teacher must embody Zen and express it in all his or her words and deeds, a Zen teacher is not exactly a guru, a Buddha archetype at the center of a student's practice. To be sure, respect for and confidence in the teacher is essential if one is to undergo the transformation in consciousness that Zen promises. But the Zen teacher is also an ordinary, conditioned human being, simply a person, however much he or she has realized of Zen. This paradox—that the teacher is to be appreciated as a realized spiritual adept and at the same time as an ordinary individual with rough edges and personality quirks—seems to go to the heart of Zen's uniqueness. Through the relationship to the teacher, the student comes to embrace all beings, including himself or herself, in this way.

In Asia, lineages through the generations tended to be separate and usually opposing congregations. It was typical in the early days of the transmission of Zen to the West for teachers of different

lineages to be scornful of each other. There were centuries of tradition behind this prodigious failure to communicate. Thankfully, in
the West there is now much more sharing between the various lineages. In recent years in America, two organizations have been created to promote warm communication among the Zen lineages: the
American Zen Teachers Association, which includes teachers from
all lineages, and the Soto Zen Buddhist Association, which is made
up of teachers of the various lineages of Soto Zen, the largest Zen
tradition in the West.

TAKING THE PATH OF ZEN IN THE WEST

I've said that Zen is essentially monastic and depends on the intensive practice of sitting meditation. In the West, however, most Zen
practitioners are not monastics. While this may seem strange, it is
not at all strange if we consider "monastic" to be an attitude and a
level of seriousness, more than a particular lifestyle. Unlike Zen
laypeople in Asia, whose main practice is to support the monastic
establishment, Western Zen lay practitioners want to understand
Zen deeply and to practice it thoroughly, regardless of what their life
circumstances may be. In this sense, all Western Zen students are
"monastic," regardless of their life circumstances. All of them do
some form of monastic-style training within the context of their lay
lives. They sit in meditation regularly, either at home or at a local
temple, attend retreats, and live their daily lives with full attention
(or at least coming as close to this as they possibly can). They take lay
or priestly vows, and even sometimes enter monastic training at one
or more Zen centers for periods of time.

While there is a great deal of variety among the many American
Zen centers, in general their programs are open to the public, encouraging all who want to practice Zen at whatever level they wish to
practice, but emphasizing committed, ongoing practice—gradually
entered into—as the main road.

For someone who is interested in taking up Zen practice in
America, the approach is not difficult: surf the Web or the phone

book, find the location and schedule of the Zen establishment nearest you, show up and keep showing up as long as it suits you. Eventually you will learn the formalities of the local Zen meditation hall (most groups offer special instruction for beginners), and if you feel comfortable you will continue to attend meditation when you can.

Eventually you will sign up for *dokusan*, a private, intense, formal interview with a teacher. At some point you will hear about a one-day *sesshin* (a meditation retreat) and you'll try it out. You'll no doubt find it a daunting and at the same time uplifting experience. After some time you'll be ready to attend a seven-day sesshin, and that experience will feel like a real breakthrough to you, regardless of how many koans you do or do not pass, or how well or poorly you think you sat. Sesshin is a life-transforming experience, no matter what happens.

From there, if you continue, you will deepen your friendships with other practitioners. These relationships will seem to you, oddly, both closer and more distant than other relationships in your life. Closer because the feeling of doing Zen practice together bonds you deeply, and more distant because you may not exchange personal histories, opinions, and gossip as you might do with other friends. As time goes on you will establish a relationship with one or more of the local Zen teachers, and you will find these relationships increasingly warm and important in your life, so much so that perhaps someday you will want to take vows as a lay Zen practitioner, joining the lineage family.

If you go on practicing, as the years go by you may attend monastic training periods at one of the larger centers. If your life permits, you might want to stay at this center for a while—perhaps for many years, or for the rest of your life, eventually taking on the teachers and lineage there as your primary lineage. Or you may come back home and continue your ongoing practice, going back to the larger training center from time to time for more monastic experiences. Or, if it is impossible for you to get away from your family and work life for longer than a week at a time, or if you do not want to do this, you will continue with the practice of weeklong sesshin, and that will be enough.

It is also possible that you do not ever want to go to a weeklong sesshin, and that Zen classes, one-day retreats, meetings with the teacher from time to time, and the application of all that you are learning to the daily events of your life are the kind of practice you really need for your life, and that nothing more is necessary.

What will all this effort do for you? Everything and nothing. You will become a Zen student, devoted to your ongoing practice, to kindness and peacefulness, and to the ongoing, endless effort to understand the meaning of time, the meaning of your existence, the reason why you were born and will die. You will still have plenty of challenges in your life, you will still feel emotion, possibly more now than ever, but the emotion will be sweet, even if it is grief or sadness. Many things, good and bad, happen in a lifetime, but you won't mind. You will see your life and your death as a gift, a possibility. This is the essential point of Zen.

The Great Failure ❧

Natalie Goldberg

*It has its philosophies, rituals, and institutions, but at its heart the practice
of Buddhism is intensely personal, even intimate. It strips you down to a
nakedness beyond nakedness, with no private territory or even a self to hide
behind. Most intimate and embarrassing of all is the relationship with your
teacher, who loves you but knows all your tricks. Natalie Goldberg offers a
remembrance of her teacher, Dainin Katagiri Roshi, and a* cri de coeur
over all that was left incomplete and unanswered by his death.

Te-shan asked the old tea-cake woman, "Who is your
teacher? Where did you learn this?"

She pointed to a monastery a half mile away.

Te-shan visited Lung-t'an and questioned him far into
the night. Finally when it was very late, Lung-t'an said,
"Why don't you go and rest now?"

Te-shan thanked him and opened the door. "It's dark
outside. I can't see."

Lung-t'an lit a candle for him, but just as Te-shan turned
and reached out to take it, Lung-t'an blew it out.

At that moment Te-shan had a great enlightenment. Full
of gratitude, he bowed deeply to Lung-t'an.

The next day Lung-t'an praised Te-shan to the assembly
of monks. Te-shan brought his books and commentaries in

front of the building and lit them on fire, saying, "These notes are nothing, like placing a hair in vast space."

Then bowing again to his teacher, he left.

On a Thursday night I flew into Minneapolis and saw Katagiri Roshi's body laid out in the zendo, dead eighteen hours from a cancer he fought for over a year. It was incomprehensible that I would never see my beloved teacher again.

My father was the only one I knew who had sneered at death's bleak face as he fought in the righteous war that marked his life. Of everyone I knew, he alone did not seem afraid of the great darkness. "Nat, you're here and then you're not. Don't worry about it. It's not a big deal," he told me as he placed a pile of army photos on my lap. "The Japanese, you have to give it to 'em. They could really fight. Tough, good soldiers." Then he held up a black-and-white. "Here's your handsome daddy overseas."

Roshi also fought as a young man in World War II. He told a story about not wanting to kill and shooting in the air above enemy heads. I told that to my father. "What a lot of malarkey," my father sneered. "You don't believe that, do you? You're in battle, you fight."

My father met my teacher only once, about a year after I had married. We had just bought the lower half of a duplex on a leafy tree-lined one-way street six blocks from Zen Center in Minneapolis. I was in my early thirties, and my parents drove out for a week in July. They were still young, in their early sixties.

In the middle of one afternoon when no one was around, we slipped off our shoes and stepped onto the high-shined wooden floor of the zendo. My parents peered at bare white walls, black cushions, and a simple wooden altar with a statue and some flowers.

I heard the door in the hall open. "I bet that's Roshi."

My father's eyes grew wide. His face swung to the large screened window, and for a moment I thought he was going to crash through in a grand escape. Pearls of sweat formed on his upper lip.

Roshi turned the corner. They stood across the room from each other. The meeting was brief. They never shook hands. My father was subdued, withdrawn, and Roshi too wasn't his usual animated self.

I remember thinking, my father has become shy in front of a Zen master—finally someone tamed him.

I got it all wrong. He didn't give a shit about that. He had just encountered the enemy face to face. After Roshi exited, he hissed, "I fought them, and now you're studying with them."

"If this were your last moment on earth," Roshi cut the silence with these words late one night, "how would you sit?" We were waiting for the bell to ring. It was the end of a weeklong retreat. Our knees and backs ached. The candle flame hissed; the smell of incense from Eiheiji monastery (the Japanese training center for Soto Zen), shipped in cartons to Minnesota, soaked our clothes.

"You've got to be kidding. Just ring the damn bell," was the only thought that raced through my head.

On other occasions when he asked similar questions, my mind froze. Me, die? Not possible.

Death was something aesthetic, artistic; it had to do with the grand words "forever," "eternity," "emptiness." I never had known anyone who had died before. It was merely a practice point: everything is impermanent. Sure, sure. But really it was inconceivable that my body would not be my body. I was lean, young, and everything worked. I had a name, an identity: Natalie Goldberg.

What a shock it was for me to see my great teacher's stiff body. This was for real? The man I had studied with for twelve years was gone? Stars, moon, hope stopped. Ocean waves and ants froze. Even rocks would not grow. This truth I could not bear.

I was guided by three great teachings I received from him:

Continue under all circumstances.
Don't be tossed away—don't let
anything stop you.
Make positive effort for the good.

The last one Roshi told me when I was divorcing and couldn't get out of bed.

"If nothing else, get up and brush your teeth." He paused. "I can never get up when the alarm goes off. Nevertheless," he nodded, "I get up."

Once in the early days I was perplexed about trees. I asked at the end of a lecture, "Roshi, do the elms suffer?"

He answered.

"What? Could you tell me again? Do they really suffer?" I couldn't take it in.

He shot back his reply.

It pinged off my forehead and did not penetrate. I was caught in thinking mind, too busy trying to understand everything.

But my confusion had drive. I raised my hand a third time. "Roshi, just once more. I don't get it. I mean do trees really suffer."

He looked straight at me. "Shut up."

That went in.

The amazing thing was I did not take it personally. He was directly commanding my monkey mind to stop. I'd already been studying with him for a while. Those two words were a relief. Dead end. Quit. I rested back into my sitting position and felt my breath go in and out at my nose. The thought about trees that evening stopped grabbing me by the throat.

With him extraneous things were cut away. My life force stepped forward. After a sleepy childhood I was seen and understood. Glory! Glory! I had found a great teacher in the deep north of this country. Maybe that had been the purpose of my short marriage: to bring me here. Both Roshi and I did not belong in Minnesota, yet we had found each other.

I positioned Roshi in the deep gash I had in my heart. He took the place of loneliness and desolation, and with him as a bolster I felt whole. But the deal was he had to stay alive, continue existing, for this configuration to work.

The third year after his death was the worst in my life. Our process had been cut short. In a healthy teacher-student relationship, the teacher calls out of the student a large vision of what is possible. I finally dared to feel the great true dream I had inside. I projected it onto this person who was my teacher. This projection was part of spiritual development. It allowed me to discover the largeness of my own psyche, but it wasn't based on some illusion. Roshi possessed many of these projected qualities, but each student was individual. When I asked other practitioners what impressed them about Kata-giri Roshi, the reported qualities were different for each person. One woman in Santa Cruz admired his unerring self-confidence. She stood up and imitated his physical stance. She said that even when no one understood his English and we weren't sure of the Buddhist concepts he discussed, he bowed in front of the altar and walked out after his lecture as though all time and the universe were backing him.

I'd never even taken note of that. What I loved was his enthusiasm, his ability to be in the moment and not judge and categorize me. He had a great sense of humor. I admired his dedication to practice and to all beings and his willingness to tell me the truth, with no effort to sweeten it.

Eventually, as the teacher-student relationship matures, the student manifests these qualities herself and learns to stand on her own two feet. The projections are reclaimed. What we saw in him is also inside us. We close the gap between who we think the teacher is and who we think we are not. We become whole.

Roshi died before this process was finished. I felt like a green fruit. I still needed the sun, the rain, the nutrients of the tree. Instead, the great oak withered; I dangled for a while and then fell to the ground, very undernourished.

How many of us get to live out the full maturation process? Our modern lives are built on speed. We move fast, never settle. Most of us grab what we can, a little from here, then there. For twelve years I had one source. I should have been satisfied. He gave me everything. I knew that when I saw his dead body, but how to live it inside myself?

This projection process also can get more complicated if we haven't individuated from our original parents. Then we present to the teacher those undeveloped parts too. Here the teacher needs to be savvy, alert, and committed in order to avoid taking advantage of vulnerable students. I have read about Zen ancestors who practiced with their teachers for forty years in a single monastery, and I understand why. There would be no half-baked characters in those ancient lineages.

But, oddly enough, Te-shan only had that one meeting with Lung-t'an, and he woke up. Of course, he was a serious scholar of the dharma for a long time. Who is to say scholarly pursuits—studying books intently and writing commentary—don't prepare the mind as well as sweeping bamboo-lined walkways, sitting long hours, or preparing monastery meals?

Zen training is physical. But what isn't physical while we have a body on this earth? Sitting bent over books, our eyes following a line of print, is physical too. So that when Te-shan had that single evening in Lung-t'an's room, he was already very ripe. Lung-t'an merely had to push him off the tree, and Te-shan was prepared to fall into the tremendous empty dark with no clinging.

Te-shan was shown true darkness when Lung-t'an blew out the light; he held at last a dharma candle to guide his way, but he still had a lot of maturation ahead of him. Don't forget the next morning he made that grandiose gesture of burning his books in front of the assembly of monks. He was still acting out, choosing this and leaving that. He was not yet able to honor his whole journey, to respect everything that brought him to this moment. Te-shan still envisioned things in dualistic terms: now only direct insight mattered; books needed to be destroyed. He didn't see that all those years of study had created a foundation that supported his awakening with Lung-t'an. Originally he traveled from the north with his sutras on his back to enlighten the southern barbarians. Here he was doing a complete reversal, torching his past and revering his present experience. Someday he would embrace the north and the south, unify all of China in his heart, and attain a peaceful mind. But he was not there yet. We see him engaged in drama, presenting a flaming pageant in front of the other monks.

His life has not yet settled and become calm.

After he left Lung-t'an, he wandered for a long time, looking to be tested and sharpened. He already had left his place in northern China to wander among what he thought were the southern barbarians. He might be the precursor to our fractured American way of searching for peace.

How can anyone survive if the way is so splintered? What we learn is it's all whole, been whole all along. It is our perception that is broken and that creates a shattered world. But each of us has to discover this in our own lives. That is what is so hard.

"I wish you'd gotten to meet him," I'd tell writing students.

"We are," they'd say, meaning they did through knowing me.

I scoffed. "You don't know what you're talking about."

At a party in San Francisco, Ed Brown, a longtime Zen practitioner and author of many books, pulled me over. "Nat, I have another story about Katagiri for you to steal."

I laughed. I'd asked his permission and acknowledged him with the last one I used. I put my arm around him. "Sure, Ed, give it to me. I'd love to steal from you again."

He began, "I'd been practicing for twenty years when the thought suddenly came to me, 'Ed, maybe you can just hear what your heart is saying. You can be quiet and pay attention to yourself.' It was a big moment of relief for me. Tears filled my eyes."

He showed me with his fingers how they fell down his cheeks. "I'd tried so hard all my life. Made such effort, lived in a monastery since I was young. And now this. Could it be that simple?

"The next day I had an interview with Katagiri. I asked him, 'Do you think it's okay to just listen to yourself?'

"He looked down, then he looked up. 'Ed, I tried very hard to practice Dogen's Zen. After twenty years I realized there was no Dogen's Zen.'"

Dogen was a strict patriarch from thirteenth-century Japan. We chanted his words each morning. He was a yardstick by which we measured ourselves.

I felt my legs buckle. I reached out for the back of a chair. Just us. No heaven Zen in some Asian sky out there.

I put my hand on Ed's shoulder. "Ed, I vow to once again misappropriate your story." He nodded, satisfied.

I was reminded again how simple, sincere, earnest Roshi was. I was happy, and then it ignited my anger. I was mad he died. I had found the perfect teacher.

I tried practicing other places. I did two fall practice periods at Green Gulch, part of the San Francisco Zen Center. While I was there, an old student told me about the early years at the Zen monastery in Carmel Valley.

Tassajara was in a narrow valley. The sun didn't reach it until late morning, rising over an eastern mountain, and it dropped early behind the slope of a western one. The practice was difficult, and the days and nights were frigid and damp. But American students of the late sixties were fervent about this path to liberate their lives. One particular winter retreat, that lasted for a hundred days, was being led by Katagiri, fresh from Japan.

One young zealous woman, a fierce practitioner, a bit Zen-crazed, was having a hard time. She was full of resistance when the four o'clock wake-up bell rang on the fifth day of Rohatsu sesshin, an intense week that honored Buddha's enlightenment and signaled almost the finish of the long retreat. Practice that day would again be from four-thirty in the morning until ten at night with few breaks except for short walking meditations and an hour's work period after lunch. It was her turn that morning to carry the *kyosaku*, that long narrow board administered in the zendo to sleepy students' shoulders. Her hands were frayed and her bare feet were ice on the cold wooden floor when she got there. She picked up the wake-up stick and passed quietly by the altar to do the ritual bow to Katagiri, the head teacher, who was facing into the room. The flame on the candle was strong. The incense wafted through the air. The practitioners were settled onto their cushions, facing out toward the wall.

A thought inflamed her just as she was about to bow in front of Katagiri: It's easy for him. He's Asian. He's been doing this all his life. It's second nature. His body just folds into position.

Though it is a rule of retreat that people do not look at each other, in order to limit social interaction and provide psychic space for going deeply within, at this moment she glanced up at Roshi. She was stunned to see pearls of sweat forming on his upper lip. Only one reason he could have been perspiring in this frozen zendo: great effort. It wasn't any easier for him than anyone else. Was she ever wrong in her assumptions. She had gotten close enough to see what no one was supposed to see. All her rage and stereotyping crumbled.

My heart jumped. I imagined the small hard dark hairs above his lip—he did not shave for the whole week during sesshins. I recalled the shadow building on his cheeks and shaved head as the days went on, how he bowed with his hands pressed together in front of him, elbows out and shoulders erect. His small beautiful foot as he placed a step on the floor during walking meditation. Though retreats were austere, singular, solitary, there was also a rare intimacy that was shared in silence and practice together.

Just two weeks before the end of my second Green Gulch retreat, in December 1995, almost six years after Katagiri Roshi had died, in a stunning moment in the zendo that shot through me like a hot steel bolt, I realized this regimented practice no longer fit me. The known world blanked out, and I was lost in the moving weight of a waterfall. For me, the structure was Katagiri Roshi. I learned it all from him. If I stepped out of it, I'd lose my great teacher. I knew how to wake at four o'clock in the morning, to sit still for forty-minute periods, to eat with three bowls in concentration, but it was over—other parts of me needed care. Structure had saved my life, given me a foundation, and now it was cracking. It was a big opening, but I wasn't up to it.

Roshi was the youngest of six children. His mother barely had time for him. He'd spoken fondly of the single hour that he once had with her when she took him shopping. No other brothers and sisters. Just the heaven of his mother all to himself.

My mother was mostly absent in my life, not because she was busy, but because she was vacant. She woke in the morning, put on her girdle, straight wool skirt, and cashmere sweater, and then sat in a chair in her bedroom, staring out the window.

"Mom, I'm sick and want to stay home from school."

"That's fine."

The next day I wrote the absentee note for the teacher, and she signed without glancing at it. I was hungrier than I knew. I wanted someone to contact me, even if it was to simply say, "Natalie, you are not sick. That wouldn't be honest. As a matter of fact, you look lovely today." As a kid I needed a reflection of my existence, that I was, indeed, here on this earth. The attention I received from my father was invasive and uncomfortable. I hoped at least for my mother's affirmation, but there wasn't any.

Roshi was the one person who directly spoke to this hunger. When I went in for *dokusan* (an individual face-to-face interview with the teacher), we sat cross-legged on cushions, opposite each other. He wasn't distracted, "aggravated," or impatient. He was right there, which inspired me to meet him in that moment. I had friends, acquaintances I interacted with, and we sat facing each other across luncheon tables, but this was a man whose life's work was to arrive in the present. The effect was stunning. Life seemed to beam out of every cell in his body. His facial expressions were animated.

I could ask him a question, and he would respond from no stuck, formulated place. I think it was the constant awareness of emptiness: that although this cushion, this floor, this person in front of you, and you yourself are here, it isn't of permanent duration. Knowing this in his bones and muscles, not just as a philosophical idea, allowed him a spontaneity and honesty.

"Roshi, now that I am divorced, it is very lonely."

"Tell me. What do you do when you are alone in the house?"

I'd never thought of that. I became interested. "Well, I water the plants," I faltered, then continued, "I wash a few dishes, call a friend." The momentum built. "I sit on the couch for hours and stare at the bare branches out the window. I play over and over Paul Simon's new album about New Mexico—I miss it there."

His attention encouraged me. "Lately, I've been sitting at my dining-room table and painting little pictures." I looked at him. Suddenly my solitary life had a texture.

"Is there anything wrong with loneliness?" he asked in a low voice.

I shook my head. All at once I saw it was a natural condition of life, like sadness, grief, even joy. When I was sitting with him, it didn't feel ominous or unbearable.

"Anyone who wants to go to the source is lonely. There are many people at Zen Center. Those who are practicing deeply are only with themselves."

"Are you lonely?" I entreated.

"Yes," he nodded. "But I don't let it toss me away. It's just loneliness."

"Do you ever get over it?"

"I take an ice-cold shower every morning. I never get used to it. It shocks me each time, but I've learned to stand up in it." He pointed at me. "Can you stand up in loneliness?"

He continued, "Being alone is the terminal abode. You can't go any deeper in your practice if you run from it."

He spoke to me evenly, honestly. My hunger was satiated—the ignored little girl still inside me and the adult seeker—both were nourished.

I understood that Roshi too had been neglected in his childhood.

Even though he had tremendous perseverance, he was human, with needs and desires. All of us want something—even the vastly wise like a good cookie with their tea and delight in good-quality tea. Maybe it was that very perseverance that broke him. He couldn't keep it up, and his human needs leaked out. "Continue under all circumstances," he barked out, so often that that dictum penetrated even my lazy mind and became a strong tool for my life. But as I grew older I understood its drawbacks: if you are crossing a street and a semi is coming, step aside. If you have hemorrhoids, don't push the sitting; take a hot bath. That one tactic—perseverance—can put you on a dead-end road, and then what do you do? Continue to march deep into a blind alley?

Touching Roshi's frailty finally brought him closer to me, unraveled my solid grief. At the end of January I had a painful backache that lasted all day. At midnight in my flannel pajamas I got up out of bed, went to the window, and looked out at the star-studded clear, cold night sky with Taos Mountain in the distance.

"Where are you? Come back!" I demanded. "We have things to settle."

I let out a scream that cracked the dark, but one raw fact did not change: nothing made him return, and I was left to make sense of his life—and mine.

Mind Is Buddha 🐚

Geoffrey Shugen Arnold

"Mind is Buddha" is a deceptively simple koan, yet among the most profound in all of Buddhism. To have confidence that your true nature is enlightenment is to be enlightened. The quandary, says Geoffrey Shugen Arnold in this commentary on Case 30 of the collection of koans known as Gateless Gate, *is how to grasp something that pervades everything yet has no form.*

GATELESS GATE, CASE 30

Mazu's "Mind Is Buddha."

THE MAIN CASE

Damei once asked Master Mazu, "What is buddha?" Mazu answered, "Mind is Buddha."

WUMEN'S COMMENTARY

If you can at once grasp "it," you are wearing buddha clothes, eating buddha food, speaking buddha words, and living buddha life; you are a buddha yourself. Though this may be so, Damei has misled a number of people and let them trust a scale with a stuck pointer. Don't you know that you have to rinse out your mouth for three days if you have uttered the word "buddha"? If you are a real Zen person, you will stop your ears and rush away when you hear "Mind is buddha."

WUMEN'S POEM

A fine day under the blue sky!
Don't foolishly look here and there.
If you still ask, "What is buddha?"
It is like pleading your innocence
While clutching stolen goods.

From the moment when we first engage the dharma we encounter the truth of our buddha nature. This is the fundamental teaching, our essential reality. In China, the concept of buddha nature took on great importance and was infused with the Chinese sense of the meaning and role of "nature." For Chinese Buddhists, nature included the meanings of being ever-present, inherent, and uncontrived, but it also carried with it a sense of obligation; something that we have a responsibility to see and understand. We often think of obligation as a burden, but to realize our true nature is to alleviate the profound weight of our confusion, anger, and fear.

Buddha nature is not something that we possess, nor is it something we can be. It is the nature of things, just as they are. To realize our buddha nature, to live in accord with this awakening, is the truth that alleviates suffering in the world. Having encountered this dharma which offers such a path, knowing that there is another way that leads out of our self-created darkness, don't we then take on the obligation to bring it to life, to make it real? I believe we do, and it's this obligation that is expressed in our Bodhisattva Vows. This is the wonderful burden we take on which only increases as we awaken to the true nature of things.

Damei asks, "What is buddha?" Damei was a disciple of Mazu. Master Mazu had over eighty disciples, making him one of the great teachers in the early Zen tradition. And "Mind is buddha" became one of his hallmark teachings. The story of Mazu meeting his own teacher, Nanyue, is very well known. He was on a mountain in a small temple doing zazen day and night. Nanyue was in another temple on the same mountain and heard about this monk sitting so diligently and came over to see him. He asked him, "Revered sir, what are you doing here?" Mazu replied, "I'm doing zazen." Nanyue said, "What are you trying to accomplish by doing zazen?" "I'm trying to become a buddha," answered Mazu.

So Nanyue went over and picked up a brick or a roof tile and quietly began to polish it. Mazu, noticing this, looked over and asked, "What are you doing?" Nanyue said, "I'm polishing this brick." "For what?" asked Mazu. Nanyue said, "I want to make a mirror out of it." Mazu replied, "You can't make a mirror out of a brick, by polishing a brick." Nanyue responded, "Can you become a buddha by doing zazen?"

Mazu said, "Well, then, what should I do?" Nanyue said, "It's like putting a cart to an ox. If the cart doesn't move, what should you do? Should you beat the cart or do you beat the ox?" Mazu said, "I don't understand." Nanyue then explained, "You practice zazen and try to become a buddha by sitting. If you want to learn how to do zazen, know that Zen is not in sitting nor lying down. If you want to become a buddha by sitting, know that buddha has no fixed form. Never discriminate in living in the dharma of nonattachment. If you try to become a buddha by sitting, you're killing the buddha. If you're attached to the form of sitting, you can never attain buddhahood."

Mazu was trying to do what all of us try to do, become a buddha. But what does that actually mean? How do you become a buddha? Should we try to become calm and serene, wise and compassionate? These are just ideas, and trying to live according to an idea doesn't lead to the reality. Why is it not possible to become a buddha?

As I was reflecting on this, I thought back many years to when I was a musician. This was something that I wanted deeply; it was what I wanted my life to be. I worked hard at it, practicing every day for hours. Yet in the midst of this I had this feeling that somehow I wasn't a musician. I wanted the music to be my whole life, and although I was filling my life with music, it was not filling me. Something was missing. At one point I was preparing for a recital performance with another musician, and we were working on some pieces together with one of my music teachers, whom I deeply respected. We played through one of the pieces, and after we finished he sat quietly, then said, "No, this is not working. Play it again." We started playing again and he stopped us and said, "No! You're doing this all wrong. It's too controlled. It has to be spirited, wild! Play it so that it's right on the edge of flying out of control." We started playing again, and he kept calling out, "Faster! Wilder! Faster!" until the whole thing started to fall apart and he cried out, "Yes! Yes! That's it!" I walked away from that experience having felt something come alive—a hint of something that I had been looking for that arose out of my forgetting the scales, the exercises, and all of the discipline that I was so diligently and necessarily developing, and yet that somehow had become an obstacle to the music filling me completely. All of my efforts and striving to become this concept I had, a "musician," were preventing me from letting go and just experiencing it directly.

Nanyue said, "If you want to become a buddha by sitting, know that buddha has no fixed form." We cannot *become* something that has no fixed form. That's our buddha nature, it has no fixed form. Don't attach to the form of sitting, Nanyue says, but this doesn't mean that we shouldn't practice zazen. If we attach to the form we can never attain buddhahood; if we don't sit deeply it is most unlikely that we'll realize our nature. Clearly, either extreme is not the true path. Seeing zazen or the dharma as a fixed object is the danger of twenty-five hundred years of tradition. We can understand it as a method, a technique, or an exercise that offers a solution or an answer, like a formula to a problem. It's not that there is no resolution, or that there is no solution to the problem, but it's not what we think it is. It has no fixed form.

So Damei comes to Mazu one day and says, "What is buddha?" Naturally, he's not asking about Shakyamuni; he's not asking about a person or someone assuming a certain form. He's asking about what is true. This is why practice can't be fixed, because everything in this great universe is formless, which is impermanence itself. Life doesn't have a fixed form; a moment has no fixed form. So if our freedom or peace is dependent upon something static—as in a state of mind or the absence of thought—then it has no power, no ability to respond in a free, formless world. Damei is asking, what is true, what is real at all times, in all conditions, in all situations?

Mazu said, "Mind is buddha." Mind alone—all-pervading, without edges—is truth. Bodhidharma said that everything that appears in the three realms comes from mind. Hence the buddhas of the past and the future teach mind to mind without bothering about definitions. A student then asks, "If they don't define it, what do they mean by mind?" Bodhidharma said, "You ask, that's your mind. I answer, that's my mind. If I had no mind, how could I answer? If you had no mind, how could you ask? That which asks is your mind. Through endless kalpas without beginning, whatever you do, wherever you are, that's your real mind; that's your real buddha.

"This mind is the buddha" says the same thing. Beyond this mind, you will never find another buddha. To search for enlightenment or nirvana beyond this mind is impossible. The reality of your own self-nature, the absence of cause and effect, is what's meant by mind. Your mind is nirvana. You might think you can find a buddha or enlightenment somewhere beyond the mind, but such a place doesn't exist."

"You ask, that's your mind." What does that mean? We ask questions all the time; we offer answers. How is this mind? How is this buddha? Bodhidharma also says that buddha means "miraculous awareness." The universe asks, the universe itself answers: this is miraculous awareness. Mind is buddha; this is the mind of the universe. It is the one great body that fills heaven and earth. Where is the self to be found?

This is why the search for enlightenment or nirvana beyond this mind is impossible. There is nothing outside of it. And that's one of the most difficult things for us because without even knowing it, we look outside. Even as we are seeking outside ourselves for the answers, we don't see this; it's so habitual and deeply conditioned. From the moment we encounter the dharma, the moment we begin doing zazen, we are instructed not to look outside ourselves. We know this is true, we believe in it, but we don't do it. We continually go outside, looking for that which is beyond our awareness. We might think we can find a buddha or enlightenment somewhere beyond this mind; we might think we can find serenity, clarity, and meaning beyond this mind, but such a place does not exist. Everything that appears is this mind, Bodhidharma says. But if it encompasses everything, then how can it be seen? That which is seen is mind, that which is seeing is mind. Seeing itself is mind. So how can it be seen? Well, it can't, and yet it must be realized.

Mind is buddha. This is not our brain; it's not in our head. It's one reason why it's so important to put our awareness in the *hara,* the lower abdomen, and get out of our heads. While Mazu's teaching that "Mind is buddha" was one of his hallmark teachings, it was not original with him. Another old master said, "To see into one's nature is to be awakened to the buddha mind. Cast all thoughts and consciousness away and see that mind is buddha. The one who realizes that their true mind is buddha is the one who has attained buddhahood. One neither practices good nor commits evil; one has no attachments to the mind. Your eyes see things, but you don't become attached. This mind that does not become attached to each and every thing is buddha mind. This is why Master Mazu said, 'Mind is buddha.'" Being attached is what prevents us from seeing, is what clouds this *miraculous awareness.* This is what we chant in the *Identity of Relative and Absolute*: "To be attached to things is illusion."

To be free of the discriminating mind is to manifest miraculous awareness—awareness that is miraculously simple, miraculously unadorned. This is the koan of *shikantaza,* "just sitting." Don't do anything; don't be passive either. Being passive is still doing. This is the heart of every koan. A traditional case koan creates the sense that you're doing something. You have a question which you drop down into your hara and inquire into deeply. You keep your mind still and stable within that question so it doesn't turn or agitate the mind, but there's still the sense that you're doing something. I remember wondering about this in my own koan study. Isn't this somehow creating a state of mind, working with something that's outside of myself? Can it be trusted to reveal the truth? It took a lot of work to see the error in my way of understanding the nature of *koan*. When the thinking mind ceases and the self falls away, there is no koan and nothing to create. That is when the koan is realized.

In the commentary Wumen says, "If you can at once grasp 'it,' you are wearing buddha clothes, eating buddha food, speaking buddha words, living buddha life; you are a buddha yourself." Here's a real point of difficulty with this koan. It seems so obvious, "Oh, I'm a buddha." But when it's just an idea, do we notice that nothing has changed? We're not actually wearing buddha clothes, eating buddha food, speaking buddha words, living buddha life. All we're doing is carrying around the thought, "I'm a buddha." We just increased our burden. So what is it to wear buddha clothes, what is it to see "Mind is buddha"? That's why Mumon says, "Damei has misled a number of people and let them trust a scale with a stuck pointer." There is no fixed form. So as soon as Mazu says, "Mind is buddha," it becomes static, like a slogan. It's a great slogan, isn't it? It's short and punchy. Yet right there the scale sticks, which is a nice image: the scale gives a weight, but it's a fixed weight. Regardless of what you place on the scale, it's not reflecting the truth anymore. It's showing something, but what it's showing is false. So to even say such a thing creates a problem.

> A fine day under the blue sky!
> Don't foolishly look here and there.
> If you still ask, "What is Buddha?"
> It is like pleading your innocence
> Whilst clutching stolen goods.

Don't foolishly look here and there. Why is this so difficult? Does it, in fact, come back to our lack of trust and faith in our buddha nature or in our ability to realize it? Having this faith, being confident in our ability, does not mean arrogance. If it's arrogance, it's something other than confidence. This faith is just recognizing what's true. So when you get stuck in your own practice, rather than creating a pit of self-pity and woe, have faith in yourself. Why shouldn't you? Being free of attachments, living a life that is joyful, is your birthright, your endowment.

> If you still ask, "What is Buddha?"
> It is like pleading your innocence
> Whilst clutching stolen goods.

This is why realizing ourselves is, in fact, an obligation. But whose obligation is it? It can't come from the outside; it has to come from within. So, please, having received the gift of this time and place, meet your obligation. If you still have doubts about your responsibility, consider the costs of confusion, delusion, jealousy, and anger in this world of ours. Take the posture of the Buddha on your meditation cushion and understand that there is one who knows. "Mind is buddha" is awakening to that truth. It's no one else's affair. Please take care of it.

The Path
of Mahamudra ☙

Traleg Kyabgon Rinpoche

If mind is inherently enlightened, why pick and choose among our thoughts, perceptions, and feelings? Why struggle to liberate what is inherently free? The Tibetan teachings of Mahamudra bypass the gradual path to enlightenment and cut right to the essential nature of mind. As Traleg Kyabgon Rinpoche explains, we don't accept or reject what arises in our mind, but develop our insight so we can see its true nature. The fruition of the path is a return to the primordial ground from which everything arises.

True Mahamudra practice is the approach of self-liberation. With this approach, we are not attempting to renounce, purify, or transform anything at all. Instead, the idea is to allow our negativities and conflicting emotions to become self-liberated. As long as we are trying to renounce, purify, or transform, we are trying to *do* or contrive something. This involves seeing ourselves as fundamentally flawed, because we have no control over our strong emotions. We feel that if we are ever going to become a better human being and be spiritually redeemed, we must do everything in our power to dispose of these undesirable states of mind. In the Mahamudra view, by deliberately trying to eradicate conflicting emotions, the source of our conflicting emotions, we are perpetuating a negative view of these things. Ultimately these emotions and conflicting emotions have no intrinsic nature, and the Mahamudra method incorporates this premise from the outset. In so doing, it is designed to cut through conflicting emotions rather than wear them out, eliminate them, or transform them.

Rather than going through the long process of elimination, purification, and transformation, we simply enter immediately into our own spiritual being or rest in our natural state, as it is said. If we can do this, liberation is automatic. Mahamudra is sometimes described as the sudden approach to enlightenment. This does not necessarily indicate that we can become enlightened instantly, but rather that the conflicting emotions that obstruct our enlightenment can become self-liberated naturally. Self-liberation is called *rangdrol* in Tibetan—*rang* is "self" and *drol* is "liberation." Self-liberation is achieved through recognizing our innate state of being, or the nature of the mind, according to the Mahamudra teachings. Self-liberation comes through resisting the temptation to deliberately try to create a particular state of mind. Instead we allow ourselves to be with whatever arises in the mind. When we allow things to come and go without fixating on them and without trying to solidify, correct, or react to them, everything can become self-liberated. It is simply a matter of maintaining our awareness (*sampajanya*).

GROUND MAHAMUDRA

The Mahamudra view is based on the underlying metaphysical concept of the nature of the mind, a term used interchangeably with the terms *ground Mahamudra* and *ground of being*. It is said that this ground has been pure right from the beginning because it has not been caused to come into existence but is spontaneously established. It is also atemporal, because we cannot talk about it in relation to the past, present, or future. We cannot attribute any form of action to it by saying it has come into being or has gone out of existence, and so on. We cannot speak about using our normal reifying concepts of existence or nonexistence, permanence or impermanence, good or evil, sublime or degraded, and so forth. It is even completely devoid of notions of samsara, nirvana, or a spiritual path. While it is the source from which all samsaric and nirvanic experiences arise, it is not subject to causes and conditions, nor is it something that can be harmed or negated. It is free from all the limitations of our ordinary empirical consciousness.

This aspect of Mahamudra reality is called ground Mahamudra because it is the innate existential condition in which we all find ourselves. In his *Mahamudra Song*, the great Kagyü master Jamgön Kongtrül Lodrö Thaye (1813–1899) describes the ground Mahamudra in these terms:

> As for ground mahamudra:
> There are both things as they are and the way of confusion.
> It does not incline toward either samsara or nirvana,
> And is free from the extremes of exaggeration and denigration.
> Not produced by causes, not changed by conditions,
> It is not spoiled by confusion
> Nor exalted by realization.
> It does not know either confusion or liberation.*

Ground Mahamudra is an open state of being that is identical to our authentic condition. It is the ground from which all our experiences originate. Our liberating experiences arise from it, as do our experiences of imprisonment, constriction, and constraint. It is completely impartial in terms of both samsaric and nirvanic experiences—pain, pleasure, happiness, unhappiness, and so on. Our authentic condition is totally open and undifferentiated. As soon as we speak of our own authentic condition as being this or that, as inclining toward nirvana and away from samsara, we introduce a dualism that simply does not exist in reality.

---

*From *The Rain of Wisdom: The Essence of the Ocean of True Meaning*, translated by Chögyam Trungpa and the Nālandā Translation Committee (Boston: Shambhala Publications, 1988).

This authentic condition is present in ordinary sentient beings as well as enlightened beings. In other words, there is ultimately no real difference between the two. The only difference is that enlightened beings have recognized their authentic condition, whereas ordinary sentient beings have not. This nonrecognition of our true condition is called ignorance, which is the reason we wander about in the cyclic existence of birth, death, and rebirth.

Mental fabrications of every conceivable kind have to be put to rest when we contemplate our natural state of being. If we try to conceptualize about it, we will think things like: "Does it exist or not exist? Does it favor our effort to realize nirvana and disfavor our samsaric tendencies? Is it permanent or impermanent?" One should resist forming ideas entirely. The point is not to develop ideas but to learn to rest in the natural state of being through the practice of Mahamudra.

In Buddhist logic, it is said that all concepts are based upon exclusion. As soon as we affirm something by saying, "It is this," we automatically exclude so many other things it might have been. By imposing a conceptual limitation we fabricate an idea. The suggestion here is that it is just an idea—it is not an open experience. The thrust of Mahamudra meditation is to allow our mind to be open so that we can ease into a more natural state of perceiving and being. This does not imply that we should not have ideas at all but that we really need to be skeptical and careful about getting overly fixated on any descriptions of the qualities of our original state of being.

A great Mahamudra master known as Jowo Gotsangpa said that we need three things in order to stay with the correct view— the correct view here being "the view of no view," because it is a view that subverts or undercuts all views. The first thing we need is a decisive understanding of our original being. The second is nonbias toward samsara and nirvana. The third is conviction, because once we have attained conviction, we cannot change our minds back again. Gotsangpa claims that this view is like a spear that shoots through open space.

Mahamudra uses the expression *ordinary mind (thamal gyi shepa* in Tibetan) to describe the nature of the mind as the mind we already have. The nature of the mind is not lurking somewhere underneath our normal empirical consciousness. Rather, we gain insight into the nature of the mind by gaining insight into this ordinary mind. If we avoid judgment of our thoughts, we will be able to attain the luminous bliss of the nature of the mind, which is the ordinary mind itself. Making this point, Jamgön Kongtrül says in his *Mahamudra Song*:

> Like the center of a cloudless sky,
> This self-luminous mind is impossible to express.
> It is wisdom of nonthought beyond analogy,
> Naked ordinary mind.*

PATH MAHAMUDRA

Ground Mahamudra is referred to as the basis of purification. The ground itself does not require any form of purification. However, even though the ground, the nature of the mind, is unsullied and pure, adventitious mental conflicting emotions have arisen. This is precisely the reason we need a path, a method to alleviate our condition. The objects of purification, then, are the adventitious mental conflicting emotions; the means of purification is the practice of Mahamudra meditation; and the fruit of purification is the realization of the ground of being—the luminous bliss of the inherent nature of the mind. In other words, the nature of the mind does not need to be purified. The ground Mahamudra and fruition Mahamudra are in actuality one and the same thing. Once the adventitious mental conflicting emotions have been purified, there is nothing to stand in the way of our realizing our own true nature.

---

*The second Jamgön Kongtrül, quoted in the third Jamgön Kongtrül's *Cloudless Sky: The Mahamudra Path of the Tibetan Buddhist Kagyu School* (Boston: Shambhala Publications, 1992).

Tranquillity Meditation

Path Mahamudra consists of the practices of tranquillity meditation *(shamatha)* and insight meditation *(vipashyana)*. First, tranquillity meditation is used to still the mind. We do not—as is done in more conventional forms of Buddhist meditation—attempt to tame the mind. In other meditative traditions, the mind is compared to a wild elephant, and meditation techniques are compared to the implements an elephant tamer uses to tame an elephant. That image is not applicable here. Rather, in tranquillity meditation, the mind is allowed to subside naturally of its own accord, using the method of self-liberation. Mindfulness is present, but there is no artifice or contrivance at all. In Mahamudra, the thoughts themselves are allowed to settle of their own accord; there is no need to force them into submission. The third Karmapa, Rangjung Dorje, had this to say about tranquillity meditation in his *Prayer of Mahamudra*:

> Not adulterating meditation with conceptual striving,
> Unmoved by the wind of worldly bustle,
> Knowing how to rest in the spontaneous, uncontrived flow,
> Being skilled in the practice, may I now continue it.

Insight Meditation

Insight meditation involves an intimate and methodical examination of what the mind is. During this form of meditation, we ask ourselves questions like: "What is the mind? What is a thought? Where is a thought? What is the nature of thought? What is the nature of emotion?" Persistent analysis of this sort will reveal that the mind is not an entity or a substance. In the Mahamudra tradition, this is viewed as a supreme realization. As Savaripa, the eighth-century Indian mahasiddha, stated:

> In the process of searching for all that manifests as mind
>   and matter
> There is neither anything to be found nor is there any seeker,
> For to be unreal is to be unborn and unceasing

In the three periods of time.
That which is immutable
Is the state of great bliss.*

By analyzing every experience that we have in this fashion, we come to realize that even our own confused thoughts—those we normally see as the very source of our mental disturbances—have the same nature as the mind itself. In this way we realize the ground Mahamudra. In Mahamudra insight meditation, everything that we experience is regarded as having the potential to reveal our true nature. Our disturbing thoughts and negative emotions are not something we try to abandon; we simply need to develop an understanding of their nature. Through the methods of the Mahamudra teachings, we can learn to use our thoughts to attain a meditative state.

Fruition Mahamudra

Mahamudra practice culminates in the four yogas of Mahamudra: the yoga of one-pointedness, the yoga of nonconceptuality, the yoga of one flavor, and the yoga of nonmeditation. Each yoga represent the fruition of a certain level of meditative practice. Je Gomchung, an important Kagyü Mahamudra master, explains:

> To rest in tranquillity is the stage of one-pointedness;
> To terminate confused thoughts is the stage of nonconceptuality;
> To transcend the duality of accepting and rejecting is the stage of one flavor;
> To perfect experiences is the stage of nonmeditation.

The yoga of one-pointedness essentially denotes recognizing the nature of the mind. One has attained this stage with the first taste

---

*Quoted in Takpo Tashi Namgyal, *Mahamudra: The Quintessence of Mind and Meditation*, translated by Lobsang P. Lhalungpa (Boston: Shambhala Publications, 1986).

of luminous bliss while in a state of deep, undisturbed meditative equipoise. The fruition is the ability to maintain meditative luminosity *(prabhasvara)*.

The yoga of nonconceptuality is attained by realizing that the mind has no root and is devoid of enduring essence. Not only is the nature of the mind devoid of essence, but everything that occurs in the mind is also devoid of essence, including the confused thoughts and disturbing emotions. If we look for where these thoughts and emotions arise, persist, and dissipate, we will find nothing. Therefore, while the first yoga is concerned with gaining insight into the luminous quality of the mind, the second yoga is concerned with insight into emptiness.

The yoga of one flavor refers to the experience of nonduality. The division between the mind and the external world, subject and object, and all other dualistic notions are overcome at this level. Everything, including the liberation of nirvana and the bondage of samsara, is equalized in this state of one flavor.

The yoga of nonmeditation signifies the genuine, ultimate fruition of path Mahamudra. It is inseparable from the ground Mahamudra, the departure point of the spiritual journey. The yoga of nonmeditation has nothing to do with not meditating per se; it simply means that the meditation state has become the natural state to be in, rather than something that we need to pursue. Therefore, there is no division between the meditation and postmeditation states.

Fruition Mahamudra is the ultimate realization of the nature of mind as having three qualities: it is empty, it is luminous, and it is the experience of bliss. When the emptiness of physical and mental phenomena is directly experienced as a subjective reality and the mind is stable and able to maintain awareness, the luminous clarity of the mind gives rise to a sense of well-being that transcends both happiness and unhappiness. This is the experience of all-pervasive bliss, the goal of Mahamudra practice. When we no longer fixate on our thoughts and emotions but let them arise without interference and without hope and fear, our minds will become blissfully clear.

If You Depict a Bird, Give It Space to Fly

Eleanor Rosch

Eleanor Rosch is one of the world's leading cognitive scientists, and a long-time practitioner of Tibetan Buddhism. She brings together, from East and West, two of history's great examinations of the nature of consciousness and perception. Here she uses her deep understanding of mind to reflect on the nature of the artistic process and how we can use art to see deeper truths about ourselves and our world.

> We are led to believe a lie
> when we see with and not through the eye
> —WILLIAM BLAKE

> Feeling is a rebound or echo from contact (contact between
> a sense organ and its object). It is symbolized by a man with
> an arrow through his eye. It is a very penetrating experience.
> —CHÖGYAM TRUNGPA RINPOCHE

What is mind? What is perception? To whom do we give the authority to show us our minds and ourselves? Increasingly, Western culture has given that authority to the sciences: psychology, neurophysiology, brain research, evolutionary theory. The portrait that they paint is of a mind inherently separate from the world, a mind which struggles continuously to build mental representations and develop skills so that it can fulfill its originating value, which is to survive and reproduce. Yet humans have a sense that they know themselves and the world in a more direct, real, alive, even meaningful, way than this. When we are deeply struck (for example, when the terrible climax of a tragedy is known and felt as incomprehensibly, timelessly perfect), we seem to have a glimpse of something else, of something other than survival—in fact, of something other than the way our mind usually functions, or the way we think it functions.

Both meditation and the arts tap into this basic intuition; thus, I will argue, meditation and art can illuminate each other and can do so beyond particular artistic styles or practices. Furthermore, in this way, both art and meditation may have a great deal to teach to contemporary society and cognitive science, more, perhaps, than vice versa.

My basic claim is that it is the special province of the arts to show people themselves in a mirror which reflects their ordinary self-image in the light of these broader and deeper intuitions. How? The arts are both created and appreciated by the activity of the senses and of the thinking mind. According to some meditation traditions—particularly later Buddhism—activities of the senses and of thoughts are inherently double-faced. They can arise from and can point back either to their surface, confused, habitual mode of operation, which is what humans are conscious of most of the time (and which is reflected in most of the portraits of mind in our psychologies), or to a deeper, more panoramic, and more immediate wisdom way of knowing, feeling, and being. Such an underlying nascent wisdom mode is said to be always available, half glimpsed, by everyone. Let us explore three aspects of this wisdom mind in relation to the arts:

1. Humans as a directly felt part of the natural world
2. Humans as beings that are part of humanity
3. Humans as part of that which is said to be inexpressible but of supreme importance

A series of contemplative exercises is the centerpiece of each of the following sections. You are invited to do as much or as little of each as you would like. Some of them may remind you of experiences that you have already had, or may trigger understanding just by reading the exercise without the need to do anything extra. The exercises are provided because the searchlight of the present topic is on the art quality of ordinary mind and of ordinary life itself.

Furthermore, this essay is intended to be evocative—like its subject matter. For example, the term "intuition" is used, not in a technical sense, but as a means of pointing the reader to his/her own experiences of these matters. Claims are broadly but briefly sketched to invite contemplation of their import. This does not mean that the essay is hermeneutical, political, or postmodern. Granted that there are great variations in what the creators and consumers of the arts in different times and cultures have thought and said about what they were doing, and granted there are many subgroups within each Eastern tradition which offer different doctrines and practices—those matters are the legitimate subject of a different sort of analysis than is being carried out here. My claim is that humans have a mode of knowing themselves and their world that is more basic and deeply rooted than the habits of mind that we usually deploy, and that art, at its best, can provide glimpses and connections to that realm of psychology. The reader interested in exploring such a perspective might want to bring to mind those works in the arts which have most deeply struck or affected him or her in the past and think about the categories that follow in relation to the experience of those personally potent works.

HUMAN AS PART OF NATURE

For both standard psychology and a certain kind of common sense, the perceiving mind is obviously separate from the objects it perceives. Is it? Where is your consciousness? Do you feel it to be confined behind your eyes, peering out at a separated world? Always?

Meditation in most traditions serves not only to calm and focus the mind, but to begin to integrate the person: to bring body, mind, and action together, to bring the senses and their objects (the seen, heard, thought . . .) together. There is a basic mode of knowing that knows the knowing self, mind, body, and environment as one panoramic whole. Don't we all have glimpses of this, independent of any formal meditation experience?

One type of intuition of one's integration with nature is the experience of one's body and mind as part of a panoramic expanse. Suggested contemplative exercises:

a. Gaze out (or imagine you are gazing out) from a height such as a highway vista point or hillside. Allow the mind to expand outward in all directions, including behind. Feel the surround and oneself in it. Keep on expanding.

b. Pick a time when you are working intensely (or relive such a time for a moment). As you finish or come to a break, stop!—and let the mind expand into the senses and environment.

c. What has given you an experience of panoramic knowing in the past? Go there.

There are many artworks that can strike the senses in such a way as to throw the mind into a momentary sense of panorama. Chinese landscape painting from its inception has specialized in visions of great mountains, rivers, valleys, and vistas among which are blended tiny houses and human figures. Architecture and landscape design can be natural modes of conveying such experiences. Narratives too, although typically verbal, have imagined settings. Perhaps because in both verbal and pictorial presentations, the setting, the figures, and the action are all presented in the same imaginative modality, such as brushstrokes or the author's words, the audience can more readily apprehend and participate in the mutual determination of figure and setting, than in real life, where our ordinary assumptions and habits hold sway.

A second kind of integrative experience of oneself and other humans as a direct part of nature arises from the energy level of experience. To know oneself as the movement of *ch'i*, or energy, is perhaps most obviously and directly the province of music and dance. If you engage in either of these forms or in a martial art, the next time you are doing your practice (or, right now, imagining your practice) you might pay special attention to the way in which mind, as well as body, appears to you. Or try the following: Deliberately do, or remember doing, something that is constraining and renders you seriously impatient. Trying to do sitting or standing meditation longer than you feel like it might be just the right trigger. Or maybe right now you're getting impatient reading this essay. Let it build up, then tune into the energy level of that impatience. Where is the energy and where does it go—and where and what is the mind?

The sense of humans and nature as *ch'i* can also be conveyed pictorially. This may be by means of content: Think of mountain landscapes with rushing streams and waterfalls, or of winds tearing at trees and human clothing. More likely it is conveyed by design and the quality of brushstrokes (think of Van Gogh). Likewise, in narrative it is the quality and style of description that paints things in their energy aspect; think of the writing style of Hemingway:

> In the late summer of that year, we'd lived in a house in a village that looked across the river and the plains to the mountains. In the bed of the river there were pebbles and boulders, dry and white in the sun, and the water was clear and swiftly moving, and blue in the channels. Troops went by the house and down the road and the dust they raised powdered the leaves of the trees. The trunks of the trees too were dusty and the leaves fell early that year and we saw the troops marching along the road and the dust rising and leaves, stirred by the breeze, falling and the soldiers marching and afterwards the road bare and white except for the leaves.*

---

*Ernest Hemingway, *A Farewell to Arms* (New York, Scribner, 1957).

Perhaps it is because humans already have the ability to know themselves directly as an interdependently arising part of the energies of nature that they would ever think to propose a naturalistic science or naturalistic philosophy in the first place—or an account of human origins such as evolution. However, when this intuition is expressed in the form of art, it appears to have the power to awaken a knowing of a different quality with different implications than does its scientific expression.

Suggested exercise: Try contemplating some scientific theory about humans that you believe. What faculties of mind do you use to do this, and how does it feel? Are you doing it with the head? The "heart"? The "spirit"? How does this compare with the faculties and feelings in contemplation of art, such as Chinese landscape painting or Van Gogh?

For many, the scientific version seems to lead the intellect to the conclusion that we are mere products of nature and as such without value or meaning; that is, it tends to cut off the rest of the knowing that goes with this intuition. (The Christianity-versus-evolution debate, which might seem to address related issues, has tended to be framed in terms of doctrine, not the psychology of knowing.) My claim is that when the underlying human knowledge of oneself as part of nature is evoked, it is anything but nihilistic. For example, this poem by Mary Oliver:

> You do not have to be good.
> You do not have to walk on your knees
> for a hundred miles through the desert, repenting.
> You only have to let the soft animal of your body
>   love what it loves.
> Tell me about despair, yours, and I will tell you mine.
> Meanwhile the world goes on.
> Meanwhile the sun and clear pebbles of the rain
> are moving across the landscapes,
> the prairies and the deep trees
> the mountains and the rivers.

Meanwhile the wild geese, high in the clean blue air,
are heading home again.
Whoever you are, no matter how lonely,
the world offers itself to your imagination,
calls to you like the wild geese, harsh and exciting—
over and over announcing your place
in the family of things.*

HUMANS AS PART OF HUMANITY

Who has not had the experience, "There but for the grace of God go
I"? Who has not felt at some point amazed at being confined to just
one small life, which somehow happens to be one's own? (As the
protagonist of Ethan Canin's story, "Accountant," puts it in the final
denouement of that remarkable character portrait: "I suppose I was
wondering, although it is strange for me to admit it, why, of all the
lives that might have been mine, I have led the one I have just described.") Who has not been deeply moved, perhaps life-changingly,
by visual images or narratives of other humans—even fictional
ones? We don't particularly need a contemplative exercise to get in
touch with feelings of connectedness to other humans, do we? Just
as the manifestations of our selves and our knowing minds are an
interdependent part of environments, so they are literally interdependent parts of other living beings. One recent account in psychology speaks of the simultaneous interplay of human interactions,
such as those between mother and infant, as "intersubjectivity."
Buddhism points to the way in which a deep realization of interrelatedness naturally manifests as compassion. As Vietnamese monk
and peace activist Thich Nhat Hanh writes:

Look deeply: every second I am arriving

. . . .

I am the frog swimming happily

---

*Mary Oliver, "Wild Geese," *New and Selected Poems* (Boston: Beacon Press, 1992).

in the clear water of a pond,
And I am the grass-snake
that silently feeds itself on the frog.

I am the child in Uganda, all skin and bones,
my legs as thin as bamboo sticks,
And I am the arms merchant,
selling deadly weapons to Uganda.

.   .   .   .

Please call me by my true names,
so I can hear all my cries and laughter at once,
so I can see that my joy and pain are one.

Please call me by my true names,
so I can wake up,
and the door of my heart
could be left open,
the door of compassion.*

But why is it that humans take such delight in identification with representational characters in *fictional* worlds? Evolutionary psychology offers some practical reasons in terms of training for real-world action. The earliest Buddhist psychology of the Abhidharma suggests an additional possibility. In the Abhidharma texts it is argued that the sense of an enduring and solid ego self from whose vantage point we usually experience life (and which is credited with causing all our troubles) is actually built up out of five *skandhas* (heaps) consisting of a dualistic sense of body, feeling, perception, habits, and consciousness. Perception (and the resulting habits and consciousness), from the point of view of the ego mind, always filters experience through personal hopes and fears. But it is

---

*Thich Nhat Hanh, "Please Call Me by My True Names," *Call Me by My True Names: The Collected Poems of Thich Nhat Hahn.* (Berkeley: Parallax Press, 1999).

taught further, and particularly emphasized in later Buddhism, that this is not necessary, that there is an underlying mode of immediate perception without the bias of hope and fear concerning one's self. Note that this is not a state of indifference (one of the egoistic states of feeling, according to the Abhidharma system), but rather an appreciative mode of knowing one's experience, whether it is positive or negative experience, as it immediately occurs in its full vividness.

The appreciator of the arts and of fictional narrative always knows, at some level, that s/he is not the character in the artwork. Thus s/he can fully identify with and participate in the vividness of that character's life and world without the pervasive filter of self-interest. By that sleight of hand, the reader or viewer may perhaps be caught off-guard by a glimpse of the potentials of a more direct way of knowing. (This is actually not complicated: the claim is simply that there is a basic mode of knowing which is direct and appreciative and is accessed whenever one's ego mind ceases to get in the way.)

Contemplation: Pick a live situation or remember one in which you were interacting with another person or group with at least some tension. Let the mind expand to include oneself and the other(s). Notice that edge of concern about oneself and "How am I doing?" in that interaction. Then do the same while reading or remembering reading a (perhaps favorite) narrative about a tense interaction. How do body and mind react in these two situations?

HUMANS AS PART OF AN INEXPRESSIBLE, UNTHINKABLE OPENNESS AND SACREDNESS

What can be said about this? It is the gist of it all. (It may sound somber, but humor is as good as haiku for flashing openness.) The problem is that, by its very nature, whenever you turn to face into or try to actively pursue this ground of the mind, this "mind of don't know," what you see is something else. But the arts can do a great job of getting through to us because they can slip it to us sideways, so to speak. This may be done by a number of means:

Timelessness

Consciousness tends to be obsessed and controlled by time: the past, the future, memories, reliving of defeats, replays of emotion—good and bad, plans, hopes, worries, fears, boredom. But there is another way of knowing time.

Contemplation: Recall an experience in which time seemed to stand still or life seemed to be complete in a single moment. It might be a moment of great personal meaningfulness, such as a near-death experience or a moment of love (Joan Baez sings, "Speaking strictly for me, we both could have died then and there"); or it could be in a completely ordinary moment, such as walking down the street. Or it might have been an experience of art. Second, although normally such experiences cannot be provoked, you might try, for a moment, "recollecting in tranquillity" some previous period of personal turmoil.

Tibetan Buddhism calls this other way of knowing time the "fourth moment" (Tibetan: *dus bzhi pa*), described thus: "All phenomena are completely new and fresh, absolutely unique and entirely free from all concepts of past, present and future, as if experienced in another dimension of time." An analogous description of time figures in many experiential reports of Zen *kensho*, or realization. *A Course in Miracles* brings a similar sense of time into a Christian context. These wisdom traditions tell us that every moment is like this, born afresh, with no past, from a timeless source. How can such experience be conveyed by the intrinsically temporal arts? Perhaps visual media inherently have the power to strike the viewer with enough force and vividness to momentarily cut through the ongoing conceptual mind. (Some Buddhist yogic systems portray direct channels linking the eyes with the heart—museum directors take note!) Verbal narratives, which by definition unfold through time, have various devices for collapsing time. One means is the climax—Oedipus gives an earthshaking cry and pokes out his eyes. Or the entire plot may be drawn together in a denouement (even good mystery stories do this). Or there may be a moment, perhaps even in one's recollection of the work, in which the perfection of the form of the entire piece strikes one vividly, as perhaps, with *Silas Marner* or the film *Rashomon*.

Can you think of other literary devices? Music may work with time in ways analogous to narrative. Many pieces of classical music have narrative like climaxes. But note: years ago a recording was released called "Great Moments in Music." It contained the death music from *La Bohème*, the death music from the ballet *Romeo and Juliet*, the climax at the end of *Emperor Concerto*, and so on. It was ludicrous! Perhaps we need "the whole catastrophe," stretched out in time, in order to collapse time and bring a sense of completeness—in Taoist terms, "rectification"—to the world of phenomena.

Realness

Contemplation: It may be difficult to evoke a sense of direct experience because it is so close. It is like looking for your eyeglasses when you are already wearing them. But you might think of this as your last moment alive. Focus on the senses: the last visual image, the last sound, the last thought, the last pain. Do the memories or perception have a different quality than usual? Alternatively, remember an experience where an artwork made you feel hyperreal—more alive, more yourself. (Curiously, it might have been a work depicting feelings of meaninglessness and unreality such as *L'Étranger* or *The Catcher in the Rye*.) Shouldn't indulgence in the arts have the opposite effect? What is going on here?

Buddhist mindfulness practice emphasizes being present. One cannot feel real if one is lost in memory, wishes, plans, autobiography—even if one amps up the stimulation, which is our culture's usual strategy for trying to make ourselves feel real. Knowing, in Tibetan Buddhism's fourth moment, is said to be direct and unfiltered. It bypasses one's personal egoistic story. Artists talk about seeing nature and people directly, in a way that is vivid, ungraspable, even "authentic." To be sure, art can lull one into mindless somnolence, but it can also capture and hold the attention, making the viewer or reader a true witness. And that witness, knowing s/he is not literally in the world of the artwork, may even be lured into bypassing the personal ego story and joining immediately into the felt, direct reality portrayed through the artist's vision, whatever that may be.

We don't generally believe talk about direct knowing, at least not with our cognitive minds. How can any experience be unmediated and free of time when we can plainly see that the present experience is the result of who I am—my beliefs, feelings, expectations, and all my past experiences? Isn't everything conscious filtered through our concepts, categories, and cognitive representations? This may be true (and wisely seen), but it applies only to the *content* of the present experience. According to Buddhist teachings, while all of the interdependent past can be causally gathered into the microcosm of the moment of present experience, that does not mean that the basic mode of apprehending the present moment is somehow filtered or distorted or abstractly representational. Think, instead, of a present experience (for example, looking at a painting in a museum) as enriched by past experience (including information in the museum catalog or painting display labels), as a harvest of the fruits of life rather than as something that corrupts the viewing experience. Consider: What debates in the art world might the distinction between the content of an experience and its mode of apprehension address or clarify?

Freedom

What could give humans an idea such as freedom? After all, psychology and cognitive science seek determinate accounts of the mind. According to later Buddhism, each moment is inherently timeless, open ("empty"), and free ("self-liberated"). Both meditation and transmission from dharma teachers are designed to point this out.

Ah, but the arts do too. Humor is one of the most immediate ways. Laughter releases! Think of times that it did this for you. Hearing about people who have everything but still feel miserable also seems to release, as in our fascination with tales of tortured movie stars (or with the life of the Buddha!). And shock releases. In real life, we may be too busy coping with the implications of a shocking experience to notice the open instant, but think of the effect of the juxtaposition of images in a haiku, or, for that matter, those beloved scenes in classic horror movies where the audience screams. As a matter of fact, every moment releases; this is one of the open secrets of life.

Contemplation: Try to catch the sense of what is happening when something strikes you as really funny. Or, can you catch moments of shock, even little ones, or remember some? What's the difference in your reaction between the shocks of life and those engendered by art?

Coming Home: Inherent Value

The values most touted by our institutions are conditional ones: success versus failure, pleasure versus pain, good versus bad. Yet there seems to be a haunting intuition that there is something more than that, or less, if you will. Take, for example, the concept of unconditional love. How many Westerners blame their mothers for not having given it to them (and, with advances in sexual equality, their fathers too)? How many theological wrangles in Western religions have been generated by the need to reconcile the illusive intuition of an unconditional God with the conceptual demands of conditional anthropomorphic imagery?

Buddhism, Hinduism, and Taoism, as well as all the major Western religions, explicitly point beyond conditionality. Later Buddhism is particularly clear in the assertion that what is unconditioned—the primordial or original mind ("no mind")—is our fundamental state, what we are right now, not any particular or special experience. That is one reason why mindfulness, rather than withdrawal from the senses, is a basic practice in Buddhism. When we realize this wisdom, it is said that the phenomenal world, including the false sense of self and all the other problems and degradations of life, are experienced as the timeless perfect radiance of that basic ground. Be that as it may, most long-term meditators (as well as POWs and the like) do report that they are kept going by some illusive sense of basic, unconditional positiveness.

Contemplation: Maybe the best we can do intentionally is to notice that tinge of resentment at the world for its conditionality— resentment of parents, spouses, children, and jobs, or the disappointment when meditations or other spiritual practices don't yield the expected experiences. Where is that intuition that there's anything else? What sort of knowledge is that?

The problem with primordial unconditionality is that, since it is not a separate thing and not any particular or special experience, it cannot be found or known by any of our usual ways of looking or knowing. It cannot be an object of the senses or of thought, since senses and their objects are part of it, and it cannot be the end result of striving for a goal, since the goal is already achieved. One traditional simile is that it is like looking for a lost horse that you cannot find because you are already riding it.

Herein lies the effectiveness of the arts. Riding the lost horse is just the activity of life itself in all its various manifestations. That is what the arts present. In daily life, even as one strains toward values projected outward, the arts can portray that very life in a way that subtly proclaims that to be alive and mortal and have experience and, yes, suffer, is already very much to the point—from Shakespeare's King Lear bellowing to the "oak-cleaving thunderbolts" to Buson's

> Sparrow singing—
> its tiny mouth
> Open

Implications

1. Artists (and everyone who spends time reading, looking at, and listening to their offerings) should feel empowered and proud. Meditation and the arts have no less than awake mind and essentially humanity itself to give to people, to society, and, yes, to our cognitive sciences. Generally the humanities are wont to genuflect before the sciences. Not here. Artists, don't ask; *Tell! Show!*

2. Meditators and would-be meditators should take note of the arts. As Eastern meditation comes increasingly into Western cultures, meditation is practiced more in lay life than monastic settings. Thus there is much discussion of "the yoga of everyday life." The arts, it was suggested here, already have a genius for presenting daily life in all its manifestations in such a way that these manifestations can be glimpsed as what meditators might call wisdom mind at play. Present-day meditators might well contemplate the arts for pointers, well polished by centuries of use, on what a yoga of daily life could practically mean.

3. Psychologists and cognitive scientists should take seriously both meditation and the arts. Are not psychology and cognitive science supposed to be about real people and real minds? Yet from the point of view of the Eastern psychologies, what they have so far studied is the habitual, "surface" mind. Finding changes in blood flow in the brain when people perform some meditation technique is fine (did anyone really think that the body was not involved?), as is being able to fit a thesis about art into a theory one already has. But these do not begin to exploit what meditation or art might have to offer. They do not allow either discipline to tell its own story. In this essay I have tried to sketch how both meditation and the arts may provide clues to a different, more inclusive, and perhaps more basic psychology.

4. Critics and scholars of the arts should notice the possible contentiousness of the claims made here. There are obviously different levels to the relationship between Buddhism and art. Meditative art doesn't have to be any particular style of art. Sophocles is as good an example as John Cage. Art that focuses on consciousness, or that fragments images, or that creates environmental installations can be excellent and potent art, but such styles are the product of our particular historical and cultural concerns. They may be one way, but surely not the only way, to tap "awake" mind, and they need not be taken as the sine qua non of Buddhist insight.

5. Of course, the arts can put us to sleep as well as wake us up, so critics (and our critical minds) should understand that, yes,

discrimination is to be much valued. What kind of art is not awake? Think about your least favorite form of art. (I have a particular vendetta against the style of fast cutting used in TV, which I feel violates the natural awake qualities of the eyes.) Discernment is needed here, just as it is in evaluating meditative or religious experiences. How can we judge?

6. Creators—and this means everyone—should feel empowered and proud. From the point of view of the mind of the present moment, we are all ceaselessly creative artists. When you talk to a friend, or, for that matter, when you pause for a moment and chatter begins in your head, are you reading those words off a teleprompter? In some forms of Buddhism, each gesture of daily life is considered art. Art at its best presents a recipe for awake daily life. May we all be able to tap into that.

The Future of Ice

Gretel Ehrlich

Adventurer and novelist Gretel Ehrlich spent a year traveling the world's coldest places, meditating on the experience of winter and exploring the effects of global warming on the polar regions. As she backpacks the peaks of the southern Andes, she contemplates the unity of nature, landscape, and human consciousness, and what price we pay for ignoring it.

Weather is all mixed up with movements of mind: a gust can shove one impulse into another; a blizzard erases a line of action; a sandstorm permeates inspiration; rain comes in the form of sleep; lightning can make scratch-marks on the brain; hail gouges out a nesting place, melts and waters the seed of an idea that can germinate into idiocy, a joke, or genius. How could it be otherwise?

A year ago I went out into the world to live in the cold and snow and to look at ice, since climate change may threaten to make the season of winter "extinct." There can be no question about global warming. We have 420,000 years of climate history at our fingertips, covering the last four glacial and interglacial cycles. Ice cores are time machines. As snow becomes firm and then compresses into ice, oxygen bubbles are trapped in the glacier, providing samples of ancient atmosphere; using these, we can compare levels of methane and carbon dioxide before and after industrialization.

In the last ten years, as industrial pollution and greenhouse gases have increased rapidly, the weather has made precipitous jumps. Our sky is now another kind of tent: not one that shelters, but kills. The biological health of our planet is in jeopardy because we manage the world only for production and profit, not for quality of life. Too few remember how to care for the planet, to be heartbroken about anything but themselves. But a broken heart is an open heart. Since we are all one, land, plants, animals, oceans, rivers, glaciers and all sentient beings share equal rights.

With that in mind, I traipsed from pole to pole and wintered in a snowbound cabin in between. My first trip took me to Tierra del Fuego and the tip of Patagonia, where a young friend and I backpacked a seventy-mile circuit around the orange, pillar-like granite peaks of the southern Andes.

Emerson said the first circle is the human eye, but so is the planet. They are linked: the one is always beholding the other. I went searching for what the poet Muso Soseki called, "This view of the world without end . . . ," the one where there is "nowhere to hide."

El Seron

Wild daisies and lenga trees and the winding, milk-green rivers that walk down to the ocean from glaciers. We too are walking. Glaciers have shaped roughly a third of the terrestrial planet. I came of age on John Muir's trail, climbing sharp arêtes, domed cliffs and the U-shaped valleys between, the floury rivers and string lakes held tight in steep canyons. Our backpacks are heavy and the wind is against us as we head up a steep rise. In my Spanish dictionary the word *senda* means not only "a path," but also "a ways and means," while the masculine *sendero* is only a footpath, nothing more. Yet the verb *sendear* means "to conduct along a path," and also "to attain by tortuous means."

Perfect. We follow the Paine circuit counterclockwise, and as the days go on, I refer to it as a path that passes with no end in itself and as a circuit of pain. Not just by bodily pain, which at times is considerable, but also the one implied by any circular route consciously taken. Perhaps "circle" is the wrong word. A wheel with broken spokes might be a better description, just a body following its feet around.

We walk from Hostería las Torres, along the Rio Paine, to El Seron. Sun gives itself over to unraveling storms. The river goes dark, then brightens to a dull celadon. Storm shadows tint tree shadows. Rain shatters and stutters; guanacos graze. Patchworks of ice—the remains of hanging glaciers—rot away before our eyes. Snow squalls fall flat like bedsheets. As we walk through them, they erase both the *sendero* and the *senda*—the path as well as the ways and means. Later, going over a pass, an 80-mph wind tips us over. Laughing, we get to our feet and look up: a pair of Andean condors jump off a cliff—a jutting arête—and float effortlessly.

At the end of the day sleep comes easily. I'm tired from traveling and a recent bout of the flu. In the morning I roll the condor feather Gary brought to me inside my sleeping pad, hoist my backpack and hit the trail. Oh, for feathers and wings! Effortless is not how I'd describe myself in the days that follow. Gary and I walk at such different speeds that I see little of him, and for the first time, the age difference between us seems appalling.

I trudge and saunter, wipe sweat from my face, and laugh at the poorly working parts of my body, while he's all grace and exuberance. Usually an hour ahead, he comes back for me at the end of the day and carries my backpack the last half-mile because he's a fair-minded man and is always looking for ways to make our differences equal. At the end of each day we pitch camp, eat soup, drink tea, share chocolate, and happily compare notes: who saw what flower, grass, plant, waterfall, bee, or bird, and how speed or slowness brought these gifts to our eyes.

Unmarked

Every day is a circle walked within the big one of the Paine circuit, its outline as unsteady and meandering as our minds and gaits. Once a Chinese master asked his head monk where he was going. Fa-yen answered: "I'm rambling aimlessly around." The teacher asked what good it did, and Fa-yen answered: "I don't know." The teacher smiled. "That's good."

Farther into the mountains the river winds in and out of valleys gone white with *romero chilco de magellanes*—wild daisies. At the center are the ceros—the towers of granite whose red shoulders spin like fresh-minted interior suns pulsing squalls of rain and wind, and lobbing heavy-bodied clouds through the sunset like torpedoes.

The tenth-century Chinese weather predictor Pu-tai wandered through the towns of Chekiang. When asked how old he was, he answered, "As old as space." When he slept outside during winter storms, no snow fell on him at all.

PANTANO

It is a fresh wound, a whole shoulder torn, with a watery ooze and a hole that's getting bigger. I'm walking through a hanging bog, one that is cupped by the upper reaches of a mountain. Stunted trees bend sideways like dislocated hands. As I walk I see how the wound has grown, seen where backpackers have climbed farther up to avoid the mud, but in so doing, tear the earth's skin more.

How fragile we are. "We" being the humans and this mountain. My Inuit friends in Greenland use the word *sila* to describe weather: the power of nature, landscape, and human consciousness as one and the same. Every scar on the landscape is also a perturbation of mind. The trees thin. Gary is so far ahead I can't see which trail he's taken, so I choose one and enter the wound, trying not to get my feet wet because there are snowclouds gathering and surely it will freeze by evening.

My foot is a knife, tormenting the mountain's body. I continue up alone. *Es muy borrascoso*—It is very stormy. Am I lost? I step on a path. It leads me out of the bog onto dry ground.

THE PASS

The way is rock-strewn and bare, with tarns the size of footbaths. I wipe daubs of mud from my face, grinning because I'm above the tree line, in wide open country. Here, the only inflorescence is rock, the way it turns in a stream and flicks light. Rock walls carry the signatures of moving ice: I see how glaciers have shaped this place. During ice ages, birds, fish, plants, trees, and animals were pushed toward the equator. What's left behind are new surfaces: kettle moraines, outwash plains, pingos, scoured barren grounds. Ice scrapes the earth as if it had claws. Look closely: this is all that is left of the world's body after ice has picked the bones clean.

The mountain pass we are supposed to cross looks close but is a few hours' walk straight up. On the way, a serac falls and the waist of a glacier—a series of accumulation crevasses—crumbles. The deep rhythm of glaciers is not something we can always hear. It is an ancient memory of sound carved in long grooves and nervous chattermarks, thundering erratics bouncing on the under-melody of shushing streams of ice. Glaciers represent what is bold, inscrutable, exposed, quiet, and glinting in us, as well as what is delicate, dynamic, and precise. Perhaps if we walk among them long enough, we can learn from them.

We walk on rubble. Ice spires are wind-sharpened. We look up at glaciers while walking on the dents and scuffmarks that ice has left behind; we walk on its walking.

Traversing the spine, we re-enter a womb made by ice and climb into the cranium where mist pivots. The sky borrows its radiance from ice, its adamantine clarity, and we spend lifetimes tracking down those elements within ourselves.

ICEBERGS

Below is a meltwater lake strewn with small icebergs. "I've got to go see them," Gary says, and glissades down a steep-sided bowl to the water. At the bottom he slides, then jumps a patch of water onto a berg. Crouching, he's pensive, studying the half-hidden explosions of turquoise of the ice. He wipes meltwater on his face and gauges a glacier's brightness by holding a piece of ice to his eye. He's looking at time and impermanence, how each snowflake, trapped for hundreds of years and compressed as ice, can be put into service to a glacier before being released at the terminus; he sees how a glacier grows by giving away almost as much as it has received. Accumulation and ablation, to get and to give: these are the balancing acts of any human or body of ice.

A waterfall peels out of a cave, rounding the granite lip over which it has traveled for thousands of years. Everything we need to know about beauty, justice, time, movement, subtlety, and surrender is here. We climb and climb. Hoarse-throated streams rush past. No scent of humans or horses here, only the tang of snow. A single flower sheltered by an overhanging rock shivers.

Late in the day we make camp a few hundred yards below the pass. We tie the tent to krumholtz—stunted trees that hardly move in the stiff wind. I gather twigs and make a fire. We finish our nightly meal of soup in spitting snow that quickly becomes a blizzard. Night comes as a white monstrosity. Shadow asks body, are you there?

We sleep on a barren womb that was once filled with ice. I have no children and I'm with a man who wants them. Is this beauty enough? I ask. When I go out to pee, I step on snowflakes, each one a singular geometry, what Frank Lloyd Wright called "the grammar and spell-power of form."

Wet snow slaps at the tent. A zipped door flutters. We slide into a pulsing darkness—not a fearful place, but a room of winter where we are quiet, lost inside each other for a long time. Later I peek out: there's been a break in the storm. Across the valley I see a scooped-out shelf where there was once a hanging glacier. Now it's an empty bowl. Lit by moonlight, it chimes.

Descanso

"Be your own lamp, your refuge," the Buddha said as he was dying. Same thing Trungpa Rinpoche told me the last time I saw him. But

I'm lost, I'm dropping straight down into a thick forest. For a moment I see a glacier's six-mile-wide roof, its blue-blasted crevasses and fluted channels, its white flank flashing. Then it disappears. I've entered a tangled labyrinth on a near vertical slope with a footing of greasy mud that does not hold me. Sometimes the trees are marked with orange paint, but there is no trail. I bend under contorted branches and let myself down by dropping two or three feet to the next foothold. The weight of the backpack punishes my knees. It takes eight hours to go 3.5 miles.

The Bath, the River, the Wall

A half moon hangs in the sky at midday. For the first time the wind is pushing us from behind. We climb out of forest gloom and treachery onto a rocky ridge and make camp overlooking the crumbling terminus of an immense glacier. Later, Gary goes into the trees to bathe. I find him crouched behind two enormous logs. A stream trickles down a staircase of rock and feeds into a shadowy pool. Leaves drip onto him. His hair is wet. He stands in a wide plié, then shifts his weight to one knee. I take off my clothes and squat at water's edge. Moss is our only washcloth. We are hidden and naked; we lower our bodies into cold leaf-broth. A soft rain comes down.

In the morning we climb a vertical wall of rock on a rickety ladder made of cut tree limbs and cable. Facing the wall, I meet a dull mirror of basalt. Who's there? An impostor. The walls have fallen from around my body. Everything about my life seems fraudulent.

Wind kicks me in the ass. Near the top the backpack shifts sideways. Hope I don't fall. There are things I'd like to do before I die: live for a year with binocular vision, speak only animals' languages, start sleep-walking again, and do away with all automobiles. I grab rung after rung and pull myself up. In Japan I met *Yamabushi*—ascetic mountain monks who climb ladders made of knives and are hung upside down by their heels in frigid waterfalls. Mountains invite us to humiliate ourselves. They offer danger and difficulty and drive beauty to the bone.

The Bumblebee

Raindrops, sun, a single cloud wheeling between two condors. Why do we walk in circles? We take a side route up to interior peaks. It rains again and we make camp quickly in a narrow gorge beside a river. Water sounds push Gary into sleep and I listen to sila—how the mind-litter rolls with chaotic weather. We are made of weather and our thoughts stream from the braidwork of stillness and storms. For years, Nietzsche searched for what he called "true climate" for its exact geographical location as it corresponds to the "inner climate" of the thinker. He might as well have gone searching for the ever-shifting North Pole.

Rio Frances roars by. Upstream there's a glacier tucked in a cirque and its edges are ragged. The trimline of lenga trees is clearly visible: leggy tree roots hang over the cliff carved away by ice as if amputations had just been performed.

A collar of ice encircles the glacier's top edge, not white, but eggshell blue. Twenty thousand years ago temperatures plummeted and ice grew down from the top of the world. Glaciers sprouted and surged, covering ten million square miles—more than thirteen times what they cover now. In the southern Andes, ice sheets fingered their way between high peaks all the way south to the Strait of Magellan and the Beagle Channel.

All along the circuit we've encountered glaciers, but worldwide they're on the wane. As a result, the albedo effect—the ability of ice and snow to deflect heat back into space—is quickly diminishing as glaciers melt and less and less snow covers the ground each winter. Snow and ice are the world's air conditioners. They are crucial to the health of the planet. Without winter's white mantle, earth will become a heat sponge, and only smoke from a volcano will shield us from incoming UV rays. As heat escalates, all our sources of fresh water—already in danger of being depleted—will disappear.

Warmer temperatures are causing meltwater to stream into oceans, changing salinity; sea ice and permafrost are thawing, pulsing methane into the air; seawater is expanding, causing floods and intrusions; islands are disappearing; and vast human populations in places like Bangladesh are in grave danger. The high mountain peoples of Peru, Bolivia, and Chile, who depend on meltwater from the snowpack for irrigation, are at risk of being lost. The Ice Age culture of the Greenland Inuit, who depend on ice for transportation and live on a subsistence diet of marine mammals, will disappear. And the early onset of spring and the late arrival of winter is creating ecosystem pandemonium in temperate climates everywhere.

No place looks as pristine as the Arctic. But some of the deadliest contaminants have congregated there. Ironically, the Arctic and its ecosystem are most vulnerable to global warming. Whereas sea ice between Ellesmere Island and Greenland was 14 to 24 inches thick in 1991, when I first went there, it is now only four.

Thirteen years ago I traveled to the high Arctic with a seal biologist who has spent twenty years of fieldwork on the ice. Recently he said, "Climate is what we talk about now because both glacier ice and sea ice are going fast, and whatever oscillation we impose on the computer models, the same linear signal shows up. That signal is the one made by industry and automobiles—human-caused pollution—and it's very strong. This warming trend is a frightening thing. As the albedo effect decreases, things will get warmer. More solar heat is absorbed and the increase in temperatures grows exponentially. Which means we lose more and more ice.

"The history of climate is cyclic and fluctuating. But there has been no other time in the history of the world when greenhouse gases, airborne methane and mercury, desertification, and deforestation have been around. The anthropogenic signal is nonfluctuating. It just goes up and up in warmth. The ironic thing is that none of these ills of so-called 'civilization' originated in the Arctic. The polar winds bring pollution from the entire northern hemisphere, including the U.S., Canada, Russia, China and Europe, to the north; precipitation rains the pollutants down; ice stores them; and when 'break-up' starts, we have toxic spring in the high latitudes."

I lie in a boulder pile looking upstream at the hanging glacier, which, if it crumbled, would take me out. Clouds slide over, banking up, one on top of the other as if trying to make the small glacier grow. But like so many others, this one is receding. Already its forehead has been torn open and is poised to fall.

It is not unreasonable to think that a whole season can become extinct, at least for a time. Winter might last only one day—a minor punctuation in a long sentence of heat. Mirages rising from shimmering heat waves would be the only storms.

We have already destroyed so much natural vegetation on the planet that the increased heat, due to bare ground, deforestation, ineffectual rainfall, and city pavement, will have particularly dire effects with nothing to modify them. Hot and toxic: those are the words that will describe where we once lived. Land-ocean-atmosphere-solar-galactic cycles are inextricably linked. One flap of the butterfly and we all fry.

Gary returns from a six-hour walkabout. We argue about how long our "short-term" relationship can possibly last. A snow squall migrates down the narrow canyon toward our tent. I grab the shirts and underwear I've washed and pull them in. The wrathful and peaceful deities at the center of the mountain complex are still spinning storms around with their hundred flailing arms, still telling us what, in Sanskrit, is called a *pariplava*, a circular story. Things between us will end when they end. Just as the fate of human life on the planet. But not yet. Storms pulse by. Behind clouds, sun strobes. If the path is whatever passes, no end in itself, why are we walking in circles? Why don't we just stand?

For a minute the clouds clear and the orange peaks burst through. A single bumblebee flies by our tent, headed into the storm. In the Arctic, at latitude 80 degrees North, the Arctic bumblebee—*bombus polaris*—shivers to keep warm. The worker bees die at the end of summer, and the impregnated queen starts a new colony when warm weather returns. I don't know this southern hemisphere bee, but it must be cold-adapted in ways that we humans are not. I wonder if it will be able to adapt to heat. Gary and I hold each other; we shiver with cold. The bee is bright orange and looks like a piece of fire.

Exploring the Great Indoors ꩜

Jeff Greenwald

Here's a different kind of travelogue, an interior one. The first time you do a meditation program, you're like a tourist visiting your own mind. Like any tourist, you discover wondrous sights, but also unpleasant truths, boredom, and a lot of hidden suffering. Here are Jeff Greenwald's notes from his first long meditation program, a ten-day vipassana retreat.

Day One—Spirit Rock Meditation Center

One hour into my ten-day retreat, I drop my bag in a cool, compact room in a dorm named Upekkha: Equanimity.

So far, so good. I accept the dry, grassy hills outside my window, the wild turkeys on the walkway, the wind curling down the valley. I accept my practical room with its small table, folding chair, and narrow bed with fuzzy pink blankets.

It reminds me, in fact, of a room I inhabited on a previous journey. In 1994, I set off on an around-the-world trip to commemorate my fortieth birthday. The idea was to avoid airplanes and perform a *kora*—a devotional circumambulation—around the Earth's surface. On the final leg of that nine-month odyssey, I crossed the Pacific aboard the *Bremen Express*, a huge container ship sailing from Hong Kong to Oakland. My residence was the pilot's cabin, a spartan room very much like this one. For fifteen days there was nothing in my life but my room, the purr of the turbines, and the ocean beneath and all around us.

The upcoming voyage seems similar: a long passage across a mysterious sea. But while the ship carried a thousand liters of beer and an impressive library of action videos, the retreat comes with an intimidating set of rules meant to limit distractions: almost total silence; no reading, TV, or radio; no eye contact with other "yogis"; and a seventeen-hour schedule of sitting and walking meditation broken only by work duty, meals, and dharma talks. There will be no iced steins of pilsener or midnight screenings of *Predator*.

This is my first ten-day retreat, and I have no idea what to expect. But I do know that the shape of my life is not as easy to accept as this monastic cell. I face the mixed blessing of a creative but solitary life. Traveling the world since my twenties, I've avoided the entrap-ments—and pleasures—of domestic life. I've no wife, children, pets, mortgage, life insurance premiums, or equity. Lately, that "freedom" has seemed akin to the sort in "Me and Bobby McGee": "just another word for nothin' left to lose."

Last spring, after my fiftieth birthday, I decided to pursue more conventional comforts. Miraculously, the perfect opportunity arose. Reggie was the kind of woman who could climb El Capitán, serve up a dinner of roast duck and cherry cobbler at the summit, and name the constellations in afterglow—but her urgency to start a family aroused my ambivalence. I waffled; she bailed. Facing ten days alone, in silence, I realize that my heart is still shredded by this sharp-edged failure.

Then comes the small stuff. Mortality, for example. Fifty, I'm fond of saying, is the new thirty. But eighty is still eighty, and it's not so far away. My career remains a sore point (especially when my mother tries to find *Tricycle* in Hicksville). And there remains the eternal hope for a partner. A whole different set of issues may well arise on the retreat—but that's the menu of distractions on Day One at Ground Zero.

As a travel writer, I sense these days will be spent in an unfamiliar, intriguing country, a land I've long dreamed of visiting, but which I know only from guidebooks. That this terrain lies within *me* makes little difference; it's likely to be as alien as Ouagadougou.

A steady wind flies down the hill and in through my screen, rustling the papers on my bed. The sky is the color of Tibetan turquoise. Live oaks and pine trees cast scraggly shadows across the dry yellow grass, and a turkey vulture circles above the residence halls. I can't believe I didn't bring any chocolate.

Day Two

A night of fitful sleep, during which I dreamed I ate a Kit-Kat bar the size of my door.

The first sitting is at 5:45 A.M. I tiptoe into the meditation hall at six, squeaking guiltily through the earnest silence. Our teachers sit on a low dais. Before them is a bowl-shaped bell, to be struck at the sitting's end. Spirit Rock's sitting hall is imposing but enclosing, a beautifully crafted room that lets in light and air while keeping out the static of civilization. I'd brought my zafu into the empty hall last night, and now find the cushion surrounded by my co-yogis: people who have dropped everything and traveled from far and wide, simply to sit in silence. Many sit cross-legged on zafus, while others meditate in chairs. The variety of folding seats, knee supporters, backrests, and zafus is astonishing. Meditation gear, like ski wear, is clearly a thriving industry.

The days will be regimented: sitting, walking, sitting, walking, from dawn until dark. Vipassana practice, teacher Joseph Goldstein reminds us, is an experiment, an investigation of how our mind works. The relentless schedule is simply a technique to remove distractions, and watch the mind with as few obstructions as possible.

My first work meditation is at 7:30 A.M. I've signed up for vegetable chopping. There are five of us, and we are quickly schooled by the cook. We wash our hands, slip on aprons, collect our knives, and receive our designated veggies. My upekkha is challenged at once: we're having eggplant for lunch.

Walking meditation is a bit like scuba diving: the part where one ascends toward the surface, rising no faster than one's tiniest air bubbles. I move into the walking room, pick a "lane"—it's a bit like lap swimming—and begin the zombie-like gait. Across the way is a Burmese Buddha in the standing pose, hands by his side, palms out. Walking toward those open arms, I feel like a child taking his first steps. How many other yogis, I wonder, have felt this same sense of learning something familiar all over again?

I carry my lunch outside, to the redwood tables below a high, round hill that immediately captures my attention. Its golden grasses shimmer in the wind, mirroring the shadow of a hovering hawk.

I've been warned about "Vipassana romance," and there are definitely some contenders: a blonde cowgirl, a doe-eyed Asian, an olive-skinned beauty who looks like Brenda on *Six Feet Under.*

It's not just them. All the women I've known come skipping into the spotlight of my concentration, dancing like Mara's daughters. Some memories are tinged with lust, others with sweetness, many with sadness.

Hardest to shake are the memories of Reggie. I imagine her here, calming her mind beneath these lovely clouds. I ask her for another chance, letting go into the safety I felt in her arms. When I let them in, these thoughts seem unbearable. But I do bear them, tears welling. I observe the texture of grief, watching it rise and fall.

Returning to my room, I spy—behind the thermostat—the brilliant orange feather Reggie wore in her hair on the Fourth of July. Why, oh why, did I bring that feather with me? I know why . . . and at some point I must bring it to one of the nearby Buddha shrines, and let it go. At some point . . . but not today.

One arrives here full of glee and trepidation, like a traveler visiting a famous city for the first time. It seems impossible to imagine that you will someday know the streets and subways, the best cafés and hidden museums.

This doubt, Joseph assures us, is natural. Have faith: the mind will calm down. This convoluted landscape may someday become a second home. Like a first-time visitor to Benares—or a hiker on the first day of a Himalayan trek—one must accept the initial agonies, and persevere.

DAY THREE

First "interview" group today, kicked off by a frizzy-haired yogi who complains of shooting pains in her joints. "Vipassana pain," our teacher, Annie, tells her. "A good sign."

My issue is pain, as well. Loneliness, agitation, even despair as my mind dishes up memories of failed loves. I reveal this to Annie, who confirms that, yes, such things *will* come up. There's no easy way to do this practice. Friends warned me of this, as well. "You'll love the first few days," my editor told me wryly. "It's like being locked in a phone booth with a raving lunatic."

This is the paradox of practice. It needs faith, to continue sitting through the boredom and knee pain and doubt. But one cannot expect anything.

While sitting, I make an effort to focus my awareness. But when thoughts come, they come hard, and the harder they come, the more they cry to be written down. Joseph shares his mantra on the subject: *For the purpose of the meditation practice, nothing is worth thinking about.* This, then, is my *Seinfeld*-like conundrum: to write a story about nothing.

DAY FOUR

Eyes move from ground to trees, from food to hill, grazing on legs and hips, chests and lips, along the way. No smiles, or outward signs. But the dance goes on. Men shave; women paint their toenails. We note who wears rings, and on which finger.

• • •

Spirit Rock is so beautiful that it is a distraction in itself. I'm obsessed with the ever-changing light on the crest of that hill outside the dining hall, with the wild turkeys in the grass, the lizards on the path, the calls of the birds who nest in the beams outside the meditation hall.

But this retreat, really, is about the Great Indoors. The sensation of a peach slice against my tongue. The tightness in my hips after exactly thirty minutes of a forty-five-minute sitting (the last fifteen are always the hardest). My bare toes against the cracks in the asphalt. The awareness of my awareness of women. The fictional dialogues and rehearsals that my mind continually invents: dialogues with friends, foes, family, ex-lovers, editors, everyone who has done me wrong, misunderstood me, judged me, or let me down. Dialogues in which my righteous view always prevails.

"You can find the entire world in your in-breath," a teacher trainee tells me in our private session. "The in-breath is like your home, the place your mind returns to after work. Pay attention. Everything is there."

Perhaps so. But for now, the whole world is also *out there*: in that hawk, the waving grass, that tall red-haired woman walking past my window.

A strong afternoon sitting. I split my "self" into two parts, and observe with detachment my monkey mind: rehearsing dialogues, churning up scenarios of attack-and-response, cultivating desire, perfecting verbal self-defense. The patterns seem so obvious, the remedy so near at hand. And then I lose it all an hour later, during Kamala's talk on the Five Hindrances.

The talk, so succinct during the first half, begins to drag on, as Kamala provides endless examples of the disguises of Doubt, Aversion, and Restlessness. I began to realize that the talk will go over an hour, and cut into my evening walk. *Cut into my walk!* How dare she?!

Kamala had earlier described anger as a fireball, and I feel one descending. It's the intense irritation I experience whenever I'm *kept waiting*. For the first time in days I find my mind on the loose, out of control. The feeling passes, of course (as soon as the talk ends), but it leaves me shaken. I look down at my hands, amazed to see that I've unconsciously bitten my nails—less than two hours after congratulating myself for breaking the habit!

Preparing tea in the dining hall, I remember the words of the Buddha, as shared by Kamala: "In this fathom-long body, all of the universe can be discovered."

DAY FIVE

Monkey mind; reptile mind. During walking meditation, I watch a big lizard capture and devour a smaller one. The victim thrashes, then remains still as it disappears into its predator's maw. Fascination; revulsion; aversion; the awareness of judgments being made. Then a placid return to walking.

The lizard is just one more metaphor, added to the countless metaphors from our instructors. There are a thousand ways to paint the mind and its discontents. And what about these "mindful" thoughts? What should I do when I'm seized by the urge to fathom the meaning of a reptile?

"Don't stop the thought—you *can't*. Simply be mindful," Joseph asserts. "Return your attention to the primary object: breathing, walking, the sensations in your body."

It's enormously difficult. Still, I have a slight advantage over my fellow yogis. Insight meditation is all about observing, and observation has been part of my training as a journalist. The skill, I'm learning, may be transferable.

I sit in silence for thirty minutes, then open my eyes. Out the window, the grassy hill looks radiant in late afternoon light. The ridgeline is a lion's back, fine brown hairs prickling on the haunches.

Every morning at 6:45, every afternoon at 12:15, and every evening at 5:15 one can see it: the World's Slowest Race, as dozens of yogis compete in a "mindful walking" sprint toward the dining hall.

This evening, a plate of cookies waits at the end of the food line. With impressive self-control I follow the unspoken protocol, and take just one. Twenty minutes later, another yogi emerges, and sits beside me. I glance at her plate. *Two cookies!* Judgment spirals through my brain. My emotions run the gamut from gall to embarrassment (for her sake), ending with equanimity and admiration. Here is a woman who has guiltlessly accepted her love of cookies.

But as I reenter the dining hall for tea, I understand all. There's a whole new tray of cookies! I take two, wrap them in napkins, and put one in each jacket pocket, planning to eat them under the stars after the day's final sitting.

When that long-awaited moment comes, I sit on an outdoor bench and unwrap the first cookie—daydreaming about how great it would be to have a cup of hot chocolate, and how I'll be sure to bring some next time. When I look down, both cookies are gone; I've eaten them in a virtual coma.

Another perfect teaching. Desiring one thing while devouring another, I'm left with nothing.

A breakthrough sitting this afternoon, during which each emerging thought is fixed with the lens of mindfulness, and viewed without attachment. One by one they bubble up from the tar pit of my unconscious mind, blossom into life, and—poof!—disintegrate. It's great; I feel like Neo in *The Matrix*.

Rarely do we realize how utterly controlled we are by our thoughts. They run roughshod over us, ponies in stampede. I can see why people devote entire lifetimes to stabilizing those rare, blissful moments when we take back the reins.

But I bristle at Joseph's warning that even these positive sittings, these rare moments when I think I might be getting somewhere, are "corruptions," and self-delusion. It often seems that our teachers delight in being obtuse and in framing practice as a wild goose chase. I'm tempted to throw up my hands, and suggest a new "mantra" for the process: "We can't tell you where you're going, but you're never going to get there."

Day Six

A good morning sitting, after a breakfast of rice pudding. Seems I sit best when well fed. My focus is on the nature of thoughts. What *are* they? Last spring, on a Point Reyes beach, Reggie and I saw thousands of tiny, dried-up jellyfish, washed onto the shore like sea bream. It seems that thoughts are much like those hapless beings: spawned by the millions, carried on the waves, and then blown away, desiccated, by the wind.

Speaking of Reggie, my mind has settled; I'm ready to make a symbolic gesture. And so, with a pang of sadness, I take her orange feather out of my room and leave it on the lap of the White Tara behind the meditation hall.

The only parts of the practice that can be described with confidence are the rough, cerebral edges. What happens at the center, when the mind quiets down, is impossible to verbalize. It's as if I were writing about the Grand Canyon, but could only talk about the rim.

Still, there are moments—especially during the dharma talks—when I experience the delight of hearing a deeply felt truth articulated for the first time. In meditation itself, I feel something even more gratifying: the notion that my mind may actually be trainable. Thoughts are endless, and they rush in to fill the yawning well of awareness. But one might learn to hold that space open, with practice. It may not stay *empty*—but one can choose what to let in.

But don't get me wrong; I'm still a bumbling novice. On Day Six, I continue to battle infinite distractions—from self-recriminations over my romantic foibles to a parade of ideas for absurd, *New Yorker*–style cartoons. Today's best-in-show: "Tourette's Syndrome Sitting Group."

It's all about openness. Being open, with equanimity, to every thought that arises. Without preferences, without identification, without attachment. It's the same mind-set required of a traveler on pilgrimage: "Whatever arises—bring it to the path."

Day Seven

"All happy families are alike," wrote Leo Tolstoy, "but every unhappy family is unhappy in its own way." Conversely: All unhappy sittings are alike, but every happy sitting is different in its own way.

Unhappy sittings are always about the same thing: collapsing into the trap of identification, clinging, wishing for things to be different from the way they are. But all productive sittings reveal new facets of the breath, or the sounds outside the window. Each opens a new avenue for insight. Every one of my "good" sittings has been transformative, highlighting a different aspect of my awareness. Every unhappy sitting is about *dukkha*, suffering—and *dukkha* is about closing down.

I've had those sittings, and plenty. This afternoon, the woman in front of me belched at reliable intervals; to my left, a stomach gurgled like a swamp. Minutes before the bell, as I was approaching a state of relative calm, someone on my right released a resonant fart. How much can a yogi bear?

For now, the important thing is just to let it all in, and to let it all out. If it can find the door.

Reggie's feather blew off the White Tara; I find it in a bush a few yards away. That won't do. I pick it up, bring it to the big stone Buddha by the dining hall, and toss it sheepishly among the feathers and talismans placed under rocks near the statue's base. Not a very good job, so far, of letting go.

Kamala recounts a time when, in Burma, she told her teacher how hard practice was. "I'm not asking you to cut down the jungle," he replied, "I'm just asking you to be mindful!" Everyone laughs; but I think it's *easier* to clear a jungle. You gather a fleet of bulldozers—or pruning shears—and get to work. After a finite length of time, it's done. That's one of the most daunting aspects of meditation practice: One has no idea when, or if, the job will be "done."

· · ·

My mind assigns personalities, develops attractions and aversions, based on the most superficial impressions. This rude woman belches every sitting; that kind man holds the door for me; that lonely woman looks like she's been weeping; that strange man bows to his zafu; that generous woman tilts the soup pot for me; that selfish man jumps the queue. And so a menagerie of characters is created, all fanciful, but oddly persistent. They demonstrate, as much as any teaching, how the mind manufactures and clings to illusion.

There's a secluded bench in a small grove, not far from the meditation hall. On the way I pass an outdoor shrine filled with memories from lost lives: photographs, amulets, poems, prayer flags, candles, bones, a dog collar, a compass, a rake. I search my pockets, but find nothing to leave as an offering. For the first time in days, I regret being empty-handed.

Day Eight

During walking meditation I take the forest trail, picking a spur between two oaks whose limbs overhang the path. I close my eyes and move toward mindfulness. Twenty steps out, twenty steps back. The crunching of leaves synchronizes with my breath as the sounds of the forest arise and recede. My eyes are closed, and I experience a moment of sublime spaciousness—which ends abruptly as my head whacks into an overhanging limb.

In September of 1994, a few days after my around-the-world trip ended, I was driving through San Francisco. Somewhere in the lower Haight, I saw a body-piercing salon. On a whim, I parked my car.

It had been a momentous week, witnessing the conclusion of a transformative journey. During my trip I'd covered nearly thirty thousand miles, visiting twenty-seven countries. Those final days on the *Bremen Express,* like this retreat, had settled my mind and prepared me for what lay ahead. Entering the piercing salon, I prepared to brand the memory of that journey onto my body.

Minutes later, I emerged with a silver hoop through my left ear-lobe. On the ring was a tiny enamel sphere. Green and blue, it looked like a miniature Earth.

It's a shame there's no body-piercing salon at Spirit Rock. I'd like a companion to that ring: something to mark fifty years, and this latest rite of passage. But how do you commemorate nothing?

Before dinner, I return to the Buddha where I'd left Reggie's feather. It's nowhere to be seen. I glance around to see if it has blown into a bush, or elsewhere. Nope; gone. I'm filled with deep regret. I watch the feeling arise, reach its emotional zenith, and dissipate into space. How can I fail to see the metaphor, the inner workings of cause and effect? Reggie had offered me everything: love, companionship, a family. I hesitated; now she's gone. It is hard to deny that, on some level, that must be what I wanted.

Just as I wanted that feather to be taken away; and so it was.

Day Nine

Of all the vegetables I've chopped this week, tomatillos are my favorite. Their firm skin, jade hue, and receptivity to the blade made prepping for lunch a true meditation. Zucchinis are a close second. Mincing dill is a delight, though one soon becomes covered with fragrant hairs. Carrots are also noble, the knife tapping on the wooden board after every cut. I love cutting kale, collard greens, and chard, though those last inches can be tricky. Green peppers I can take or leave. Onions I strictly avoid, as well as tomatoes—for though I enjoy them as much as the next yogi, I loathe the slimy mess on the cutting board.

I imagine my fellow yogis wondering who will get which slice of each vegetable. Will this be eaten by the motionless man on my left? By the woman with the silver toenails? Or—yikes!—by one of the teachers themselves?

It's a good feeling, feeding people. A delightful surprise, this "chopping for Buddhists."

Silence will soon be broken. A few announcements are made, and we are told that speaking will be allowed for two hours (until dinner) in a few outdoor locations.

Nearly all the yogis race outside to chat. I remain seated, glad for some time alone. But within minutes, bedlam ensues—right outside the meditation hall windows. I recall a description of the human race from Kurt Vonnegut's *Galapagos:* "My God, were they ever loud."

I leave my cushion and move into the woods, walking until I reach the Grove of Memories. This time, I'm not empty-handed. I reach up and, for the first time in ten years, pull carefully but steadily on the silver band through my earlobe. It opens reluctantly, then falls into my hand.

There, on the arm of a laughing Buddha, I leave my forties.

A final meal by the grassy hill, where I've eaten every meal. I'm still captivated by its ridgeline, that protean edge where the rippling grasses meet the sky. With its ever-changing play of light and motion, this hill has taught me much about presence, change, and nonattachment. It belongs to me—but only on a moment-to-moment basis. Soon, even those moments will be gone.

Day Ten

I sit by the stone Buddha, unable to believe it is ending.

The world has rushed back, a flash flood into a box canyon. The yogis, so mysterious and inaccessible when silent, now step forward with their stories. The man with splotched pants, whom I took for a painter, is a paralegal; the zaftig, thick-haired woman who looked so sad is a spunky therapist; the tall man who seemed so serious is an animated Irishman, who hugs me with a grin.

Out of silence, these yogis still shine.

My mind is clear as I contemplate the most important insight gained during this long, strange trip: I am not, in truth, the distracted, dissatisfied person I often appear to be to myself and others.

The obstacles to my happiness are not insuperable. I have the tools to remove them entirely; how I use those tools, and how often, is up to me.

But if I'm comforted, it may be (as the teachers implied) because I don't know the deeper truth. My demons are still down there. For one reason or another, they kept their silence. I made no effort to dare them awake.

My car, waiting down the hill, seems a world away. As I drive south, banking around precarious curves, I recall a quotation from one of Joseph's talks. It is by the Dalai Lama, and seems uniquely appropriate to this moment of departure:

"Changes in attitudes never come easily," the Tibetan monk states in *Tibetan Portrait: The Power of Compassion.* "[Their] development is a wide, round curve that can be negotiated only slowly—not a sharp corner that can be turned all at once."

I take a few long breaths, watching the play of light and shadow on the road ahead.

Sunset Boulevard ﹚﹚

Erik Hansen

*As he drives to his weekly meditation group, Erik Hansen ponders
a two-mile strip of sex, money, and power—and all the temptations
and distractions it represents—and wonders just how American
American Buddhism should be.*

Wednesday evenings, on our way to our weekly meditation group
in Los Angeles, my wife and I must traverse the section of Sunset
Boulevard that runs from Hollywood to Beverly Hills. Our approach
to this famous strip is signaled by an enormous billboard—it used to
be the Marlboro Man, now it's a fifty-foot silhouette of an Absolut
Vanilla Vodka bottle—jutting up at the point where Sunset first
starts to bend, before snaking along the foot of the Hollywood Hills.
Once past the Absolut bottle, it's 1.9 miles of sex, money, power,
glamour, glitz, and sleaze. Okay, perhaps it's not the prelude most
conducive to an evening of meditation, but I think it serves as an apt
metaphor for some of the challenges facing American Buddhists on
the path to enlightenment. You can look, or you can look away, but
you cannot avoid the impact of our culture.

In our larger American sangha, we often consider the evolution
of Buddhism in this country, and in the West at large. But we might
also consider the flip side: to see what insights Buddhist practice
can offer into the experience of being American. This is the exercise

I've set for myself as we drive past strip joints, liquor stores, tattoo parlors, and sushi bars, past the Roxy and the Whiskey and Hustler's sex emporium. I know that my deepest mirror mind is stainless, but what about the rest of me? Can I cruise this stretch without the clouds of dissatisfaction and desire obscuring my mind's innate brilliance?

No, I can't. That's the short answer. Take this moment, for example: I'm keeping pace with a silver-blue Lexus RX300 SUV, my dream vehicle. I know that elsewhere in the world there is terrible deprivation—shouldn't that knowledge inform my values? But alas, at this moment all that distant suffering is just a faint shadow in a corner of my mind, while this beautiful Lexus is a tantalizing, tangible presence.

A million messages await me along this strip, and I decode them instantly. A billboard depicts a lean woman stretching in designer spandex, and no words are needed to remind me how important it is to wear nice clothes and stay in shape.

I sometimes think of my Zen practice as a process of "de-hypnosis," reversing the developmentally necessary but contrary process— begun years ago by parents and teachers, schoolyard chums and siblings, screenwriters and advertising executives—of turning me into a good little American. They succeeded wonderfully. Before I knew much else, I knew that Trix were for kids.

So, as I cruise down Sunset, forty-five years of conditioning locked away in my brain and nervous system, you might say I'm hardwired for America. Moment by moment, from this latent field of prior conditioning, "America" and "self" spring into existence, summoned, for example, by the billboard across the street advertising the next George Clooney movie. For a moment, I get to experience that subtle, compound being which is me-as-an-American-sharing-a-world-with-George-Clooney. I recall that he was on *Letterman* two nights ago, speaking with warmth and modesty about his beautiful costar, his latest project, his villa on Lake Como, and I was the guy who sits on the couch with his wife and listens to movie stars talk about their lives. No doubt I'd be wise to toss my TV, unplug the radio, and cancel my subscription to *Newsweek*; the bite into a Big Mac, the trip to Wal-Mart, the casual chat around the water cooler will always zap me into this time and place, this realm of values, this American self.

My Zen teacher, Dr. Edward Wortz, sometimes says, "There's no fixed way to be [a Buddhist, an American, a human being], but there are consequences." No fixed way to be. Could this be true? It would mean that all judgments of ourselves and others—all moral absolutes—are merely human constructs. It would mean there's no place in the universe where judgments reside, except in the human mind. But before we get carried away, let's remember Dr. Wortz's second dictum: There are always consequences. No judgments, just karma. Freedom bound to personal responsibility.

That's why, at the end of this long drive, I am so happy to settle onto my zafu cushion, exchange smiles with friendly, familiar faces, and prepare myself for zazen. I feel my priorities reorder themselves along the axis of what is real. From the safety of my zafu, I wonder: Should I come a different way? I surely could do a better job of insulating myself from this clamorous culture. But it seems to me that this practice is not about forcing change or becoming an idealized version of ourselves. It's about life as it is, accepting who we are, American twang and all. In fact, total acceptance might be the most radical practice there is.

I contemplate the wonderful "okay-ness" of being American. Imagine, even *that* is acceptable. Yes, there are consequences, but if I want to take in a mind-numbing action movie, play games on the Web, or have a Heineken with my *Monday Night Football,* it's okay. "No fixed way to be" means that in each of us the American and the Buddhist come together in different ways. Labels never quite fit; contradictions are okay. Including this one: Like a jewel in Indra's net, my mind reflects not only all other sentient beings, but also *Gilligan's Island* reruns, presidential debates, Victoria's Secret ads . . . sex, money, power, glamour, glitz, sleaze . . . and Sunset Boulevard.

Waking Up at Work ⥎

Michael Carroll

*Traditionally in Asia, serious meditation practice was the province of
monastics and yogis who could devote their lives completely to Buddhism.
A unique feature of Buddhism in the West is that most meditators are
laypeople, with jobs and families. Rather than separating from conventional society, they must learn how to bring their meditation practice
right into it. This is in many respects uncharted territory. The practice
is difficult, but potentially it can be of great benefit. Here, businessman
Michael Carroll explains how Buddhism can help us deal with the chaos
and challenges of life at work.*

In 1980, at the age of twenty-six, I set aside my worldly ambitions—
and cashed in all my savings—to attend a Buddhist Seminary in
Alberta, Canada, led by the renowned Tibetan meditation master
Chögyam Trungpa Rinpoche. In Seminary we sat in meditation for
seven to eight hours a day, studied Tibetan and Indian texts, and discussed timeless Buddhist teachings among ourselves and with Rinpoche. The training was rigorous and thorough, and the time spent
in those long, regal stretches of the Canadian Rockies was delightful.

For me, a young, enthusiastic spiritual seeker, I felt that I had
arrived at the inner sanctum. I was living the cloistered life, studying ancient teachings with a renowned master. Surely this was as

momentous as life could get! I had left behind the world of materialism, and I was studying meditation techniques that would lead me to wisdom and bliss. However, despite my lofty ambitions, I was soon to discover that I was being trained for something much more practical and profound.

As the weeks passed I decided with firm conviction that I wanted to devote myself to spiritual study and meditation for the rest of my life. I contemplated the details of such a venture. Where would I live? How would I pay the bills? What bills would I even have? Could I wander from place to place, or should I find a monastery to take me in? How would my girlfriend feel about my living the life of a monk? She'd probably be relieved, I thought. It was all very exciting. I was convinced I was making the right choice.

Toward the end of seminary, I requested a meeting with Rinpoche, and I planned to let him know my intentions. One could never be quite certain what he would say, but I was pretty sure that he would give me advice on how to proceed. Maybe he would suggest that I join a monastery or direct me to go on an extended meditation retreat. Maybe he would see my true potential and send me to Sikkim to study at the feet of the Karmapa, one of the most revered teachers of Tibetan Buddhism!

As seminary drew to a close, we all gathered for a graduation celebration. Rinpoche joined us for the festivities and took a seat at the far end of the large spacious ballroom. That evening the sadness of the many farewells, the budding Canadian spring, and the graduation party were mingling into a perfect ending to a truly defining time in my life, when a young man said to me, "Rinpoche will see you now."

"Now," I thought, "in the middle of a party?" I finally had my chance to speak with him, but I didn't feel prepared.

I was escorted to Rinpoche, and after the customary bow and then the typical silent, awkward moments, I began to explain my plans to become a full-time meditator. He patiently listened to my reasoning, smiling, nodding his head and studying my face. I explained to him that I had left my job, given up my home, and cashed in my savings to come to Seminary. I was devoted to getting to the heart of the teachings, committed to meditation, and prepared to spend the rest of my life focused exclusively on the Buddhist path. Now I just needed a little advice, a tip or two. So I asked: "How should I proceed?"

"Go home and get a job," he replied instantly. I stammered and tried to get my footing; my mind was racing. "Maybe he thinks I'm not good enough to be a monk. Or maybe he thinks I am someone else. That's not unusual; with so many students, he could make a mistake like that." I grabbed for a story line—any story line. I didn't expect him to tell me to get lost—to go get a job!

Then I thought, "Maybe I haven't been clear. Maybe he misunderstood me." I got control of myself and repeated my rationale once again. And again, Rinpoche patiently listened to my reasoning, sipping from his glass and sitting solidly in his chair. Finally he sat back and with a wide, mischievous grin said, "You can do it. Give it a try." The interview was over, and my monastic career was on the rocks. The tables had been turned, and I was, in many respects, out in the cold.

So it was with mixed feelings that I left Canada and returned to New York City. But my brief conversation with my teacher marked the beginning of a spiritual adventure more fulfilling than I could have imagined at the time. Instead of seeking out a monastic life, I was to live in New York and find my spiritual footing in the bowels of capitalism, on Wall Street. Here I would come to learn that what I thought was trivial, the so-called conventional world, was in fact sacred; and what I had considered profound, the "spiritual path," was simply my own naive fantasy. I was to learn my spiritual lessons at work, not in a monastery.

Throughout my twenty-two-year career on Wall Street and later in publishing, I gradually came to understand the wisdom of my teacher's instruction. The daily grind, the successes and failures, the hard work and stress, all gradually unfolded as a profound teaching. And central to that teaching was the realization that the spiritual path is nothing other than living our very life, fully and confidently, in the immediate moment—and that nothing can be excluded, especially not our jobs. Scrubbing a floor, writing an e-mail, leading a country, feeding a hungry child, are all noble steps we take on our path to becoming completely *who we are, where we are.* Work becomes our spiritual journey when our destination is no longer just becoming more successful or more wealthy, or getting a paycheck, promotion, or job security, but when we also work to resolve a most fundamental question: Can we be at home in our lives—can we be open, honest, and at ease under all circumstances, moment by moment?

Being at ease with ourselves at work can be a challenge indeed, because, try as we might, we cannot control work. It is chaotic, fickle, and messy. We may have a passion for becoming a superb doctor or a dedicated teacher. Or we may work hard at being an effective lawyer or outstanding dancer. But somehow complications always seem to get in the way: malpractice insurance, rebellious students, tough bar exams, tired ligaments. Work is never quite what we expect, and being successful at our jobs is never as simple as we hope.

Work's untidy complications can be distressing, at times even alarming. Our work lives unfold amid countless uncertainties and upsets that leave many of us feeling disappointed, stressed out, and even under siege. Today's business culture would have us believe that such complications are mere roadblocks to achieving what *really* matters: a paycheck, promotion, profitability. Business requires, indeed, often fiercely demands, that the path to success be as smooth as possible.

But such is never the case. Success is often elusive and work *by its very nature* is unruly and at times unfair—and deep down we know it. We know that career troubles and conflicts are inevitable, that stubborn personalities and poor decisions are par for the course. Yet, oddly, we keep treating such difficulties as bothersome detours and unwelcome intrusions.

If we want work to be more than just an annoying imposition in our lives, if we are intrigued by the possibility of being both successful *and* spiritually engaged at work, we will need to pause and examine our basic attitude toward our jobs. Maybe we're missing something. Maybe problems arise at work not as interruptions or intrusions, but as invitations to gain real wisdom. Perhaps, in some sense, work's "complications" are exactly what we're looking for.

At first glance, such a suggestion may appear strange. Yet, if we examine work closely, we will notice that whatever gets messy with our jobs demands that we slow down and pay attention. The difficulties go to the front of the line, so to speak, and stare us straight in the face. But all too often, rather than responding with the resourceful attention that the situation requires, we dig in and resist.

Sometimes we resist in small ways. Maybe we avoid a difficult coworker or make a harsh remark under our breath: "Here comes that knucklehead Frank again." Sometimes our resistance becomes all-consuming: a lawsuit turns into a lifelong battle or an offhanded remark becomes an eternal grudge. By recoiling from any of work's problems, we inevitably find ourselves in hostile territory—often feeling lonely, imprisoned, confused, even at battle with our jobs, protecting ourselves from work rather than achieving its objectives.

The sober reality we face is this: resisting work's difficulties and hoping for smooth sailing is pointless. Work, indeed all of life, is often disappointing and uncertain, and it is futile to expect otherwise. Being hostile toward any of life's difficulties only amplifies our discomfort, and we end up at war with ourselves, arguing with our lives rather than living them.

I still work in the corporate world today, and I also teach Buddhist meditation and lead seminars on work as a spiritual practice. I often begin my seminars by asking participants to list three adjectives that best describe work for them. Inevitably, the responses are the same: "stressful," "discouraging," "difficult," "worrisome," "frustrating." Occasionally a few positive adjectives are thrown in, such as "challenging," "stimulating," or "creative." But for the most part, work is experienced as a burden, a threat, an inconvenience—a place where we are held captive by life rather than free to enjoy it.

Fortunately, we can stop feeling imprisoned by work. We can stop hoping for smooth sailing, and we can stop experiencing work as hostile territory. We can, instead, discover a profound sense of freedom and fulfillment in our jobs. But in order to do such a thing we will need to make a simple and profound shift in how we engage work: *rather than resist, we will need to slow down and open up.*

Rather than rejecting work's difficulties as bothersome interruptions, we can instead acknowledge work, with all its complications, as an invitation to wake up and live our lives honestly and fully. From this point of view, the problems that arise in our jobs are not inconvenient speed bumps or demoralizing battles but valuable experiences worthy of our wise attention. We can learn to welcome whatever stares us in the face—whether disappointing, exhilarating, confusing, or routine—confidently and fully.

If we take a moment to slow down and open up to our work circumstances, we will discover that work is continually inviting us to help, not hide; to listen openly, not close up; to connect, not detach; to perfect our skillfulness, not put it in question. But in our impatience to succeed and become better, faster, and more profitable, we overlook the fact that work, with all its pressures and problems, is encouraging us to be engaged, resourceful, and alive—right here, right now. And, maybe that is what we've really wanted all along: to simply be *awake at work.*

Engaging our jobs intelligently and without resistance does not require that we redefine our entire approach to our livelihood. We can engage our jobs sanely and openly without giving up on success or disregarding our feelings or ambitions. What is required is surprisingly ordinary: simply to be *who we are where we are,* to subtly shift from *getting somewhere fast* to *being somewhere completely.* By taking such an approach, we discover not only a larger view of work but also a basic truth about being human: by genuinely being ourselves in the present moment, we naturally become alert, open, and unusually skillful.

When we are willing to shift from getting somewhere fast to being somewhere completely, we discover that we are not just making a living but we are living our lives on the job, right here, right now, in all the present moment's vivid and remarkable immediacy. When we are on the job completely, we do not forget to live our lives. Whatever comes along is not dismissed as an annoyance or an obstacle, or pursued as a comfort or relief, on our way to somewhere else. Whatever comes along *is our life,* and we actively appreciate it and respect it for being so.

To be awake at work is to acknowledge, maybe just briefly at first, that work only offers us the present moment, which is fleeting and fickle and constantly surprising. Work, with all its pressures and successes and confusion, unfolds on its terms, not ours, and we can be awake as it unfolds or we can resist—a choice we can and will make moment by moment for the rest of our lives

Whether we are rich or poor, Christian or Sufi, CEO or hairstylist, we can accept work's invitation to wake up. We can learn how to engage every aspect of our lives as a spiritual practice and in turn live life confidently without fear or anxiety. But in order for our lives and jobs to be just such a spiritual path, rather than a fortress or a prison or a vacation, we must be willing to set out deliberately on a journey.

In order for us to journey with inspiration and delight, we will need to work with our minds. By this I mean making a gentle, firm, and utterly powerful gesture toward ourselves, not just once but throughout the entire journey, a gesture that cultivates sanity and well-being each step of the way. This gesture is *mindfulness*, and it is central to our ability to be awake at work. Mindfulness, in Buddhism and many other spiritual traditions, is essentially learning to be fully alert and available in the present moment. Whether we are pouring a cup of tea, changing a light bulb or a diaper, or holding the hand of a dying friend, we glimpse through our mindfulness that our life is happening *now* and cannot be taken for granted. By being mindful, we face the ordinary, fresh immediacy of our experience and discover that simply being human is profound beyond our hopes and fears and preconceptions. Such mindfulness will be our vehicle for traveling the path; it will show us how to move forward and to trust ourselves step by step, moment by moment.

So we embark on our journey. Our work now becomes our frontier, and we become pioneers of the unfamiliar. Gradually, we can stop struggling with our jobs and begin exploring them as uncharted territory. We can learn to acknowledge that anything can and does happen at work—which can be both shocking and delightful. When the phone rings, we may notice the fresh mind that we bring to such a simple and immediate invitation. When our boss is upset and overbearing, life will be uncomfortable. But we may also notice that we are sharply alert and intelligent at such moments—if we are *mindful*. And, by just showing up at work, we may also notice that we have already begun our spiritual journey and work's invitation to wake up is staring us right in the face.

Learning to be awake at work is straightforward and very practical. It is not wishful thinking; we can't just hope ourselves awake and leave the rest to chance, with the vague idea of attaining a state of bliss on the job. Nor is it some new "technology of the mind" that we enthusiastically inflict on ourselves and our colleagues. Awakening on the job is learning to drop our resistance and be intelligently and energetically alert to our lives at work. This process is very personal and demanding. It means learning to live our lives nobly and without fear, coming down to earth and into direct contact with our experience. This takes effort and discipline.

You may think of discipline as a boot-camp mentality or as a kind of punishment. Maybe discipline brings to mind images of denying yourself your favorite foods, running long distances, or saluting your superiors and performing your duty. However, in this case discipline is not punishment or denial or obligation. Rather, the discipline required to be awake at work is learning to be completely honest with ourselves and overcoming any pretense or deception about our work circumstances.

Such honesty requires that we approach our jobs with a sharp and clear-minded intelligence that is neither gullible nor hardheaded.

Being disciplined at work requires that we stop kidding ourselves—stop trying to defend our jobs, our prestige, our smooth path to success—and commit to being attentive to and honest about our actual experience. This willingness sets the stage for engaging work skillfully as it unfolds, without trying to secure our well-being or gather false guarantees. Such honest discipline is the essence of mindfulness, and it does not simply appear but must be cultivated over time.

Buddhism has a rich tradition of mindfulness practices that have been developed and handed down from teacher to student for centuries. The most common practice taught in most schools of Buddhism and some non-Buddhist traditions is called *mindfulness-awareness* meditation, or sitting meditation. In sitting meditation we learn to be still, directly experiencing our minds and hearts and the present moment. We explore very precisely and gently who and what we are, gradually seeing through our self-deceptions, becoming aware of our experience, and glimpsing a fundamental wakefulness that is in fact always available. With sitting meditation we begin to relate directly with the simple power and flexibility of being ourselves right here, right now.

Sitting is deceptively simple: We sit up straight, either in a chair or on a cushion on the floor, and remain attentive in the present moment. Our eyes are open, our hands are placed gently on our thighs or in our lap, and our gaze is soft and slightly downward. We breathe normally and sit still. Essentially, this is all we do. Just sit. It seems very simple, but a lot goes on.

When we sit still, we will inevitably notice the vividness of the moment, even if for just a brief second. Perhaps we may notice the sound of a fan or the wood grains of the floor. Maybe we detect the faint echo of traffic off in the distance or sense the cool humidity of the rain gently falling on the roof. When we sit, we glimpse the simple, clear *now*ness of sights, sounds, and physical sensations.

We may also notice that we are thinking. We may be recalling a TV show that we found memorable or rehearsing a difficult conversation we are expecting to have with a loved one. Our thoughts may be restless and cranky, meandering and dull, or colorful and engrossing. This bright and shifting quality of the mind is not a problem; it is what we work with.

In sitting we attend to our thoughts and our sensations by cultivating a precise yet gentle awareness of the breath. When we notice we are thinking, we make a slight shift. We deliberately note our thinking and gently bring our attention back to our breath. In sitting meditation, we learn to lightly "ride" the breath in this way to stabilize our attention in the present moment. By sitting in such a way, we feel the rhythm of our minds and engage emotions and thoughts of all kinds. Rather than getting lost in our thoughts and emotions, however, we learn to touch our feelings and *let go*, bringing our attention back to our lives in the immediate moment, right here, right now.

If you aspire to relate to work in a more open, wise, and enlivened way, I believe you will be greatly helped by taking up a regular sitting meditation practice. Many people before us have practiced sitting meditation and discovered a natural wisdom that transformed their lives, and such possibilities are open to us as well.

Of course, being mindful won't make our jobs any less messy. Cranky customers, computer viruses, and overly competitive colleagues don't suddenly disappear because we are mindful and alert to the immediate moment. And neither does our resistance to work's difficulties. We might still feel annoyed by "knucklehead Frank," who criticized our sales presentation, or uneasy at the prospect of losing our job or resentful toward our employer. Being mindful in the immediate moment will never eliminate work's real and neverending problems or all our resistance to them.

But mindfulness does make us increasingly curious about our predicament. The more we attend to work in the immediate moment, the more our mindfulness begins to develop a keen edge of curiosity. We go about our jobs, but now we are more attentive to how work gets messy and how we resist. Our annoyance with our client or hesitations to be candid with our boss are no longer an irritating undertone but become sharply apparent and interesting to us. It's as if we're haunted by our heightened mindfulness. We are continually noticing more, pausing in the midst of the hectic pace, opening to the rawness of our daily work experiences, and becoming more and more candid with ourselves.

Developing mindfulness, then, is really our central task at work. But not because we prefer to develop ourselves spiritually rather than get the job done. Being mindful at work doesn't turn our jobs into a Himalayan retreat or a meditation cushion. In fact, mindfulness becomes central because we finally want to do our jobs properly rather than protect ourselves from work's unpleasantness. We are mindful at work—indeed, in our entire lives—because once and for all we want to live life well, without anxiety and resentment.

Making Friends
with Ourselves))

Gaylon Ferguson

*A sad fact of Buddhism in America is that its appeal has been largely
limited to a small demographic: educated, middle class, and white. That's
particularly unfortunate because some African-American Buddhists, such
as Charles Johnson, bell hooks, and, here, Acharya Gaylon Ferguson, have
argued that Buddhism's teachings on kindness and respect toward ourselves
are precisely what people of color need to counter the feelings of low
self-worth that come from internalized racism.*

Recently, a friend of mine was daydreaming out loud about a future
in which there would be meditation centers in every neighborhood—as common as convenience stores are now. "Instead of Stop
and Shop," she suggested, "they could be called Stop and Stop!" The
Buddha's third noble truth—that suffering can end—can be
summed up in that one word: "stopping."

As it says in Chögyam Trungpa Rinpoche's *Cutting Through
Spiritual Materialism,* a classic guide to the path of Buddhist meditation: "There is no need to struggle to be free; absence of struggle is
itself freedom." Stopping the inner battle is the basis for peace and
nonaggression in our world. Only when we stop the battle within

ourselves can we lay the groundwork for the truly compassionate activity of helping others to overcome suffering.

This is the heart of cessation: stopping the fight with ourselves. Traditionally, the opposite of making war on ourselves, endlessly judging and harshly criticizing ourselves, is spoken of as "making friends with ourselves"—the practice of loving-kindness, *maitri* or *metta. Maitri*—a Sanskrit word that sounds like "my tree"—means friendliness, loving-kindness or, simply, love. Just as compassion begins at home, a loving relationship with others radiates out from an inner affection, a friendly and fundamentally kind relationship to ourselves. This is a deep friendship with ourselves—not at all the same as those superficial relationships with what we call "fair-weather friends." We can all appreciate ourselves and our companions in moments of victory and shining success—but what of the times of loss and defeat, of discouragement and uncertainty?

What does it really mean to be kind to ourselves in this deeper sense? How is it different from indulging our every whim and desire for entertainment and escape? When does making friends with ourselves become mere indulgence? The essence of meditation is non-struggle—not fighting with ourselves inwardly, developing a welcoming attitude toward our thoughts, our feelings, our bodies and minds altogether.

The founding Zen master of San Francisco Zen Center—Shunryu Suzuki Roshi—calls this welcoming approach a "spacious meadow." It involves welcoming our thoughts, our emotions, the sensations of the body, and the sights, smells, colors, and tastes of our world with an open-armed embrace. It means letting ourselves fall in love with the colors and sounds of ocean and sky, of freeways and streetlights. This can be as simple as really noticing the taste of orange juice in the morning—or as surprising as getting up to close the window against the noise outside and noticing that actually we enjoy the music floating in.

The disciplined freedom of cessation is much like the experience of leaving a stuffy, crowded room and stepping through an open doorway into fresh air. We give up editing ourselves—our minds and our emotions particularly—and simply let ourselves be as we are. We are neither exaggerating our potential—with wishful thinking of how great we are or will soon become—nor are we minimizing our faults out of fear that if we look too closely we won't like what we see. We are not dramatizing our emotions through elaborate fantasies of acting them out—how delicious continuing this love affair will be or how sweet the revenge on that person who hurt my feelings will feel. Nor are we repressing our emotions— our passion, anger, jealousy, feelings of puffed-up pride, lonely fear, and sadness. We simply let all this be and this letting be is cessation—the struggle to tightly control our experience stops, if only for a moment.

The heart of the problem is the constant attempt of all people to "fix" ourselves. In everyday life, we take things to be fixed because they are in need of repair—something is wrong with our car, for example; it needs more of this and less of that. Often, we regard ourselves in the same way—something about us is wrong or inadequate, in need of a little more this and a little less that. There is almost always room to indulge this view since, after all, who is perfect?

But the view of the Buddha is that we are, all of us, fundamentally whole and complete as we are. In some traditions this is called our basic goodness or "Buddha nature." As Suzuki Roshi says, Buddha nature is just our human nature. We all possess an inherent, natural wakefulness. Our deepest longing is to reclaim this fundamental heritage of human goodness, basic compassion.

Cessation is celebrating this fundamental goodness, uncovering an inner strength and confidence that cannot be weakened or corrupted by the sometimes disorienting ups and downs of outer successes and failures.

Now, the widespread human tendency to regard ourselves as in need of a good "inner fix-it" repair job is particularly important for us as people of color. People of color in the West grow up in societies saturated with ideas and values that invalidate their very existence. As Cornel West has written, affirming exclusively Eurocentric standards of beauty often goes hand in hand with the denigration of the moral and intellectual capabilities of Europe's "Others." This is but one thread in a cultural fabric of white supremacy interwoven with the strands of gender domination, homophobia, and pervasive economic exploitation. Everyone reading this will have their own scars and stories to tell from bruising encounters with that demonic trio of societal "isms"—sexism, racism, classism. We are all survivors of many battles and many wars. We all have our own sense of the meaning of Jimmy Cliff's "many rivers to cross." As Charles Johnson phrases it: "The black experience in America, like the teachings of Shakyamuni Buddha, begins with suffering."

The focus of the Buddhist practice of meditation is the internalized nightmare of these outer battles. In *Rock My Soul*, bell hooks has written movingly of the challenging issues of self-esteem facing many of us. She points out: "Most discussions of black people and self-esteem start by identifying racism as the sole culprit. Certainly the politics of race and racism impinge on our capacity as black folk to create self-love rooted in healthy self-esteem, sometimes in an absolute and brutal manner. Yet many of us create healthy self-esteem in a world where white supremacy and racism remain the norm." What makes such recovery of basic healthiness possible in the midst of the speed and aggression and everyday assaults on human dignity of twenty-first century social life? I want to acknowledge from the outset that the path to liberation is not easy and will not be a smooth journey from confusion to clarity. But is it possible that the ancient teachings of the Buddha—including instructions on working with gentleness and insight into our own hearts and minds—can be part of a path of liberation, which begins, as he taught, with self-liberation?

Yes. The teachings and practice of meditation allow us to activate the intimate yet public connection of the personal and the political. Outer change proceeds alongside inner revolution. As hooks emphasizes, there has historically been some reluctance to include the psychological dimension in our collective efforts to establish a more just and sane society: "Throughout our history in this nation, black people and society as a whole have wanted to minimize the reality of trauma in black life. It has been easier for everyone to focus on issues of material deprivation as the reason for our continued collective subordinated status than to place the issue of trauma and recovery on our agendas." Yes, there are real and pressing material priorities, but unless these go hand in hand with what Dr. Martin Luther King, Jr., called "the inner treasures" of the spirit, we will wake up to find that, again in King's prophetic words, "we have foolishly minimized the internal of our lives and maximized the external."

Of course, the church has traditionally been a place for healing the wounds of daily life, a safehouse for solace and recovery. It has also been in the arts—particularly the music of the blues and realistic fiction—that we find the exploration of the jagged edge of this connection between the intensity of private experience and the vast forces of historical change sweeping us from the Middle Passage through the horrors of enslaved life, the joy of emancipation, Reconstruction, Jim Crow and racial apartheid, the Civil Rights era and on into this, the new millennium. In Toni Morrison's masterpiece *Beloved*, the elderly Baby Suggs, surrounded by her congregation, preaches a sermon of profound self-acceptance in a clearing in the woods: "Here—in this here place, we flesh; flesh that weeps, laughs; flesh that dances on bare feet in grass. Love it. Love it hard. Yonder, they do not love your flesh. They despise it. You got to love it, you." We have all, all of us, heard this message before. hooks says of her own mother's wisdom and skillful means, her "motherwit": "Having lived in the midst of white supremacy all her life, Mama recognized that it would be dangerous for us to live our lives trying to please racist white people, letting them set the standards for our identity and well-being."

The truth is that freedom is possible through our own self-determination. The opportunity for making friends with ourselves is an invitation delivered to our doorstep every day. According to tradition, the Buddha's last words were: "Work out your salvation with diligence." The third noble truth of cessation—of stopping the inner battle that undermines our confidence and well-being— is followed then by the fourth truth of the path—the way of experiencing the natural freedom of our basic being itself, freed from external additives. Again, the key point here is that we are not victims of our states of mind; we are agents in our own making, in the emancipation of our minds and hearts from the internal prisons of fear, anger, jealousy, and endless craving.

This is precisely the issue of an inner "decolonizing" of the mind and spirit: any external or conceptual standards that we impose on ourselves will eventually have disastrous consequences for our own sense of self-worth. Just as the menu should never be confused with the meal we are actually eating, we cannot rely on any set of ideas—or feelings based on those ideas—to tell us who we really are. Stopping or cessation means letting go of the mistaken idea that judging ourselves and comparing ourselves to others is the way to increase our wisdom, insight, and compassion. In a powerful teaching from Chögyam Trungpa Rinpoche, we find this startling line that sums up the essence of the third noble truth: "I awaken into the wisdom with which I was born, and compassionate energy arises without pretense." Stopping means declaring a ceasefire in the battle of ego, freeing ourselves from vicious cycles of judgment and painful negativity. It is discovering the liberating message that we are, just as we are, originally good, fundamentally wise, and basically sane and loving.

Awakening the Mind of the Buddha

Gehlek Rimpoche

Buddhism is the path of radical selflessness, in both senses of the word. It teaches that none of us really has a self, and it asks us to act completely without self-interest—to take in the suffering of others and give to them whatever we can. The surprise is that in giving it all away, we gain everything in return, because the mind of selflessness is the mind of the Buddha. Gehlek Rimpoche teaches us how to awaken this compassionate, enlightened mind through the practice of "give and take."

> "Give and take" mounted on the breath is the magic device
> Bringing love, compassion, and the special mind.
> To save all beings from this world's great ocean,
> Please bless me to awaken true bodhimind.
> —from "An Offering Ceremony to the Spiritual
> Masters," by the First Panchen Lama

As the First Panchen Lama suggests, the practice of *tonglen*—give and take—is a major way of subduing our self-cherishing, ego-pleasing thoughts. Ego is our biggest obstacle to developing bodhimind, the enlightened heart and mind of the Buddha. When we try to destroy ego, we are training our mind—the mind that ignores all other people, the one that thinks we are the most important person of all. Once we have been able to destroy our selfish, egoistic thoughts, we begin to act as our true selves and we have a real ability to benefit ourselves and others.

Right now, the ego blocks our capacity to help not only others but also ourselves. We have to understand that we cannot really help anyone until we have learned how to help ourselves. But the ego prevents us from helping ourselves by presenting a false notion of what it really means to help ourselves. What does our ego want? Ego wants us to be superior to everybody else; ego wants me to be the best of all. If you are a meditator, your ego would like you to be the best meditator, and if you are an artist, your ego would like you to be recognized as a creative genius. If you're a businessman, you want to be the most prosperous, wealthy and efficient, and to that end you will do whatever it takes to destroy your competition. Your ego always demands supreme superiority. In Tibetan, we call this attitude *dag zin*, "holding tight to the self."

The more successful you become, the more the demands of your ego will increase. In the beginning, you simply want to succeed, but your ego will not be satisfied. When you become a little more successful, your ego wants to kill your competition. And when you become even more successful, it wants to make you the universal king. There is no telling what ego wants because our desire doesn't have any limit; therefore, its demands continually increase.

Our ego is so interesting. Just watch your mind when you say, "What do I want? What do I want to take? All the best! Whatever anyone has, I want it!" And what do you want to give? "All the problems and the misery." That's ego talking. But it's not the real you. You are a good and wonderful person. You are kind. You have a compassionate nature.

To free ourselves, we need to turn the tables on ego's demands. So whatever ego wants, you should turn around and do the opposite. If ego tells you, "Go up," make sure you go down. If ego tells you, "Go down," go up. That's how you have to treat your ego. If ego tells you, "Get all the best!" it means it is time for you to take all the worst. And if ego tells you, "Give all the miserable things," then take all the miserable things. That is the premise of the practice called tonglen.

Tonglen practice is united with the flow of the breath. The breathing system we have is to inhale and exhale air. That is basic human nature. We breathe in and out, and if we stop doing either of them, we're gone. Tonglen uses this basic human function to develop compassion and love. As we breathe in and out, we try to develop love and compassion: compassion-oriented breathing in and love-oriented breathing out.

One important difficulty you might encounter is thinking, "It doesn't make any difference to me that all these people are suffering. Why should I care?" That is worse than thinking, "I need to help but I can't."

Ego's trick is to make us lose sight of our interdependence. That kind of ego-thought gives us a perfect justification to look out only for ourselves. But that is far from the truth. In reality we all depend on each other and we have to help each other. The husband has to help his wife, the wife has to help the husband, the mother has to help her children, and the children are supposed to help their parents, too, whether they want to or not. You may say, "My mother and my father were supposed to nurture me. It's okay to help them because they were supposed to help me." Or you may say, "I don't really like this difficulty, but it involves my mother, so I can't look away." It is very similar to the feelings some people have when they are divorced. A woman might say about her ex-husband, "He's my daughter's father"—she dislikes him, she's angry, upset, yet he is still "my daughter's father." She can't cut that part out. Even when she's dying to cut it out and tear it into pieces, he's still her daughter's father.

This is reality. The connections between people are so serious, so strong and so long-lasting that we cannot remove them. Our changing lives have made it so that we don't recognize each other, but we do have a tremendous amount of connection. We have dealt with each other so many times in our previous lives. We put trust in each other, we consult each other, we try to gain some wisdom from each other, and we try to solve personal problems for each other. We also try to help the future generations. All these things we do together, and as a result we have a tremendous amount of connection. We are karmically connected. Even though we may feel we cannot connect to "all sentient beings" right at this moment, we are still very much connected to them.

Interdependence is reality, but we human beings have taken an "I couldn't care less" attitude. Environmentalists have been telling us about the idea of interdependence, so we have begun to understand it on that level. The environment isn't the only connection, though. The major connection is among the people. Buddha has presented the idea of interpersonal connection and how important it is, how relevant it is to our lives, and how much our lives depend on it. Great compassion, responsibility, and caring are based on interpersonal relationship. The most important interpersonal relationship is bodhimind—caring about and committing to others. That's not a perfect definition of bodhimind, but that's what it boils down to.

We are connected in a way that is similar to the connections between the parts of your body. If you get a thorn in your foot, your hand will go and take it out. If your foot is suffering from the thorn and your hands say, "I don't care. I don't have suffering. It's the foot that has suffering," or if the left hand gets a thorn and the right hand says, "I don't care. It's you who are suffering, not me," in the end the foot will suffer and the hands will suffer. That is how we function. Likewise, whether it is a personal problem, group problem, or international problem, we should address it, talk about it, and try to solve it together. If you don't care about other people, it is a spiritual problem. If you don't care about them, they won't care about you, and we'll all suffer and the problems will continue.

Tonglen practice is based on this connectedness, but when we practice tonglen—giving and taking on the breath—are we really helping others? In the long run, the answer is yes, we are helping others. No, it is not an *immediate* help for them, but it is helping us. At this moment we are not even taking their suffering; we are taking our own future suffering. So, we are also giving our positive karma to ourselves first. We try to materialize it, so that we don't have to suffer. Then we do the same with the people that we care about. Then with the people they care about. Then with their family, children, spouses, and so forth. That's how we extend our practice when we involve ourselves with it seriously.

THE PRACTICE OF TONGLEN: GENERAL INSTRUCTION

If you are a reasonable person, you want to make those nearest and dearest to you happy. What makes them unhappy? Their mental, physical and emotional suffering. Normally that's what our lives are all about. When we have physical pain, we say, "Ouch!" When we have mental or emotional pain, we have a long face. When we hear and see pain in those we love, we try to make them happy by removing their suffering. To make use of that urge, we do a mental exercise. The tool we use is our breath. The power of inhalation lifts their suffering. The power of exhalation gives them our joy, and the cause of that joy, our virtue.

You breathe in from the left nostril. While breathing in, you take their suffering. You take it completely, without any fear, without any hesitation, and you don't leave anything out.

Breathing out from the right nostril, you give all your happiness and the causes of your happiness, your compassion, everything. Without any attachment, without any hesitation, without any miserliness. It reaches them in the form of light, and all become happy and joyful.

The visualization that accompanies the breathing is very important. It makes a big impact on our consciousness. When practicing tonglen, it is recommended to imagine people with faces and names—actual living human beings. You may think, "That way we will only care about human beings. What about the others—my cat, my dog?" This is your cat or dog, but in this tradition you visualize them with a human face and body, simply because it is easier to deal with human beings. And it may also contribute to linking up with a certain good karma, so that the cat or dog may become a human being in its next life.

In your visualization, your friend, your companion, and all the people you care for can be the most important ones, right in front of you—face to face, if you want. They are the object of meditation. When I say "each and every person with a face and name," this doesn't mean that you have to keep on thinking, "Oh yeah, he's here and she's there and he's there." Your major focus can be on one or two people, but at the same time, you think that all the space is filled up with people. I very strongly object to visualizing nameless, faceless dots, but somehow it easily becomes that. If you have to keep on remembering everybody, going through all of their names and thinking of all their faces, that would be quite difficult. If we do it the simple way, we imagine that everyone is there, and when we are specifically thinking of somebody, they appear with a name and face.

At first, you may not have that much difficulty, but when you begin to think about it seriously, you may become afraid. You may have fear of taking or you may have hesitation in giving. That's the ego-controlled part of our human nature. When you begin to take the suffering of people on yourself, your mind is going to have a tremendous amount of resistance. If you don't think much about it, your attitude may be, "Whatever it may be, so be it." That's occurring on a very superficial level, where there are no problems. When you begin to think seriously about this, then you start to encounter resistance. You'll say, "Why? Why me?"

THE PRACTICE OF TONGLEN ON SELF

If you are afraid of taking somebody else's pain, start with taking your *own* suffering. If it's in the morning, you take the suffering you are going to experience in the evening; or you take the suffering you are going to experience tomorrow, next week, next month, next year, or next life. If we take in suffering that will come to us in the evening a little earlier, it might not become quite so big. It is much easier to take on your own suffering and problems in advance than taking on someone else's. It is good to keep training your mind in that way.

While breathing in, take your own suffering from yourself. For example, say to yourself, "I'll take my own suffering of this evening into me now, and tomorrow's suffering, and next week's, next month's, next year's, next life's, and the sufferings of my lives thereafter." Take your own pain into yourself, make it come a little quicker, so that you settle for a smaller problem rather than the heaviest difficulties.

Before we take any suffering, either our own future suffering or the suffering of another person, the question arises, "What do I do with this now? Where am I going to put it within me?" We have to be prepared for that. We need a garbage can, someplace to throw it. It so happens that we have an enemy inside: Mister Ego. That becomes our target. This method of making ego our target is called "special give and take."

Collect your own negativities, which are the deeds of your ego. Collect your negative emotions, which are the thoughts of your ego. Then visualize your ego in the form of whatever you dislike—a big spider or a heap of darkness. Collect all of it. Don't leave any part of your body or consciousness out. Just collect it all, somewhere at the center of your body, at the heart level.

What we are taking from the others is not only their suffering but also causes of their suffering, such as attachment, hatred, and ignorance. All of these things come in through the breath. When these gather, it has an effect like lightning striking a rocky area; or—as we see on television these days—bombs exploding; or a cyclone picking up everything in its path. In that way it hits our ego, shreds it completely, and destroys it. Not even a trace is left. Nothing! We don't have to keep what we took inside us, feeling it and saving it there, and suffering. Not only do we not have to do that, we *shouldn't* do it.

THE PRACTICE OF TONGLEN
ON A ONE-TO-ONE BASIS

Step 1. Visualize and connect. Visualize the person right in front of you, and think of their suffering—the disease they have, or the mental, physical, and emotional pain they are going through. When you really see your friend suffering with unbearable pain, tears will come to you. That is true caring. It may not be great compassion, but it is a true feeling of compassion.

If you don't feel anything when seeing the person you really love the most, then you need to change the focus and try to recollect the suffering you have gone through yourself. Think about when you experienced similar difficulties, or if that's not possible, any other difficulties: "How unhappy I was, how much pain I went through, how much anxiety I had, and how many times I woke up in the middle of the night with a heavy heart."

Think of that, and then try to understand that this other person is going through the same kind of pain. Anyone can say, "Poor little thing!" but if we have no feelings, it isn't very good—it is being out of touch. Being out of touch with compassion doesn't work. We have to have the feeling. We can only understand and develop that feeling if we think about a time when we went through something like that. If we think that way, we get a better understanding of what the other person is going through.

This particular feeling is not necessarily just for tonglen. It is important to use it within your family and apply it to all relationships: between husband and wife, between children and parents, among all members of the family. If you don't understand the other person's problems, you have to sit down, calm your mind, and think about when you had that pain and how you felt. If you can remember that, then your attitude toward your family members will be different. You will no longer be that short-tempered, snappy person. It will give you a better understanding of what other people's pain is all about. Otherwise there is a danger of falling into merely saying, "Oh, the poor little things, how they are all suffering!"

Once you have that feeling, once you can really appreciate and understand what the other person is going through, you are giving rise to real caring. You would like to offer some kind of immediate solution. Right now you would like to destroy that pain. "If I can do something about it, let me do it right away, to make that pain go away." That desire, anxiety, and eagerness are what you need. Normally, when you see your child suffering tremendously, you will anxiously ask yourself, "What can I do?" You need that type of anxiety. You have to train your mind up to that level. When you have that anxiety, you will say, "Let me take the pain. Is there any way I can take it?"

Step 2. Take. When you come to that level, you can visualize it. Take it and lift it up by your own sincerity, by your own compassion, by the power of the truth, by the blessings of the enlightened beings: "I'm here now to take all the pains of that person." Take it in the form of an undesirable color and breathe it in. Breathe it in—whatever that pain might be, including cancer. Take in the pain itself and the cause of the pain. In your visualization literally pick it up and bring it in. Like a powerful lightning bolt, it will hit that mountain of ego, that heap of darkness you have at your heart level, and destroy it. That is the taking in.

Step 3. Give. Then you give. You give love, affection, virtue—everything—without any hesitation. You give your own positive karma, your own body. Whatever the desire or need of the person may be, you give it to them. You are giving three things: your body, your wealth, and your virtue. That's the best we have to offer, so we give that. And whatever the need of the person might be, the giving comes in that form. The person becomes free of pain and happy, just as you wanted them to be.

The moment you have any hesitation, the moment you attach a condition, it is not good. People appreciate generosity, but when it is attached to a condition, it becomes difficult to accept it. I remember living in India, which is such a poor country. In the seventies and eighties, America gave a lot of aid but it came with strings attached. India didn't appreciate it. India kept on saying, "We'd rather have trade than aid." They even forced the U.S. aid office to close. If aid comes with strings attached, you become a puppet that has to dance on a string. Even India can say no to that. They are very proud of it, actually. And that is a good thing.

The quality of generosity involves not looking for return. There is no attachment, no hope of gaining something back, no looking for gratitude, and certainly no looking for control, influence, or power. When you give, give without any hesitation, without any reservation. Just give.

To do tonglen on a one-to-one basis is very helpful. It is a tremendous opportunity.

You can do this between partners. You can do this between teacher and student. You can do this between caregiver and patient. For the caregiver it is a great opportunity for practice. For the patient it is an opportunity to thank the caring people. For the therapist it is a good opportunity to make the therapy work better. For the patient it is a good way of expressing gratitude to the therapist.

Expanding the Practice to All Beings

From the traditional Buddhist point of view, we are expected to expand our object of focus. First, we can focus on the human level and whatever suffering we encounter there. We begin with one individual and expand our focus to two, three, four, or five and multiply that. Eventually, in our Mahayana practice, the focal point becomes all beings, without leaving anyone out—*all* beings with the physical appearance of the people we know, with all their difficulties, with their normal egoistic characteristics.

The traditional teachings will tell you that when you are focusing on the hell realms, you take the suffering of the hell beings completely. You either do the eighteen hell realms one by one, working with their eighteen different characteristics, or you work with them more simply by dividing them in two, taking the hot hells and the cold hells separately. You could also take them all at once, taking the hot and cold hells all together. You do it according to whatever time you have and whatever is convenient for you. Then you move to the hungry ghost realm, then to the animal realm, the demigod realm, and the god realm. You cover all six realms, or even eighteen realms, whatever you want to do. But you always begin with the people you know and recognize.

Visualize those who are suffering in the hot-hell realm. Visualize that light rays of your body manifest there as a cold shower or a rainfall that has tremendous cooling power. You take their suffering: the heat, the fear, the pain. You take the causes of their suffering: the karmic cause as well as the delusional cause—in particular the anger and hatred—together with the imprints. When you give your light, it goes out and reaches to the hell realms, and just by the touch of the light, it purifies the environment. This is extremely important, because most hell-realm people suffer because of the environment. So purify the environment, and take their hot and cold sufferings. Bring it in and use it to destroy your ego. And then give. Empty the hell realms completely; close the hell realms altogether. All those people become free of suffering.

Similarly, you meditate on the cold realms. There, your body's light rays will manifest as powerful sunshine, something to make them warm. Not only do you separate them from the pain of being cold, but also you give your body to them and they become human beings. You can also transform your body into houses—not shabby old houses but good solid ones. Transform your body into food to satisfy them; give it as clothes for them to put on, as medicine, whatever they need. You can also visualize manifesting your body as a teacher giving them teachings. They are ready to become buddhas.

Similarly, you give food to the hungry ghosts, wisdom to the animals, weapons to the jealous demigods, and lovely flowers to the gods. Whatever their needs are, you fulfill them. For human beings, however, you take a different approach. Human desires are limitless. You cannot make a blanket statement about what they want. So you give them whatever they want, whatever they desire. Manifest your body in that form and give it to the human beings.

Give your wealth and your virtues. You give body, wealth and virtues to your teachers and the buddhas, in the form of offerings so they may have long life and prosperity. You give all your virtues of the past, present, and future. You give your body and wealth of the present and future—you can't give those of the past, which is gone.

COMPASSION IN ACTION

Training in compassion is a mental activity. But our mind should also be brought to the level where every action we take is influenced by compassion. That means engaging ourselves in compassion in action. The Judeo-Christian tradition has tremendous examples of compassion in action. In the West, people have built hospitals and schools in peacetime and have also relieved the suffering of people in war. There are groups who look after refugees and address human rights issues. There is a tremendous amount of work being done on social and environmental issues. If this is done with kindness, it is an example of compassion in action. If we get personally involved in such activities, it is compassion in action. If we don't, it is only compassion at the meditative level. That may not be sufficient.

If we only practice on the mind level, we run a great risk of our compassion being just talk. As we know, talk is cheap. To develop true compassion, we have to put our money where our mouth is. That is why we need to combine the mind training practice of ton-glen with compassionate action. We are fortunate to live in a society that provides us with many opportunities to put our compassion into practice. That is what will really make a difference in freeing ourselves from the tyranny of our ego-cherishing thoughts. That is what will help us to gain true control over our lives so that we can be of real benefit to ourselves and others. That is how we awaken true bodhimind.

Listen to the Cries
of the Universe

Barbara Rhodes

Sometimes love comes through practice. Sometimes it just breaks over us.
Often love comes through feeling our own suffering, and thus feeling the
suffering of others. For when we truly feel their suffering, how can we help
but love them? Packed in this brief story by the Zen teacher Barbara
Rhodes is a lot of beauty and deep emotion.

In January 2003, I began a hundred-day solitary retreat. It was my
third such retreat and I had waited seventeen years for the opportunity to practice this way again.

The silence and the retreat schedule were the two pillars that
supported me for the hundred days. My cabin sat among evergreens
and oaks and they generously sheltered me. I felt grateful for the
silence, a silence which included sounds such as the ticking from
the wood stove, the hoots of owls, a squeaking pump, the crunch
of footsteps, and the wind. These types of sounds were all I heard
for one hundred days. The schedule was divided into five sessions.
Each session included 108 prostrations, hatha yoga, chanting, and
meditation.

Another vital support was the simple diet I ate every day—
seaweed, squash, beans and rice, fruit, nuts, spice tea. These foods

were much more than enough and reminded me again how unnecessary and burdening is excess.

Before entering this retreat, many people asked me, "Why?" To my Zen friends I would say, "To strengthen my practice." If I was speaking to one of my coworkers at the hospice, I would say, "I need to pull off the road and rest" (nurses understand that metaphor). For myself, I completely trusted the practice handed down to me by Zen Master Seung Sahn.

The first twenty-one days were the most difficult physically. I started out with thirty extra pounds of body weight and was not in a condition to do all those prostrations and the hours of sitting, cutting and chopping wood, cleaning and washing clothes, hauling water and cooking. (Those are the activities that make up my version of pulling off the road.)

But after twenty-one days, my legs stopped aching and my effort felt as if it started to carry me, instead of my carrying it. The hardest thing for me—it always has been—was the sitting. I wanted to get up and do something: wash the floor, do more yoga, find another dead oak to saw down. I knew one of the reasons I sent myself to the cabin was to learn to sit quietly and let go of the restlessness.

One of the five sessions started at midnight. The alarm would go off in the dark silence. I'd put on socks and pants, stoke the fire and start bowing. All warmed up, I'd then do yoga. A single candle lit up the entire cabin. At midnight, it seemed to take less effort to sit than during the other sessions, probably because I thought there was nothing else to do. My practice was to ask, "What am I?"—to relax and allow the "not knowing" to be enough. The key to awakening is just allowing and resting. Just this.

So practicing in that way every day allowed this tired, overweight, middle-aged woman to remember to have gratitude for it all.

During the third week, I had what seems to have been my last menstrual period. I experienced the most severe contractions and abundant bleeding I'd ever had, except for the time my first baby miscarried at six months.

At 2:00 A.M., forty-nine days into the retreat, I read this quote from the mystic poet Rumi: "This rain-weeping and sun-burning twine together to help us grow. Keep your intelligence white-hot and your grief glistening, so your life will stay fresh." I climbed into my sleeping bag, and with a warm brick on my stomach, I cried. Away from all my family and responsibilities, away from schedules, expectations, and distractions, I felt a depth of grief I have never felt before. There was something about being cradled in the sleeping bag, the cabin, the woods, and this Buddhist practice that allowed me to cry until my heart ached. But because of the tremendous support of the retreat, I didn't need to protect myself or anyone else—there was no self.

We have all heard the directive to "go with it"—to go with whatever feelings come up for us in our lives. Well, that night I went with it with no brakes applied until I very naturally coasted into *Kwan Se Um Bosal*, the ancient chant that simply means, "Listen to the cries of the universe." Just listen. There is no "my grief" or "your grief." Grief becomes just grief. Grief brings us to awakening, brings us to our vow–our vow to wake up and listen. That night I finally forgave myself for not being able to hold my baby until she was old enough to breathe on her own. I realized her breathing has really never started or stopped. Here was white-hot intelligence and glistening grief. Here was *Kwan Se Um Bosal*. How may I help?

We can't "make" these moments of recognition or resolution in our lives. But we can practice with the difficulties. And we can take some time out of our entrenched, habit-forced life to sit with silence and let it bring us home to our wisdom.

Meeting Myself
in the Cell House ☽

Scott Darnell

Here is a plainly told story, without artifice or pretension, of what Buddhist practice can do for somebody. Prisoner Scott Darnell gives a moving account of how, through group therapy and then Buddhist practice, he came to understand the forces that drove him to commit a terrible crime and to feel deep repentance for the suffering he had caused. There is a lot of skepticism about stories of people who've "seen the light" in prison. I think you'll believe this one.

July 2004 marked the twenty-fifth year of my life spent behind bars. When people find out how much time I have served, I usually get looks of shock and disbelief. Their eyes grow big. Their mouths drop open. Invariably they have to ask, "How?"

It isn't an easy answer to give. I was a boy of fifteen when I first entered the system. By the time I had gone through court and was given a natural-life-plus-thirty-year sentence, I was all of sixteen years old. The rest of my teen years were spent in a juvenile facility, battling myself and everyone around me until, after a botched escape plan a few months shy of my twenty-first birthday, I was transferred to the adult division of the Department of Corrections.

As any recovering alcoholic or drug addict will attest, sometimes you have to hit rock bottom before you can begin to make your way up again. I hit rock bottom the moment the cell door slammed shut behind me in the Receiving and Classification Unit, where inmates are first sent to determine which institution is most appropriate for their placement.

It's amazing what the mind will do to occupy itself when the ready distractions of the outside world are not available. For two very long months I had nothing in R&C but my own thoughts and feelings to occupy my time. Memories long forgotten or intentionally suppressed came bubbling up to the surface unbidden.

I found myself going through fits of depression over the life I knew I would never have. Suicide briefly occurred to me. Then I became angry at myself over all the despicable, abusive, self-serving things I had done throughout the years that ultimately landed me behind bars.

Toward the end of my stay in R&C, I went through a mandatory evaluation process with a counselor assigned to the cell house I was in. For the first time in my life, I confided in someone, no holds barred, explaining the circumstances of my crime, my memories of abuse from childhood, and my rebellion through delinquent and outright criminal behavior.

By the end of my two months in R&C, I decided that if I had to spend the rest of my life in prison, at least I would not live it in the same destructive, self-deluded manner that had caused so much grief.

With the counselor's help I was transferred to an institution where I could enter a volunteer therapy program. For the next six years, for six to twelve hours a week, I attended this program with the single-minded goal of making my decision a reality.

In the Twin Verses of the *Dhammapada*, we are told, "All that we are is a result of what we have thought. It is founded upon our thoughts; it is based on our thoughts." I realized this fundamental truth for the first time in therapy, or "group," as its members commonly referred to it.

Every session in group was spent learning how to identify the myriad thoughts and feelings that shaped the way I saw and dealt both with myself and the world around me. Our first ideas about ourselves naturally originate in the treatment we receive from parents or other primary caregivers. As a child I never found it acceptable just to be myself—I saw myself as unworthy of love, undeserving of tenderness.

My mother's influence especially helped shape these core ideas I had about myself. She was only sixteen when she had me, and she was very sick, stricken from an early age with diabetes. A disease manageable with proper care these days, diabetes was not as easily treated during my mother's childhood in the fifties. While most kids were out playing, my mother was all too often undergoing tests in the hospital or confined to her bed at home.

Unfortunately, when she was allowed out, she tried to make up for lost time, regardless of the consequences. By her early twenties she found herself saddled with a child (me), married, divorced, and married again. On top of that, she was facing the prospects of dialysis, possible blindness, and an early death.

All of this was a heavy burden for her, as it would be for anyone under similar circumstances. Unfortunately, my mother was ill-equipped to manage that burden. When things got too rough for her, I was the one she usually lashed out at.

My mother's favorite word to scream at me in fits of rage and frustration when my four-year-old fingers failed to tie my shoe, or when my toys weren't properly put away, was "retard." I took it to mean loser, helpless, unlovable.

The word was all too often accompanied by threats to have the police come and take me away, as I didn't deserve to live in the same house as normal people. Other times it was hurled at me with heavy blows that left me cowering in the corner or under the bed in tears.

When I was seven, my mother died of complications associated with diabetes. She was twenty-three. In my child's mind, I blamed myself for her death. She had left me because I wasn't good enough.

She would rather have died than be forced to live with a retard like me.

In Tolstoy's classic story "Resurrection," he writes, "Nobody can wholeheartedly do anything unless he believes that his activity is important and good." To see ourselves as less than important or good becomes so intolerable a situation for the psyche to handle that some type of solution, no matter how warped and bizarre, must be found to enable us to go on with our daily lives.

With the faulty logic of a seven-year-old, I believed that if I emulated the behavior I had learned and became the abuser, I would become the type of person my mother would have respected. Not to mention of course that being the abuser instead of the victim meant power and control over others. Although deep down I felt that I could never hope to be a truly good person, I could at least be good at being bad.

At first this seemed to work out fine. The more I skipped school, ran away from home, shoplifted, or got into fights, the better I felt about myself. I certainly couldn't be a "retard" if I could outsmart the truant officer or slip past a store clerk with a carton of cigarettes. I certainly couldn't be a victim cowering in fear when I could bully schoolmates and make them cower instead.

Other people even seemed to give me more attention when I was bad. In the beginning the attention was positive, as relatives tried to counsel and support me. But their efforts were in vain. Deep down I still believed myself the "retard" and constantly had to prove to myself that I wasn't.

By the age of ten, I was carrying and brandishing a knife at school. I was stealing anything I could get my hands on, from spare change to neighborhood bicycles. At one point I stole a handgun from my stepfather's room and robbed a woman on her way home from the grocery store.

The attention I received grew progressively more negative as I came into contact with law enforcement and finally, the prison system. Yet even then, negative attention was better than no attention.

In group, I received a different type of attention. It was based, as

strange as it may seem for a prison setting, on the idea of unconditional love. We were told that the things we believed about ourselves
weren't necessarily true and that we could become people worthy of
the love and respect we sought.

Group was run by a prison psychologist named Mike, and about
sixty of us participated. We met in sessions of fifteen to twenty
men each. We ranged in age from twenty to seventy years old.
Almost half were civil commitments, men deemed by the courts
"sexually dangerous persons" because of a mental defect that engendered a propensity for them to sexually offend. SDPs, as they were
commonly known, had an indeterminate sentence, and their eventual release depended solely upon their continued progress and
eventual completion of the therapy program.

The rest of us were felons, serving sentences anywhere from ten
years to double natural lives for crimes that included everything
from armed robbery to child molestation, rape, and murder. The
majority, whether civil or criminal, voluntarily participated in the
program with the intention of gaining insight into and changing the
behaviors that had led to our incarceration in the first place. Our
group motto was "No more victims." It was a goal each of us aspired
to wholeheartedly.

Mike taught us step by step how to be aware of and question our
thoughts and feelings. Through his persistence we slowly learned
how to map out our patterns of negative behavior and recognize circumstances in our lives which could eventually trigger violent or
other antisocial responses.

Mike, unlike many psychologists and psychiatrists who had
passed through our lives, was never distant, condescending, or quick
to prescribe the latest psychotropic medication as a substitute for
what might otherwise be achieved through therapy. We were not
"cases" to him. We were people.

When Mike thought something was funny, he would laugh
uproariously with us. When someone broke down in tears relating
an incident of childhood abuse, he would often be crying right
along with him. He never gave up on anybody in group, sometimes

waiting years for someone to turn the corner and begin to deal with the issues necessary for his well-being.

For the first year and a half I was in group, I neither understood nor appreciated any of these things. I fought Mike and, by extension, everyone in group who tried to get past my defenses and help me deal with my problems. At nearly twenty-one years old I had the emotional maturity of a seven-year-old. The idea of giving up anything that might leave me exposed to another person was terrifying. The seven-year-old had been terrorized enough.

On more than one occasion I stormed out of group, cursing everyone along the way. As I slammed the door behind me, I told myself that I was a victim, being unduly harassed by a bunch of know-it-alls who were trying to make themselves look good at my expense. When I found myself confronted with my relationship with my mother, I would often defend her as though she had been a saint. "She was sick," I'd explain. "It was my fault for not listening."

When arguments failed me, I would slide down in my chair and refuse to speak, trying my best to look hurt and misunderstood as group carried on.

Eventually it began to dawn on me that it wasn't group I was fighting as much as myself. Group wasn't trying to hurt me. All of my nonsense arguments and petulant behavior didn't keep me safe; it kept me separate from the very people trying to help me. In time I began to trust and confide in them. Little by little, the seven-year-old began to grow up.

Group became my first experience with sangha, a place of refuge where I could confront the delusions of my life and find release from the suffering I had created for myself in so many ways. In time I came to understand my mother's problems and how they had led her to deal with life. I in turn allowed myself to feel the pain and suffering she had initially caused me as a child, and now, as an adult, I began to deal with it in a way that brought forgiveness, closure, and release.

Thanks to group, I let go of the lies I had accepted about myself and began to believe that I was in fact worthy of such things as love, friendship, trust, loyalty, and happiness. It was an awakening of sorts. My life, for the first time, took on meaning and an inner quality it had never had before.

Still, every coin has two sides. As necessary for healing as it was to face the abuse I had suffered, it was equally important for me to face up to the abuse I had inflicted on others. Until group, my actions were completely self-centered. I never had any real consideration for other people's feelings unless it somehow served me. Empathy had no part in the equation. In our group, when we finally allowed our defenses to completely fall away and we were confronted with what had been done to the people we had victimized, the entire incident got relived in minute detail. Only then, in touch with the abuse and suffering in our own past, did we become capable of empathizing with those we had abused. For the first time, those we had hurt became actual flesh and blood human beings in our eyes.

When I allowed myself to see what I had done to my victim, I simply fell apart. I sat there, crumpled in a chair, oblivious to everyone around me. All I could do was cry, shaking uncontrollably at the horror of my actions and what I had put the victim of my crime through.

At one point I got up and beat my fist bloody against the wall. If several of the larger members of group had not put me back in my chair, I would probably have hurt myself worse. All I could see was the face of the person I had murdered.

That day, and for days afterward, I walked the prison yard like a zombie, bursting into tears at the slightest thought of my crime. I couldn't eat. My sleep was fitful at best. Everywhere I looked I could only see reminders of what I had done, and how the person I had murdered would never experience anything good again.

I truly believe the only reason I made it through that side of therapy without just lying down in the dirt and giving up was the support and dedication of my fellow group members, many of whom had already gone through or were going through the same process I was in order to get well.

In or out of group I found myself surrounded by friends. They would sit with me, sometimes in silence, their mere presence enough of a comfort to get me through. Other times they would try to draw me out in conversation, reminding me of how proud they were of me, or how much courage they thought I had to have faced up to what I had done. My experience encouraged others in group to begin taking the first tentative steps in coming to terms with their own crimes.

This in turn gave me the strength and courage to move on. I realized how much I owed to others. It wasn't just about me and dealing with my life. It was about trying to help others, paying back some of what I owed to a group of men who had invested themselves so fully in me, by investing myself back into the group.

For the next several years, I did just that, sharing my personal experiences with my fellow group members in order to help them break their own cycles of abuse and ultimately become decent, healthy human beings.

As life-altering as the group experience was for me, and as much as I learned and grew as a human being over the years, all things truly are impermanent. Overcrowding and the need for reorganization of the prison population eventually led to my transfer to another institution.

This was a difficult time for me. Group had become my family. I missed them dearly, thought about them often, and on more than one occasion shed tears over the loss of their companionship. But, for the first time in my life, separation from the people I loved and cared about was not confused in my mind with abandonment. I could move forward with a sense of well-being and confidence in myself.

Not long after my transfer I was lucky enough to get an inmate job assignment as a cell house clerk. I took care of records, made sure inmates who needed to see a counselor or a doctor had an appointment, and generally tried to keep the galleries assigned to me running smoothly and efficiently.

It was during this time that I had the good fortune to meet an inmate who practiced Soto Zen. He was the first Buddhist I had ever met, and through him I was introduced to the teachings of the Buddha. It was an introduction I welcomed, as much for the growing friendship between us as for the hours of study and lively conversation it provided.

The four noble truths, the noble eightfold path, and the *Great Heart Sutra* were among the first things I committed to memory. The teachings of Buddha reminded me of many of the things I had learned in group. For example, suffering due to false ideas of self and the idea of karma and its negation made perfect sense to me.

When I finally read those lines in the Twin Verses of the *Dhammapada* about how we are a result of our thoughts, I was forever hooked. Soon after, I took refuge, with my friend as a witness. At the time, there was basically just me, him, and the practice of sitting. But that was enough.

Later I began to correspond with a gentleman associated with the San Francisco Zen Center who regularly shared his own experiences and insights with me. He encouraged me to continue to grow in my personal practice and reminded me through his many letters that even though I was locked away behind bars, I was never alone.

I have been a practicing Buddhist now for nine years. Each day is a welcome journey. Some days, of course, are easier than others. Prison is certainly no country club. Prison is gun towers and razor wire. It is months at a time on lockdown status in a tiny cell. There are tactical teams with billy clubs and pepper spray, and convicts by the thousands ready to take advantage of any perceived weakness they might exploit.

Even worse, prison is the separation from family and friends. Children grow up and move on without ever having known us. Holidays filled with sparkling lights and family dinners are only experienced through a card or a photo filled with smiling faces we cannot touch.

While an inmate may serve time, prison is a denial of time both for him and his family. When my stepfather died on the operating table during open-heart surgery, I was reminded of how true this

was. There were things left unsaid and undone between us. I regretted not being there for him during his illness. I regretted not being
able to attend or speak at his funeral. I wish he could have known the
kind of person I've tried to become.

I know men who spend their years inside thinking of little else
but revenge over what they have lost or given up. They fixate on it,
facing decades behind bars with no other purpose. Their despair
drains them of hope and leaves behind an empty shell.

Still, there *are* those who choose to live, right here, right now.
They don't give in to despair, but allow themselves the possibility of
change and of being a positive influence on the people around them.

Granted, they are few and far between in this environment. But
they are most certainly here. Some of them I was fortunate enough
to meet years ago in group. Others I have met since then. Currently,
five of us meet in the prison chapel each week for an hourly sangha
meeting.

The meetings themselves are simple enough. We have no formal
rituals to speak of. We simply remove our shoes and perform *gassho*
before a colored-pencil drawing of the Buddha set up on a makeshift
altar. After bowing, we sit on the floor or on old prayer benches.

During our hour together in sangha, we encourage one another
in practice. We offer emotional support and advice on how to deal
with the day-to-day challenges that occur in a prison setting.

Several weeks ago one man came to the sangha with a question
about charity. He was well known for his habit of helping out anyone on his gallery who would ask for something. A bag of coffee, a
candy bar, or soda—whatever was asked for he freely gave with no
strings attached.

Lately, however, he felt himself being used, and wondered
whether or not he should continue giving, or should at times refuse
requests. His concern was that, should he refuse, he would only be
protecting his sense of pride and attachment to material objects.

By the end of our hour we all had a chance to weigh in with our
opinions, coming to the conclusion that to continue to give selflessly
should remain the goal. But a person could also be selfless in refusing

a request if he felt the request was exploitative. By refusing selflessly, he wouldn't be enabling or strengthening patterns of exploitative behavior that, in the long run, would only lead to negative karmic consequences. Whether to give or not to give, the primary goal should be to act with the other person's best interest in mind.

Some of us here once thought that money would bring us the happiness we craved. Others found momentary respite from their problems in drugs or sex. The adrenaline rush of a burglary or the comfort and companionship of a street gang did it for a few of our members. Through our individual practice and each other's support, we are learning that these things only lead to further suffering and, ultimately, incarceration, whether physical, mental, or emotional.

These days my thoughts and actions are far different from when I first came to prison. Whether facing a wall during meditation in my cell, performing gassho in our sangha, or scrubbing a floor on a job assignment, I find hope, purpose, even quality. I see a little more clearly that whether it's a roshi or a counselor, a prison sangha or a therapy group, freedom or incarceration, Buddha nature lies at the heart of every moment lived in awareness and engagement.

While the hard truth of the matter is that I will in all likelihood spend the rest of my life serving a prison sentence, my life has become far more than a prison sentence. Now, here, this moment, is something more. It is the freedom of heart and mind that comes with letting go of my fears and self-deluded ideations. It is Buddha, dharma, and sangha, and where possible, the opportunity to give something back to a world from which I took so much.

The Great Love

Lewis Richmond

Some people wonder whether there is a contradiction in Buddhism between wisdom and compassion. Buddhist wisdom says that beings are insubstantial, empty of a real identity. Why, then, feel compassion toward people who don't really exist, over suffering that doesn't really exist either? But there's an even bigger paradox, as Lewis Richmond tells us: when we realize beings' impermanent and insubstantial nature, we love them even more.

If, as the Buddha taught, the nature of the self and of other beings is insubstantial, impermanent, and fundamentally "empty of own-being," then why and how should we love one another? Or to put it more simply, what is the role of love in Buddhism? Vimalakirti, a householder with a wife and children, talks about this in the *Vimalakirti Nirdesa Sutra*.* He begins by describing to Manjushri, one of the great luminaries, the insubstantiality of beings:

> Manjushri, a bodhisattva should regard all living beings as a wise man regards the reflection of the moon in water, or as magicians regard men created by magic. He should regard them as being like a face in a mirror, like the water of a

---

**The Holy Teaching of Vimalakirti: A Mahayana Scripture*, translated by Robert A. F. Thurman (University Park: Pennsylvania State University Press, 1987).

mirage, like the sound of an echo, like a mass of clouds in the sky, like the previous moment of a ball of foam, like the appearance and disappearance of a bubble of water . . . like the track of a bird in the sky . . . like dream visions seen after waking . . . like the perception of color in one blind from birth. . . . Precisely thus, Manjushri, does a bodhisattva who realizes ultimate selflessness consider all beings.

When we first encounter this kind of teaching, it may feel quite maddening: if people are like bubbles of water or balls of foam, why should we care about them? Are Buddhists people who wander through life seeing others as nothing more than dreams or mirages? What does this mean for us in terms of our daily life and ordinary human relationships? Manjushri helps us frame our questions when he says to Vimalakirti, "Noble sir, if a bodhisattva considers all living beings in such a way, how does he generate the great love toward them?"

Like Manjushri, when we hear Vimalakirti's description of living beings as balls of foam, a serious question should immediately arise for us. We should ask, "How can this be, that living beings are like clouds or foam? My whole life involves other people. They seem completely real to me. My relationships with them depend on that. So what is Vimalakirti talking about?"

If we fail to ask this question, then we might jump to a nihilistic conclusion: "Well, living beings are quite insignificant after all, like clouds in the sky. I shouldn't have any particular feeling about them; they're all just insubstantial." We might think we shouldn't care about other people. But, like Manjushri, we know intuitively that compassion is the essence of the dharma. We know that not caring cannot be the right understanding.

Vimalakirti says, in response to Manjushri's question, "How does a bodhisattva generate great love"?:

Manjushri, when a bodhisattva considers all living beings in this way, he thinks, "Just as I have realized the dharma, so

should I teach it to living beings." Thereby, he generates the
love that is truly a refuge for all living beings.

If we're alert, we notice the abrupt shift in Vimalakirti's point of
view. He has just finished saying that living beings are as insubstantial as a ball of foam. But when he's challenged to explain how we
could love them, suddenly he begins talking about "living beings" in
a much more conventional way. In other words, *people* are back!

As Kumarajiva, an early translator of this sutra, points out,
living beings feel real to themselves—they have "the living-being
feeling." So, as bodhisattvas who want to help them, we immediately
inhabit that realm—we go back into that "living-being feeling" too.
In Vimalakirti's words, *we generate the love that is truly a refuge for
all living beings.*

Vimalakirti continues:

> Thereby, he generates the love that is truly a refuge for all
> living beings; the love that is peaceful because free of grasp-
> ing; the love that is not feverish because free of passions . . .
> the love that is nondual because it is involved neither with
> the external nor with the internal; the love that is imper-
> turbable because totally ultimate.

Before, when he was likening living beings to balls of foam, Vimalakirti was talking about the *understanding* of a bodhisattva. But
in this passage, with its description of various kinds of spiritual love,
we are clued in to the *feeling* of a bodhisattva. So this hints at an important terrain of practice that has to do with our emotional life,
with establishing a purified sense of radical openness and compassion. In this passage and the one that follows, Vimalakirti evokes
how a mature dharma practitioner actually feels:

> Thereby, he generates the love that is firm, its high resolve
> unbreakable, like a diamond; the love that is pure, purified
> in its intrinsic nature; the love that is even, its aspirations

being equal; the Tathagata's love, that understands reality; the Buddha's love that causes living beings to awaken from their sleep; the love that is spontaneous because it is fully enlightened spontaneously; the love that is enlightenment because it is unity of experience; the love that has no presumption because it has eliminated attachment and aversion; the love that is great compassion because it infuses the Mahayana with radiance; the love that is never exhausted because it acknowledges voidness and selflessness; the love that is giving because it bestows the gift of dharma free of the tight fist of a bad teacher; the love that is effort because it takes responsibility for all living beings; the love that is wisdom because it causes attainment at the proper time; the love that is without formality because it is pure in motivation.

Each of these phrases represents some commentary or teaching about the emotional transformation of a realized person. They are clues begging us to ask, "What is the quality of our emotional life? What is the quality of our feeling for people?" They also help us recognize what qualities we should be looking for in a teacher.

Now let's examine just a few of these phrases more closely.

The love that is enlightenment because it is unity of experience; the love that has no presumptions because it has eliminated attachment and aversion.

This provides a clue about how our way of encountering others is transformed through practice. It says that an awakening to the insubstantiality of beings and things—a "unity of experience"—actually opens us up emotionally. We might think it would somehow distance us from living beings, but it actually does the opposite. Or, as Vimalakirti says, we feel *the love that has no presumptions because it has eliminated attachment and aversion.* In ordinary people, attachment and aversion are constantly confusing us. So when these are cleared up, there is no sense of separation between ourselves and others. In that realized state, at last we can truly love without confusion.

My teacher, Shunryu Suzuki, liked to talk about how Dogen, the thirteenth-century Japanese Zen master, loved plum blossoms. Dogen would watch the plum blossoms budding in early spring. He would gaze at them, appreciating their beauty. An ordinary person might see the plum blossom with "attachment and aversion"—attachment to the plum's beauty, aversion to its impending fading away. Dogen's way was "detachment," Suzuki Roshi said—it was an attitude *that has no presumptions*.

"Detachment," Suzuki Roshi continued, "means to live with people the way you see the beauty of the plum: if you want to appreciate the living flower—or the living being—you cannot be selfish. Your mind should be instead in a state of selflessness."

Often I'm asked, "What is this detachment thing in Buddhism? It sounds cold and hard." Actually, as Suzuki Roshi explains, detachment in Buddhism means just the opposite of cold and hard. The plum flower in spring is opening very slowly and steadily, but at the same time it's dying. To fully appreciate the plum blossom—to love it—we need to give up our sense of wanting the flower to be beautiful, or wanting it to linger—both of which are involved with our own ideas and desires. We need to appreciate the way the flower actually is. So detachment means love in its true sense—love, as Vimalakirti says, which has eliminated attachment and aversion. We see the plum blossom and tears come to our eyes: it's beautiful, and it's dying. We're completely one with that.

It infuses the Mahayana with radiance.

Usually, love is thought of as being something passionate, something we have to struggle to control. But, as Vimalakirti says, through the realization of emptiness, love is transformed into *the love that is great compassion*. Why is that? *Because it infuses the Mahayana with radiance*. A teacher mature in dharma radiates. You can see it, and you can feel it. It's very much like the radiance of falling in love, but it's not the ordinary falling in love where we're still involved in attachment and aversion; it's a radiance that is *imperturbable because totally ultimate.*

Earlier in the sutra we learned that Vimalakirti is able to take his consummate wisdom anywhere. He goes to racetracks to enlighten gamblers; he goes to bars to enlighten drunkards. He's a business-man among businessmen; he participates in government. He goes to schools to educate the children; he goes to hospitals to care for the sick. He goes everywhere. So Vimalakirti embodies that level of practice in which, not only is he imperturbable wherever he goes and whatever he does, but there's a kind of radiance about him.

Without the radiance, Buddhism can seem rather dry. Man-jushri is an example of that: in this passage he comes off as a little dry in his understanding; he's not completely opened up emotion-ally. He doesn't radiate the way Vimalakirti does.

The love that is without formality because it is pure in motivation.

The best teachers teach as the situation presents and requires; they don't stick to some formal method. I'm reminded of a story that Ed Brown, a fellow student of Shunryu Suzuki, tells in one of his books. There was a beautiful rock in front of the office at Tassajara Zen Monastery—everybody loved it; it was a great rock. Ed didn't have a stepping-stone for his own cabin, and so getting into his place was often awkward. One day, though, Ed went to his cabin and the beautiful office stone that everybody loved was there, now as a step-ping-stone for Ed's cabin. He asked around and found out that Suzuki Roshi had ordered it moved there.

When Ed asked Suzuki Roshi about it, Roshi said, "Oh, well, you needed a stone." Ed was embarrassed, and said, "But Roshi, that's the office stone. Everybody loves that stone." Suzuki Roshi replied, "We can get another stone for the office. I wanted you to have this one."

It's that quality of noticing. Think how cared for, how loved, Ed must have felt at that moment. The thing that mattered to Suzuki Roshi was taking care of Ed, his relationship to Ed. He was not so concerned about the stone that everybody liked so much. The plum blossom of Ed was right in front of the teacher, and so the teacher acted without formality. It wasn't as though there was a big ceremony around it; he just moved the stone.

The love that is wisdom because it causes attainment at the proper time.

Is there some proper time for attainment? Let's take a look at one of the classic Zen koans, the one about wild geese. Ma Tsu and Bai Chang were standing together and some geese flew over. Ma Tsu asked, "What are they?" and Bai Chang said, "They're wild geese." Ma Tsu continued, "Where have they gone?" and Bai Chang said, "They've flown away." Ma Tsu reached out, then grabbed Bai Chang's nose and twisted it. He said, "They've been here from the very first."

Bai Chang had a spiritual realization at that moment.

This is Bai Chang's enlightenment story, one of the best known in Zen. It sounds very wonderful, quite spontaneous. But actually, these two people have been intimate, in a teacher-student sense, for a long time. Both of them know each other well. This moment of the geese comes, and it looks like an "opportune time." But we should not think of this "moment" as a moment in the ordinary sense. The moment that happens between Ma Tsu and Bai Chang is a timeless moment—it has "been there from the very first." A commentary to this passage in the *Vimalakirti Sutra* about "attainment at the proper time" says, "It causes attainment at the proper time because it is always the proper time." Every moment is the proper time, but usually we can't see it.

There is a term in Buddhism—"self-secret." It means there aren't actually any secrets. It's all completely open to us right now. The problem is, we create the secret through our attachment, through our inability to see through things, our hesitation to open up. So, practically speaking, the dharma appears to be a secret. But it's a secret only because we make it so.

"Self-secret" is a very accurate term to describe what's going on in this sutra. We get the sense that when Manjushri questions Vimalakirti about the bodhisattva's great love, it's a bit of a self-secret to him. Manjushri doesn't quite get it because it's not something you get—it's something you have to open up to, that you *feel*.

Children of a certain age like to play a game where they put something over their head and then think they're invisible. They put a bag on their head and say, "You can't see me!" Well, actually, we can see them, it's just that they can't see us. Self-secret is something like that. We walk around with a bag over our head and we think there's some secret we have to discover so that we can see. Sometimes we're desperate to find out that secret. And all that's required is to take the bag off our head.

The love that is spontaneous because it is fully enlightened spontaneously.

This means it's always available. We can lift the bag off our head anytime. The geese fly over every day, all the time. Any time is a good time for things to open up for Bai Chang. And who is Bai Chang in the story? Bai Chang is you or me.

The moment of opening up is the so-called "opportune moment," but it is always there. Every day there are geese, every day they are flying by, but how can we really see them just as they are, the way Dogen saw the plum blossom? When we notice the geese afresh, we realize, as Ma Tsu says, that they've been there from the very first.

This passage helps us remember that, in the end, practice really isn't about getting something we didn't already have from the very first. We might say to ourselves, "I'll be different once something big happens to me—I'll be better, happier, more OK." This understanding is not wrong, exactly, but it is a little narrow. That way of thinking is still inside the self-secret, some mumbling from inside the bag.

> *The love that is nondual because it is involved neither with the external nor with the internal.*

Once the bag comes off, we're opened up and can experience *the love that is nondual because it is involved with neither the external nor the internal.* In an ordinary state of consciousness, our love is conditional—it has presumptions. We think, "I'm here and you're there." That's the sense of "internal and external." We fall in and out of that kind of love. The love that is nondual, however, doesn't have a sense of "I'm here and you're there." The love that is nondual embraces living beings unconditionally.

From our ordinary point of view, hearing Vimalakirti describe living beings as balls of foam or clouds in the sky may seem like a putdown, but actually it's the opposite. It's a celebration of livings beings as they actually are—each of them wonderful and beautiful like Dogen's plum blossom, opening in the early spring sun, expanding into its fullness as a flower, and starting to wilt and fall even before we know it. Yes, plum blossoms—living beings—are insubstantial and always changing. But that is precisely what makes them beautiful, and why we want to help them. That is why we generate *the love that is truly a refuge for them.*

Manjushri's wisdom is good, but until it's opened up emotionally with the great love—the great *metta* that Vimalakirti evokes, there's something incomplete about it. It's only when we have this kind of sparkling care for living beings that we can be complete and open in our relationships with other people. And then the dharma comes alive—not as something to understand, but as something to live, wherever we go, whatever we do.

Daughter Time

Rick Bass

Would that we all felt toward others the love of a parent for their young child. We would gladly give them our happiness and do anything to ease their pain. The world would be a paradise. (Note how similar parental love is to the tonglen practice taught by Gehlek Rimpoche.) A loving father, novelist Rick Bass, goes picking berries with his daughters and ponders how to make the most of this precious childhood time, which seems to pass so quickly. Bass is not a Buddhist but writes frequently for Buddhist magazines. I think that's because his writing, like this lovely personal meditation, is permeated with the love and poignant sense of impermance that mark Buddhism.

After fifteen years of listening and watching and hiking around and hunting Montana's Yaak Valley—fifteen youthful years, no less—we're starting to learn some things. We'll never know enough, nor even a fraction of what we'd like to, but we know where the wild strawberries are sweetest, in the tiny little lanes and clearings no larger than a house, where little patches of soft, filtered, damp light fall down from the midst of the old-growth larch forests, little clearings where the snowshoe hares come out of those old forests (despite the protestations of timber company biologists who say the rabbits—and their primary predators, lynx—don't live back there) to nibble on those new sweet berries in July.

Late in July, we like to try to get into some of those patches just before the legions of rabbits do, and pick a little basket of berries. The girls, Mary Katherine and Lowry, have a tiny doll's basket (the berries are no larger than the nub of a pencil eraser but contain more concentrated sweetness than an entire bushel of the mega-irradiated, supermarket jumbo-giants), and because I'm colorblind, I can't find the tiny strawberries and have to rely on the girls to do the harvest.

They're delighted by my weakness, and by their sharp-eyed superiority, and delighted also, as junior hunter-gatherers, to be providing for me. We all three have little baskets—in the dimming blue light of dusk, I absolutely can't find a single berry—and from time to time the girls take pity and come over to where I'm down on my hands and knees, searching, and drop a few into my basket.

And as is their habit, they eat far more than they pick, not even really hunter-gatherers but more like wild animals, feasting in the moment, letting their bodies do the hoarding, rather than jars or cabinets—the girls more a part of the forest, in that manner, in that moment—and by the time it is too dark to see well, we must walk back to our truck. The baskets have barely enough strawberries to drop into our pancake batter for the next morning, but they will be memorable pancakes, and it will be enough.

Just as we reach the truck, some friends come driving by, and they stop to visit for a while in the dusk, with the old sentinel larches so immense all around us. Our friends' own children are grown now, and they reminisce about picking wild strawberries with their children when they were Mary Katherine and Lowry's age.

They keep telling me what everyone has been saying since the day each of the girls was born—about how fast time flies—and I agree, and thank them for their counsel. They keep looking at the girls' little baskets of berries and smiling, and saying that same thing again and again throughout the course of the lazy-dusk conversation—and yet I don't know what to do about that truth, that inescapable flight, other than to go out into the patches of light scattered here and there along the edges of the old forest and pick strawberries with them in the evening, just as we're doing. And while I'm very grateful for the advice, I also wonder often if it, the time of childhood, doesn't sometimes pass faster for the parent by considering and noticing the speed of its passage, as opposed perhaps to a sleepier, less attentive, less fretful awareness of that passage and its nearly relentless pace.

Either way, it's going to go fast. I know I'm doing what I can to slow it down. Reading to them in the evenings; cooking with them; taking them on hikes, to swim in the mountain lakes.

Any activity I do with them could be done faster and more efficiently, but only recently have I come to understand that the slower and more inefficiently we do these things, the greater is my gain, our gain; the less quickly that galloping stretch of time passes. Taking three hours to fix a single, simple meal is a victory. Coming back from two hours in the woods with only a dozen strawberries left over is a triumph. Chaos and disorderliness can be allies in my goals of spending as much time as possible with them. If I'll only watch and listen, they'll show me—for a while—how to slow time down: instructing me in a way that I could never otherwise learn from the caring counsel of my friends.

Still, it's good to hear it, even if bittersweet. I know not to argue with them, or deny it. I know, or think I know, the sound of the truth, and it's wonderful to have their support in the matter.

We say our leisurely good-byes and part company in the hanging dusk, which is turning quickly now to darkness, so that we need to turn our lights on, traveling down the road on our way through the old forest. On the way home the girls would eat every single one of the last of the berries, if I let them—would run right through the last of our supplies in only a minute or two—and so I put the little straw baskets in the cab of the truck, just out of reach.

A couple of days later, after an afternoon spent at the waterfall, we're walking along a gravel road, again at dusk, and again the girls are finding the tiny wild strawberries. It's the 27th of July: hot days, cold nights. It's a couple of miles back to the truck, and the girls alternate between running and walking slowly; and again I try to relax and release, and give myself over to what seems to me to be the irregular, even inscrutable logic of their pace, their seemingly erratic stops and starts. Stretching their freedom, then coming back.

They run pell-mell for a while down the road, then slow to a saunter. Lowry stops at one point and looks up at the sky for long moments.

"What are you doing?" I ask.

"Listening to the leaves," she says. And she's right: just above the louder sound of the rushing creek, the drying leaves of the riverside cottonwoods are rattling slightly, and sounding different, dryer—autumnal already. She's four! It pleases me deeply, so much so that I don't even say anything, other than offering some mild concurrence.

Farther down the road she stops again and announces, "It smells good here." She's talking about the scent of the creekside bog orchids, which are intensely fragrant—almost overpoweringly so, like cheap perfume—and both girls walk out into the orchids to smell them better. Lowry tells us that they "smell better than the shampoo with the silver cap."

They run for a short distance, with me trailing right behind them, for safety—giving them their freedom, yet guarding them in lion country—and they stop yet again. And when I ask what they're doing this time, Low says quietly, as if from dreamland, "Listening to water."

They're both just standing there, staring at a glade below in the dimming light, mesmerized, it seems, by the very fabric of the landscape, the interlocking of all those different species and sizes of trees: I realize with a wonderful bittersweetness that I really don't have a clue as to what either of them is thinking or feeling, only that they are fully suspended in the business of being children—that they are in a place where I want them to be, and yet where I cannot go. Though even as I am thinking this, and thinking about how totally oblivious they are in the moment to my adult presence, Low turns her gaze from the mountains and tells me she thinks I'm standing too close to the edge of the road, and the steep slope leading down to the river.

"Don't slide down there," she says, taking my hand. "I don't want to lose you."

We resume our journey. Not too far from where we've parked, we encounter a dead garter snake in the road, tire-struck, but intact. The girls are fascinated, of course, both by their instinctual, archetypal fear of snakes and by the archetype of death, and they examine the snake, the specimen, like little scientists, stirring it gently with a stick—it still looks alive—and Lowry sprinkles a little dust on its head, as if in some pagan ritual.

We pass on, then, though she's quiet all the way to the truck, and when I ask her what the matter is some fifteen minutes later, she says, "It makes me sad when things die."

What do I know about girls, or anything? Would not a little boy—a boy such as myself, perhaps—have wound the dead snake around his wrist to wear as a bracelet, an amulet, or tossed it on his sister?

All I can do, often, is watch, and listen. So often it feels as if I'm treading behind them, observing, listening and learning other rhythms, rather than being out in front, as if breaking trail for them, the way I had always assumed it would be, being a parent.

Again and again, watching the girls watch this landscape—or anything else, for that matter—helps me see that thing more fully, and in new ways, whether down on my hands and knees at ground level or staring off at the horizon.

There's still time for me to learn some of what they see and know and feel. It's not too late. I can still learn, or relearn, some, if not all, of what they seem to know intuitively about our engagement with time. When to walk, when to run, when to rest, when to dream. When to be tender—more often than not—and, by extension, when and what not to be.

I want to believe that my bitterness and cynicism, and my fears for the environment and the coming world, fade when in their company; that such worries leach away, as if back into the soil of the landscape itself, where they might even be absorbed by the rattling cottonwoods and the scented orchids. It is probably not that way at all. But some days, after a time spent in the woods with the girls, that is how it feels. And I rarely come away from such days without feeling that I have learned something, even if I'm not sure what it is, and that although time certainly has not ceased or even paused, at least it has not accelerated in that awful way it can do sometimes, time slipping out from beneath you as if you've lost your footing on ice or some other slick surface.

I guess it's better to be aware of the briskness of its passage than not, after all. It's going to go fast, either way. But if you're aware of its brevity, then at least you'll be aware too of the eddies and slow stretches.

But my friends who stopped and visited the other evening when we were picking berries were right: it's going to go real fast, either way. The best I can do is try and keep up.

Drink and a Man ☙

Joan Duncan Oliver

Joan Duncan Oliver's struggle was with alcohol, and a man. It was a particularly acute manifestation of the battle we all wage with craving and attachment. Through her addiction, she sought an end to separateness, but only when she was finally sober did she discover wholeness and joy.

Only two things have I ever craved as much as life itself: drink and a man. To save my life, I had to give up the drink. To give up the drink, I had to give up the man.

My desire for both was total, visceral: passion seeking its own DNA. The bond was physical, emotional, spiritual, chemical—drink, man, and I locked in a ménage à trois.

It began, however, as a folie à deux. Alcohol was my first love: a constant, if feckless, companion in negotiating the scary home life of my teens. Early on I fell into the addict's faulty logic: I felt "normal" only when I was high.

For a while, it worked. A few drinks and I was prettier, sexier, more assured, less bookish and aloof. In no time, the desire for that state of mind became a craving for the only vehicle I knew could get me there—alcohol. By age seventeen, I was hooked.

In a sense we're all hooked, the Buddha taught. Not on alcohol but on a desire to be happy—which often means a desire for things to be other than they are. According to the second noble truth, desire, or craving *(tanha* in Pali, *trishna* in Sanskrit, translated as "thirst") is the source of *dukkha,* dissatisfaction. For an addict or alcoholic, that thirst is literal and all-consuming. (A Chinese proverb describes the cycle: *Man takes a drink; drink takes a drink; drink takes the man.*) Overdoing alcohol, drugs, food, or, for that matter, gambling, sex, shopping, even TV-watching, Net-surfing, and checking e-mail, gradually erodes choice, until we're left with little more than our desires and our efforts to satisfy them.

But where is the line between ordinary human longing and addictive craving? Even among specialists, what constitutes addiction remains a matter of debate. Narrowly defined, addiction is "chronic or habitual use of any chemical substance to alter body or mind states for other than medical purposes." Certain substances—cocaine, nicotine, and the painkiller OxyContin, among them—are known to trigger tenacious physical dependence. Alcoholism runs in families, and a genetic link has been established. But there is a saying in Twelve Step circles—"Alcoholism comes in people, not in bottles"—suggesting that addiction is more nuanced and holistic, and in large part as the Buddha saw it: a mental affliction. The fifth precept, one of the ethical guidelines originally set out for monks and nuns, calls on practitioners to "refrain from intoxicants that confuse the mind, causing heedlessness and lack of restraint." That is precisely why I drank: to be more spontaneous and uninhibited. As I saw it, more alive.

In my teens, I took a line from the poet Marianne Moore as ultimate truth: "satisfaction is a lowly/thing, how pure a thing is joy."* Satisfaction was the opiate of the masses, I declared, and joy the nectar of the gods. I wanted nectar. That's where the man came in.

We met one July afternoon forty years ago, in Harvard Yard. It sounds quaint now, but a friend and I were trying to liven up the weekly mixer for summer school students by spiking our fruit

---

*Marianne Moore, "What Are Years?" *Complete Poems* (New York: Penguin Books, 1994).

punch with whiskey smuggled into the Yard. Soon a merry group had gathered around us, to the envy of the other students. A few approached to ask why we were having so much fun. "We're punching the Yard punch," we sang out gaily, offering them a splash.

I don't recall when T. appeared. But within minutes the conversation had sailed into deep waters, too intimate for turning back. The recognition was instant—karmic, some might have said. I was Dante encountering Beatrice:

> The moment I saw [him] I can say in all truth that the vital spirit, which dwells in the inmost depths of the heart, began to tremble so violently that I felt the vibration alarmingly in all my pulses, even the weakest of them. As it trembled it uttered these words: Behold a god more powerful than I who comes to rule over me.

I was already in thrall to the Dewar's god; that day T. joined the pantheon. Though our relationship, unlike Dante's, was earthy, it was never earthbound. We lived in different cities, and when we met, which wasn't often, it was always over a steamy brew of sex, talk, drink, and sometimes pot. For the next decade, through other affairs and vague talk of marriage, nothing came close to the raw, ravishing desire I felt for T. It was as mind-altering and addictive as any drug.

Then, as I turned thirty, alcohol turned on me. The demon lover, it was all I could think about, though no amount I drank was ever enough. The Buddha understood this: that desire, whatever its object—a substance, a person, an experience, a state of mind—is insatiable. The addict's hope is to become too sick, or sick of hurting, to continue. "Hitting bottom" is karmic grace: a moment of awakening in which the only desire is to stop desiring, and hence, to stop suffering.

Quitting—so simple, so logical to those who've never tried it— throws an addict unarmed into the pit with desire. Long after physical craving abates, longing may remain. Actor Robert Downey, Jr., described it for a *New York Times Magazine* article: "the arm's been cut off, but the phantom limb is still twitching." Issues and insecurities masked by the addictive behavior are laid bare, along with other cravings. Smoking was up next for me, and even harder to quit than drinking. I stared down the true nature of desire while living at a Zen monastery. Despite sub-zero weather, snow, and gale-force winds, I would stand outside on the deck barefoot and smoke, stashing the cigarette butts in the sleeve of my meditation robe before returning to the zendo. Back on the cushion, every urge to smoke felt like Mara tempting Siddhartha on his long night under the Bodhi tree. Or Mara's daughters—*kama-tanha* (sexual desire, in Pali), *bhava-tanha* (desire for things to be a certain way), and *vibhava-tanha* (desire to avoid losing what we have).

Siddhartha's steadfast practice saved him, and by dawn he was the Buddha, "one who is awake." What can we do when Mara and his daughters come calling? Both Buddhism and the Twelve Step recovery program propose a similar response: develop resolute awareness, generate wisdom and compassion. Craving creates tunnel vision: we see only what we yearn for. Mindfulness allows us to see that and much more, giving us the choice not to act on our desires. The one-pointedness with which we fixated on the object of desire can be turned to an object of contemplation, such as the breath. This helps stabilize "monkey mind," the racing thoughts that beset most meditators at times, but make withdrawal especially hellish. Through Vipassana, or mindfulness practice, we begin to know things as they really are. When we see our craving and the devastation it has wrought, what we crave no longer seems so desirable. Through loving-kindness practice, we can begin the long process of self-forgiveness, and of healing relationships damaged in pursuing our desires. The driven ego-self that knows only "I want" begins to ease its grip.

Psychiatrist Carl Jung famously wrote a letter to Alcoholics Anonymous cofounder Bill Wilson in which he described the craving for alcohol as "a low level of the spiritual search of our being for wholeness, expressed in medieval language: the union with God." Fourteen centuries earlier, in "Drinking Alone in the Rainy Season," the Chinese poet T'ao Ch'ien hinted at the drawback of this method:

"One small cup and a thousand worries vanish; / two, and you'll even forget about heaven." I often drank alone late into the night, desperate to dissolve a chronic sense of separation from life and from myself. Only after I sobered up and began practicing zazen did I experience true *samadhi,* union.

"A tenth of an inch's difference, / And heaven and earth are set apart," wrote the Ch'an patriarch Seng-ts'an in a classic poem we recited at the monastery. For me, not drinking was the tenth of an inch's difference between life and death. Not returning a phone call was the face-off with Mara.

I had been sober less than a month when T. left a message that he was back in town. His voice on my answering machine set off desire so bald, so breathtaking, that I wondered how I had survived it all those years. This time, I knew I wouldn't survive; I would drink. I didn't call. Months later, I phoned to tell him I was sober. We never spoke again.

It wasn't that my desire for T. was gone; just banked. I clung to a certainty that someday we would reconnect, this time for good. Eighteen years went by. One night as I was watching the Academy Awards on television, I heard T.'s name announced. He had won an Oscar—posthumously, the presenter said. Death has been a frequent visitor in my life since childhood, but this loss somehow trumped the others, as if the dashed hopes and missed opportunities of all those earlier deaths had been rolled up into one. Desire for the absent living is one thing; like addiction, it feeds on possibility, hope, denial. Desire for the dead has no such illusions. In mourning T., I had to put to rest the champagne fiction on which our relationship (my obsession, really) had subsisted. I kept thinking of the final *gatha* of the *Diamond Sutra:*

> All composite things are like
>   a dream, a fantasy, a bubble, and a shadow;
> Like a dewdrop and a flash of lightning—
> They are thus to be regarded.

Buddhism teaches us that desire, for all the agony and ecstasy, is no match for the truth. Addiction exacts a terrible price, but for the addict who recovers, there is the promise of a far more rewarding high: the "divine intoxication" that the Sufis speak of. Unleashed from my attachments to the drink and to the man, I could finally taste what I'd been craving all along: Joy.

Cultivating
Wisdom ⟫

His Holiness the Dalai Lama

The signature truth of Buddhism is known as shunyata, *emptiness.
It's the doctrine that nothing in our lives—not our mind, feelings,
body, or environment—is a permanent entity. Emptiness sounds like a
philosophical exercise, but if you really see and accept it, your experience
of life is transformed. In Tibetan Buddhism, there is a strong tradition
of reasoning to address whether things are existent or not, and His
Holiness the Dalai Lama is one of the greatest teachers of the logic
known as Madhyamka, which seeks a middle way between the extremes
of existence and nonexistence. Here he works with the chapter on wisdom
from Shantideva's* The Way of the Bodhisattva *to deconstruct the self
piece by piece. See if at the end you can still find anything to call a self.*

In *The Way of the Bodhisattva* (Bodhicaryavatara), Shantideva's
presentation of the identitylessness, or selflessness, of phenomena is
explained first by means of the four mindfulnesses—mindfulness of
the body, of feelings, of mind, and of phenomena.

So, according to Shantideva's text, first we reflect upon the
nature of our own body. This is done by contemplating the body's
general and specific characteristics; for example, the aging process

and the impure substances that constitute bodily existence. Generally speaking, meditating on the mindfulness of body, reflecting upon the nature of our own body, is the approach explained in the Hinayana scriptures. However, we can extend this contemplation to the nature of the body, feelings, mind, and phenomena of all beings, who are limitless like space. Then it becomes a training of the mind according to the Mahayana path. When we contemplate the emptiness of these four factors—body, feelings, mind, and phenomena—we are practicing a mindfulness meditation focused on the ultimate truth.

MEDITATING ON EMPTINESS: THE BODY

The Way of the Bodhisattva gives us a systematic practice for these four mindfulness meditations on emptiness. Let us take as our example the human body. It is composed of many different parts—head, arms, legs, and so on. There is also the whole—the body as a complete unit. Generally when we think of body, it appears to our mind, at least on the surface, as if there is a single entity that we can point to as a tangible, unitary reality. Based on this common-sense view, we can speak of various characteristics and parts of the body. In other words, we feel as if there is fundamentally a thing called "body," and we can speak about its parts. Yet if we search for this "body" apart from its various parts, we come to realize that it is actually not to be found.

This is what Shantideva means in the following verses.

What we call the body is not feet or shins,
The body, likewise, is not thighs or loins.
It's not the belly nor indeed the back,
And from the chest and arms the body is not formed.

The body is not ribs or hands,
Armpits, shoulders, bowels, or entrails;
It is not the head or throat:
From none of these is "body" constituted.

We have a concept of our body as a unitary entity, which we hold to be precious and dear. Yet if we look more carefully, we find that the body is not the feet, nor the calves, the thighs, the hips, the abdomen, the back, the chest, the arms, the hands, the side of the torso, the armpits, the shoulders, the neck, or the head, or any other parts. So where is "body" to be found? If, on the other hand, the body were identical to the individual parts of the body, then the very idea of the body as a unitary entity would be untenable.

If "body," step by step,
Pervades and spreads itself throughout its members,
Its parts indeed are present in the parts,
But where does "body," in itself, abide?

If "body," single and entire,
Is present in the hand and other members,
However many parts there are, the hand and all the rest,
You'll find an equal quantity of "bodies."

If this unitary, single entity called "body" is identical to, or exists separately in, each individual part, then just as there are various parts of the body, the body too will become multiple.

Therefore, continues Shantideva, the body does not exist as identical to the individual parts of the body, nor can it exist separately and independently of these parts.

If "body" is not outside or within its parts,
How is it, then, residing in its members?
And since it has no basis other than its parts,
How can it be said to be at all?

Thus there is no "body" in the limbs,
But from illusion does the idea spring
And is affixed to a specific shape,
Just as when a scarecrow is mistaken for a man.

So how can this body be autonomous, independent, and self-existent? If we carefully examine the nature of the body, we find that the body is nothing more than a designation that we assign on the basis of the aggregation of various parts. We might ask, "What then is the body?" Due to circumstantial conditions such as the lighting, appearance of the object, and so on, we can sometimes mistake a certain shape as a human being.

Similarly, says Shantideva, as long as the appropriate conditions and factors are assembled that give rise to the sense of there being a person, then we can conventionally posit the concept of body on that basis.

> As long as the conditions are assembled,
> A body will appear and seem to be a man.
> As long as all the parts are likewise present,
> It's there that we will see a body.

However, if we search for the true referent behind the term "body," then we will find nothing. The upshot is that we arrive at the conclusion that "body" is, in the final analysis, a conventional construction—a relative truth—that comes into being only by depending on various causes and conditions.

This above analysis can also be extended to the individual parts of the body, as Shantideva does in the next verses:

> Likewise, since it is a group of fingers,
> The hand itself is not a single entity.
> And so it is with fingers, made of joints;
> And joints themselves consist of many parts.
> These parts themselves will break down into atoms,
> And atoms will divide according to direction.
> These fragments, too, will also fall to nothing.
> Thus atoms are like empty space—they have
>   no real existence.

When we speak of a hand, we find that it also is a composite of various parts. If a hand existed intrinsically and independently, this would contradict its having the nature of being dependent on other factors. If we search for a hand itself, we do not find a hand separate from the various parts that form it. Just as with a hand, a finger too is a composite that when dissected loses its existence. So with any part of the body, if we search for the true referent behind its name, nothing is to be found.

When we dissect the parts even into their elemental constituents—molecules, atoms, and so on—these too become unfindable. We can carry on dividing even the atoms themselves, in terms of their directional surfaces and find, again, that the very idea of "atom" is a mental construct. If we carry on still further, we find that the very idea of matter, or atoms, becomes untenable. In order for anything to be characterized as material, it must have parts. Once we go beyond that and dissect further, what remains is nothing but emptiness.

To our commonsense view, things and events appear as if they have some form of independent and objective status. However, as Shantideva points out in the next verse, if we search for the true nature of such phenomena, we eventually arrive at their unfindability.

> All form, therefore, is like a dream,
> And who will be attached to it, who thus investigates?
> The body, in this way, has no existence;
> What is male, therefore, and what is female?

So, we can see that there is nothing absolute about the objects of our anger and attachment. Nothing is desirable or perfect in the absolute sense; neither is anything undesirable and repulsive in the absolute sense. Therefore, in reality there is no ground for extreme emotional reactions to things and events. Since the body cannot be found when sought through critical analysis, so the designations we make on the basis of the existence of the body—such as differences of gender and race—are also ultimately devoid of essence. So now, what grounds do we have to generate extreme and volatile emotional responses to people of different gender or race?

How Do Things Exist?

When we examine the phenomenological experience of emotions coming and going within us, there is, generally speaking, the appearance that all things and events each have an independent and objective reality. This is especially so with a strong negative emotion like hatred. We impose a kind of concreteness upon the object such that the object appears to us in sharper contrast, with a very solid reality of its own. In reality, there are no such tangible, concrete objects.

However, we have to ask, if *these* objects are unfindable, does this mean they do not exist at all? This is not the case. Of course they do exist. The question is not *whether* they exist but how they exist. They exist, but not in the manner in which we perceive them. They lack any discrete, intrinsic reality. This absence, or emptiness, of inherent existence is their ultimate nature.

The analytic process that seeks the true referents of our terms and concepts is not so complex, and it's not that difficult to arrive at the conclusion that things and events are unfindable when sought through such a process. However, this absence we arrive at after discerning the unfindability of phenomena through such analysis is not the final emptiness. Once we have arrived at this unfindability of things and events, then we can ask in what manner they actually do exist. We would then realize that the existence of things and events must be understood in terms of their relativity. And when we understand things and events as dependent for their existence on causes and conditions—and also as mere designations—we come to realize that things and events lack independence or self-determining authority. We see their nature clearly as dependent on other factors. And as long as anything exists only in dependence on other factors—governed by other forces—it cannot be said to be independent. For independence and dependence are mutually exclusive; there is no third possibility.

It is critical to understand that Madhyamaka does not say that things are absent of inherent existence merely because they cannot be found when sought through critical analysis. This is not the full argument. Things and events are said to be absent of inherent or intrinsic existence because *they exist only in dependence on other factors.* This is the real premise. This style of reasoning eliminates two extremes—the extreme of nihilism, because one accepts a level of existence in terms of interdependence, and the extreme of absolutism, because one denies the intrinsic existence of phenomena.

The Buddha stated in sutra that anything that comes into being through dependence on conditions has the nature of being unborn. What does "unborn" mean here? Certainly we are not talking about the unborn nature of a nonexistent entity, such as the horn of a rabbit. Likewise, we are not denying the origination of things and events on a conventional level. What we are saying is that all phenomena that depend on conditions have the nature of emptiness. In other words, anything that depends on other factors is devoid of its own independent nature, and this absence of an independent nature is emptiness.

In his *Fundamental Treatise on the Middle Way*, Nagarjuna says that things and events, which are dependently originated, are empty, and thus are also dependently designated. He says dependent origination is the path of the Middle Way, which transcends the extremes of absolutism and nihilism. This statement is followed by another passage, which reads:

> There is no thing
> That is not dependently originated;
> Therefore there is no thing
> That is not empty of intrinsic existence.

Nagarjuna concludes there is nothing that is not empty, for there is nothing that is not dependently originated. Here we see the equation between dependent origination and emptiness.

When we read the passages in *The Way of the Bodhisattva* dealing with the unfindability of things and events, it is crucial not to let ourselves be drawn into nihilism. This is the false conclusion that nothing really exists and, therefore, nothing really matters. This extreme must be avoided.

Beyond the Intellectual Understanding

An intellectual understanding of emptiness is different from a full realization of emptiness, wherein there is no cognition of the dependent origination of things. The Buddha states in a sutra cited in Nagarjuna's *Compendium of Sutra (Sutrasamuchaya)* that if in our meditations on emptiness we have even the slightest affirmative element—for instance, "This is emptiness," or "Things must exist"—then we are still caught in the web of grasping. As far as the cognitive content of our meditative experiences of emptiness is concerned, it must be a total absorption within the mere negation, the absence of intrinsic existence. There should be no affirmative elements within that meditative state.

However, when you have gained a very deep understanding of emptiness, you will get to a point where your very concept of existence and nonexistence changes. At this stage, even with regard to familiar objects, you will see a marked difference in your perception and your attitude toward them. You will recognize their illusion-like nature. That is, when the recognition dawns that although things appear to be solid and autonomous they do not exist in that way, this indicates that you are really arriving at an experiential understanding of emptiness.

This is known as *perceiving things as illusion-like*. In fact, when you have gained a deep realization of emptiness, there is no need to make separate efforts to attain this perspective. After your own profound realization and experience of the emptiness of phenomena, things will appear spontaneously and naturally in the nature of illusion.

As your understanding of emptiness deepens and becomes a full experience of emptiness, you will be able not only to confirm the emptiness of phenomena by merely reflecting on dependent origination, but also your ascertainment of emptiness will reinforce your conviction in the validity of cause and effect. In this way, your understanding of both emptiness and dependent origination will reinforce and complement each other, giving rise to powerful progress in your realization.

You might think that when your understanding deepens in this way, you have reached such a high level of realization that you are at the threshold of becoming fully enlightened! This is definitely not the case. At this initial stage, on what is called the *path of accumulation*, your understanding of emptiness is still inferential. In deepening your understanding of emptiness further, it is essential to develop another mental factor—the faculty of single-pointedness. It is possible that we can, by using the analytic approach, arrive at a single-pointedness of the mind, but it is more effective and easier to first have stability of the mind, and then, using that stability, reflect on the empty nature of phenomena. In any case, it is essential to attain tranquil abiding. Once you have gained tranquil abiding, you then use that stable mind to meditate on emptiness. In this way you arrive at a union of tranquil abiding *(shamatha)* and penetrative insight *(vipashyana)*.

You have now arrived at the *path of preparation*. From this point onward there will be a gradual reduction in dualistic appearances during meditative equipoise on emptiness. This gradual diminishing of dualistic appearances will culminate in a direct and utterly nonconceptual realization of emptiness. Such a state, free from dualism and grasping at intrinsic existence, is known as the *true path*. At this point, you have become an arya, a "superior being."

The true path results in the attainment of true cessation—the cessation of certain levels of deluded states and afflictions. This is when we have an unmediated, experiential knowledge of the true dharma, one of the three objects of refuge. Only at this stage do we really have the first opportunity to say hello to the true dharma jewel. We have yet to tread the subsequent stages of the path in order to attain full enlightenment. During the first two paths of accumulation and preparation, the first incalculable eon of the accumulation of merit is completed. Through the first seven bodhisattva levels, which begin upon reaching the true path, the accumulation of merit of the second incalculable eon is completed. At the eighth bodhisattva level, we finally overcome all the afflictive emotions and thoughts. We then progress through the *pure grounds*—the eighth, ninth, and tenth bodhisattva levels—which are pure in that they are free from the stains of afflictions. It is during these three levels that the accumulation of merit of the third incalculable eon is perfected. So you can see that it takes a long time to attain complete enlightenment!

At the last instance of the tenth bodhisattva level, we generate an extremely powerful wisdom of emptiness that acts as an antidote to remove even the habitual patterns, predispositions, and imprints formed by all our past afflictions and deluded states of mind, and this then culminates in the attainment of full omniscience, or buddhahood.

THE CRUCIAL SENSE OF COMMITMENT AND COURAGE

We can see that there is a systematic "plan" for attaining enlightenment. You don't have to grope around in the dark without any direction. The layout of the entire path and its correlation to the accumulation of merit over a period of these incalculable eons illustrate a clear direction. Practitioners need to be aware of this fact and on that basis try to develop a deep determination and commitment to their spiritual pursuits. If you then supplement your practice with tantric Vajrayana methods, your approach will definitely be sound and well-grounded.

If, on the other hand, when thinking of three incalculable eons, you become totally disheartened and discouraged and then try to seek an easier path for yourself through tantric practice, that's a totally wrong attitude. Furthermore, this would reflect that your commitment to dharma practice is not strong. What is crucial is a sense of commitment and courage that is prepared—if necessary—to go through three incalculable eons to perfect the conditions for full enlightenment. If on the basis of such determination and courage you then embark on the Vajrayana path, your approach would be well-grounded and powerful. Otherwise, it is like building a large structure without a firm foundation. Without doubt, there is great profundity in the tantric approach. However, whether that can be utilized depends on the capacity of the individual.

Of course, I am speaking here on the basis of my own personal observation. I too used to feel that three incalculable eons was too long. This time frame seemed unimaginable, something that I could not accept, whereas the time frame envisioned for enlightenment in tantra seemed more manageable. Understandably, the swiftness of the Vajrayana path held a particular attraction. However, gradually my feelings have changed, especially toward the time frame of three incalculable eons. I have slowly grown to feel attracted toward the sutra approach and have actually begun to see the tremendous beneficial effects it can have in deepening our dedication to spiritual practice.

Mindfulness on the Emptiness of Feelings

Next is the meditation on the mindfulness of feelings, which Shantideva presents by analyzing the emptiness of feelings. We read the following:

> If suffering itself is truly real,
> Then why is joy not altogether quenched thereby?
> If pleasure's real, then why will pleasant tastes
> Not comfort and amuse a man in agony?
>
> If the feeling fails to be experienced
> Through being overwhelmed by something stronger,
> How can "feeling" rightly be ascribed
> To that which lacks the character of being felt?
>
> Perhaps you say that only subtle pain remains,
> Its grosser form has now been overmastered,
> Or rather it is felt as mere pleasure.
> But what is subtle still remains itself.

If, through presence of its opposite,
Pain and sorrow fail to manifest,
To claim with such conviction that it's felt
Is surely nothing more than empty words.

If the sensations of suffering and pain existed independently, they would not depend on other factors, and joyful experiences would be impossible. Similarly, if happiness existed independently, it would preclude grief, pain, and illness. And if the sensations of joy and pleasure existed intrinsically, then even if a person were confronting an agonizing tragedy or pain, that person would still derive the same pleasure from food and comforts that he or she normally does.

Since feeling is in the nature of sensation, it must exist in relation to circumstances. We also find in our personal experiences that sensations can overwhelm one another. For example, if we are gripped by strong grief, that can permeate our entire experience and prevent us from experiencing any joy. Similarly, if we feel intense joy, that too can permeate our experience such that adverse news and mishaps do not cause us serious concern.

However, if we were to insist that underlying all of this is an independent event called "feeling," the Madhyamika would respond, "Wouldn't that event depend on other factors, such as its causes and conditions?" So the idea of an independent feeling is only a fiction, a fantasy. There is no independently existing feeling that is not in the nature of pleasure, pain, or neutrality. There cannot be sensation or feeling that is not in the nature of any of these three basic patterns of experience.

Having established the absence of intrinsic existence of phenomena, Shantideva goes on to say that we should use this understanding as an antidote to our grasping at true existence—in this particular case, our grasping at feelings as if they had an independent, concrete reality.

Since so it is, the antidote
Is meditation and analysis.

Investigation and resultant concentration
Is indeed the food and sustenance of yogis.

Such single-pointed meditation on the emptiness of feeling is
like the fuel for generating penetrative insight into emptiness. At the
beginning of this chapter, Shantideva stated that first we must cultivate single-pointedness of mind and attain tranquil abiding, and
then generate penetrative insight. Through the combination of
tranquil abiding and penetrative insight, the meditator will be able
to engage in the profound yoga focused on emptiness. "The food
and sustenance of yogis" refers to meditative absorption arrived at
through contemplation on the emptiness of feelings.

Feelings, then, arise due to contact, which is their cause.

If between the sense power and a thing
There is a space, how will the two terms meet?
If there is no space, they form a unity,
And therefore, what is it that meets with what?

However, if sought through critical analysis, the contact that
gives rise to feelings does not exist in any absolute sense either. This
verse presents an analysis of the nature of contact. "Contact," a mental factor, is defined as the meeting point between a sense faculty and
an object. It arises when consciousness, the object, and the sense faculty all come together. Shantideva asks, "If there is an interval of
space between the sense organs and sensory objects, where is the
contact?" For example, if two atoms are totally intermingled, then
they become identical; we cannot speak of a distinction between the
two. So we read in the following verses:

Atoms and atoms cannot interpenetrate,
For they are equal, lacking any volume.
But if they do not penetrate, they do not mingle;
And if they do not mingle, there is no encounter.

For how could anyone accept
That what is partless could be said to meet?

And you must show me, if you ever saw,
A contact taking place between two partless things.

Not only that, Shantideva continues, but also, since consciousness is immaterial, how can we define it with the word "contact," which relates to matter? "What can come into contact with consciousness?" he asks:

The consciousness is immaterial,
And so one cannot speak of contact with it.
A combination, too, has no reality,
And this we have already demonstrated.

Therefore, if there is no touch or contact,
Whence is it that feeling takes its rise?
What purpose is there, then, in all our striving,
What is it, then, that torments what?

Who could be harmed by painful experiences, since there is no such thing as intrinsically and absolutely existing painful sensations? Therefore, by examining contact—the cause of sensation—and by examining the nature of sensation itself, we find no intrinsically real sensation or feeling. The conclusion is that these exist only in dependence on other factors, and that nothing whatsoever can exist independently and intrinsically.

Through such analysis, we arrive at the important conclusion that neither the experiencer nor its object—the feeling—is truly existent. Once we have recognized this truth, the next logical step is to avert craving. This is presented in the following verse:

Since there is no subject for sensation,
And sensation, too, lacks all existence,
Why, when this you clearly understand,
Will you not pause and turn away from craving?

Furthermore, says Shantideva, when we think of the nature of sensation, what grounds do we have to claim that an independently existing feeling or sensation arises? The consciousness, or mind, that is simultaneous to the sensation cannot perceive such an autonomously real sensation.

> Seeing, then, and sense of touch
> Are stuff of insubstantial dreams.
> If perceiving consciousness arises simultaneously,
> How could such a feeling be perceived?

> If the one arises first, the other after,
> Memory occurs and not direct sensation.
> Sensation, then, does not perceive itself,
> And likewise, by another it is not perceived.

> The subject of sensation has no real existence,
> Thus sensation, likewise, has no being.
> What damage, then, can be inflicted
> On this aggregate deprived of self?

Nor can the moments of consciousness that precede and succeed the sensation perceive that sensation. The preceding moments are no longer present and remain only as imprints at the time of the sensation. And during the subsequent moments of consciousness, the sensation remains only an object of recollection. Furthermore, there is no experiencer of the sensation as such. The conclusion we draw from this is that there is no sensation or feeling with independent reality. This completes the meditation on the mindfulness of feelings.

Mindfulness of the Emptiness of Mind

Next comes the meditation on the mindfulness of mind. It begins with the negation of any independent or intrinsic reality of mental consciousness.

> The mind within the senses does not dwell;
> It has no place in outer things, like form,
> And in between, the mind does not abide:
> Not out, not in, not elsewhere can the mind be found.

Something not within the body, and yet nowhere else,
That does not merge with it nor stand apart—
Something such as this does not exist, not even slightly.
Beings have nirvana by their nature.

The mind cannot exist within the body, as the body, or some-where in between; nor can the mind exist independently of the body. Such a mind is not to be found, and therefore the mind is devoid of intrinsic existence. When beings recognize this nature of their mind, liberation can take place.

Although we know that consciousness exists, if we analyze and try to locate it within earlier or later moments of its continuum, the idea of consciousness as a unitary entity begins to disappear, just as with the analysis of the body. Through such analysis we arrive at the absence of intrinsic existence of consciousness. This applies equally to sensory experiences, such as visual perceptions, as they also share the same nature.

If consciousness precedes the cognized object,
With regard to what does it arise?
If consciousness arises with its object,
Again, regarding what does it arise?

If consciousness comes later than its object,
Once again, from what does it arise?

If a consciousness, such as a sensory perception, arises simulta-neously with its object, then they cannot be maintained as sequen-tial—that is, the object exists and then consciousness cognizes it. If they were simultaneous, how could an object give rise to a cognition?

If, on the other hand, the object exists first and then conscious-ness of it comes later, cognition comes only after the cessation of the object. If this were the case, what would that cognition be aware of, for the object has ceased to exist? When we subject sensory perceptions to this kind of critical analysis, they too are revealed to be unfindable, just as in the case of mental consciousness.

Mindfulness of the Emptiness of All Phenomena

> Thus the origin of all phenomena
> Lies beyond the reach of understanding.

Generally, the argument used to establish the substantial reality of phenomena is that things and events have functions; that is, specific conditions give rise to certain things, and particular circumstances lead to particular events. So we assume that things and events must be real, that they must have substantial reality. This principle of functionality is the key premise the Realists used in asserting the independent existence of things and events. If the Madhyamika is successful in negating the intrinsic existence of these functional entities, then—as Nagarjuna put it in his *Fundamental Treatise on the Middle Way*—it becomes easier to negate the intrinsic existence of more abstract entities, such as space and time.

Many of these arguments seem to use the principles of the Madhyamika reasoning known as *the absence of identity and difference*. For example, the divisible and composite nature of material phenomena is explained in terms of directional parts. In the case of consciousness, its composite nature is explained mainly from the point of view of its continuum of moments. With regard to such abstract entities as space and time, we can understand their composite nature in terms of their directions. So, as long as a thing is divisible—as long as we can break it into composite parts—we can establish its nature as dependent upon its parts. If, on the other hand, a thing were to exist intrinsically as a substantial reality, then that thing would not be dependent upon its parts; it would instead exist as an indivisible and completely discrete entity.

The Infinite Dot
Called Mind ⤳

The Dzogchen Ponlop Rinpoche

Here's another teaching on the four foundations of mindfulness, this one not through logical analysis but direct experience. Body, feeling, mind, and phenomena are basically the total of how we experience ourselves and our world. Transforming our experience of each of them, we transform our life. The Dzogchen Ponlop Rinpoche looks at the four mindfulnesses from the general Buddhist and Mahayana points of view. While the Dalai Lama aimed to deny the validity of all concepts, this discussion is based on a positive assertion: the existence of buddha nature, the enlightened nature that we all inherently possess. This understanding is the basis of the Vajrayana, or tantric, school of Mahayana Buddhism, and this excellent teaching by The Dzogchen Ponlop Rinpoche is imbued with the tantric view.

In the Mahayana tradition, mindfulness is regarded as wisdom, transcendental knowledge, which is known in Sanskrit as *prajna*. Mindfulness is also a method of working with our mind. It is the method of recollection, of watchfulness, which develops into the stage of awareness. But if you look at this mindfulness and awareness, you will see that there is not much difference between them. Once you have developed the discipline of mindfulness, awareness is simply the continuity of that mindfulness.

There are several stages we progress through in our study and cultivation of prajna. These become the means for integrating our understanding into our experience, and progressively developing that experience into the full state of realization. In this essay I will discuss the four foundations of mindfulness as they are understood and practiced in the general Buddhist approach and in the Mahayana tradition.

FOUR OBJECTS OF MINDFULNESS PRACTICE

In the path of the four mindfulnesses, there are four objects of meditation. The first is *body*, the second is *feeling*, and the third is *mind*. The fourth object is called *phenomena*, or dharmas in Sanskrit.

We have different samsaric relationships with each of these four objects. Through clinging to these four objects and relating to them in a most neurotic way, the whole universe, the whole world of samsara, is created. But by using these four objects as the objects of our meditation, we can develop a sane relationship with them. We can transcend our usual relationship with these four objects and develop more direct and profound ways of dealing with them.

The object of body serves as the basis of clinging to oneself as an existent, permanent ego. To that we add feeling, something to be experienced by this self. Then we have mind, which is what we relate to as the real self. When we try to point to the self, the ego, we usually point to our consciousness, our basic sense of mind. That is the actual object of self-clinging, which cannot exist without body (or form in general) and feeling. Mind cannot really express itself without the body and feeling. Therefore mind, in the third stage of mindfulness, is the basic idea of consciousness, of awareness.

Finally, we have the fourth object, phenomena. Ordinarily, we relate to phenomena as the basis of confusion. However, from this perspective, phenomena are seen as the basis of both confusion and liberation, of samsara and nirvana. Samsara and nirvana appear and are experienced on the basis of phenomena.

Our misunderstandings and unhealthy relationships with these four objects lead us into the vicious circle of samsara. Samsara's game of illusion arises from a lack of prajna in our relationships with these four objects. Therefore, we develop prajna so we can relate with them more profoundly, as well as more basically.

THE ESSENCE OF MINDFULNESS

What is mindfulness? The essence of mindfulness is the prajna of seeing—the wisdom that understands and experiences the true nature of form, the true nature of feeling, the true nature of mind, and the true nature of phenomena. To practice this means to focus, place, or relate your mind closely with these four situations or objects. Relating with these four objects directly with our prajna means experiencing them without any labels. This is what we call the practice of mindfulness.

The essence of these practices is experiencing these four objects without any barrier between you as the knower and the experienced object. The absence of any barrier is prajna. Prajna is also without coloring; therefore, we see the objects' basic state and relate with that. The fundamental simplicity of the object is the essence or nature of mindfulness.

If you examine these four mindfulnesses, you will recognize that they involve working with the five skandhas. The mindfulness of body relates to the skandha of *form*. The mindfulness of feeling relates to the skandha of *feeling*. The mindfulness of mind relates to the skandha of *consciousness*, which is the fifth skandha. And the mindfulness of dharmas, or phenomena, relates to the other two skandhas, which are *perception* and *formation*, or concepts. Keeping this in mind helps us to understand these four mindfulnesses.

THE FIRST FOUNDATION: MINDFULNESS OF BODY

The method of practicing the four foundations begins with mindfulness of the body. There are two ways of viewing the practice of the mindfulness of body. The first is the general Buddhist approach, which is the most fundamental way of looking at this mindfulness. The second approach specifically reflects the Mahayana point of view.

The mindfulness of body, or form, relates to our fundamental sense of existence, which is normally unstable and ungrounded due to our samsaric tendencies. Our existence is very wild, like a mad elephant. That's why we work with form as the first stage of mindfulness practice. In particular, we work with three different levels of form. These are the outer form of our physical existence, the inner form of our perceptions, and the innermost form, which is related to the Mahayana understanding of the selflessness of body.

The Outer Form of Body

In the general Buddhist approach, we work with the outer form of our physical existence. We try to understand what this existence is, what this physical form is. Usually, we experience our physical body as existing "out there" somewhere. We feel that our body exists outside of our mind. Also, we feel that it exists in a definite, very solid way. That is our fundamental experience of body, and it goes wild in our usual situation of life. Through the practice of mindfulness, we calm down the wildness of our physical existence and bring it to a certain level of groundedness. By bringing it into the present, we bring it to what it actually is, rather than thinking about what it is.

For example, we may ponder such questions as, "Is the body matter or mind?" However, forget about such philosophical or theoretical divisions. At this point, we simply relate with our physical sense of existence—that is the mindfulness of body. If we approach this with too much philosophy or analysis, it becomes complicated. Trying to see if body is mind or matter, if it's a projection or not, prevents us from relating directly to what it is. The Buddha talks about this basic approach in the sutras, when he says things like, "When you see, just see. When you smell, just smell. When you touch, simply touch. And when you feel, simply feel."

We are using very basic logic here to relate to the most fundamental level of our experience. For example, when we sit down on a meditation cushion, we experience various physical sensations, such as gravity, which are basic to our existence. Just being there with that is what we call mindfulness of body, and that mindfulness also involves a certain prajna, an understanding of what actually is.

The Inner Form of the Body

That experience takes us to the inner state of physical existence, which is seeing the reality of the relative existence of self. That is a very simple experience. In the general Buddhist approach, we simply sit and be with our body, not with our mind, so to speak. In this exercise, it's possible for us to have a sense of the profound presence of our body, the profound experience of just being, whatever it is. That experience is the inner experience of the physical self.

At this stage, we go further into the subtlety of our physical nature. We see our own impermanent nature, which is the subtle experience of the mindfulness of body. That experience is a profound realization. The Buddha said that of all footprints, the deepest imprint is the footprint of the elephant. Similarly, the Buddha said, the most precious and deepest impression that any thought can make on the progress of our path is the thought of impermanence. Therefore, the realization of the impermanence of our body is a very profound mindfulness practice.

The Innermost Form of the Body

At the Mahayana level, we go beyond the simple physical presence of body. At this point, we relate to the way the body is experienced. The way we experience our body is simply our perception, our reflection, our projection. As far as the Mahayana path is concerned, there is nothing solid beyond that—there is no real existence of an outer physical body.

Through the practice of reflecting on our physical existence, our discipline of mindfulness develops into seeing with awareness— we are seeing a much deeper level of the physical self. We're discovering the true nature of the experience of body. Here, we're approaching the level of absolute reality, rather than remaining on the relative level where we see only the relative nature of mind, body, and mindfulness. We are going to the depths of mindfulness, which is the absolute truth. Therefore, when we talk about this mindfulness in the Mahayana sense, we are talking about the selflessness of the body, which is very different from the general Buddhist approach.

The Dream Example

At this level we are dealing with our projections. We see that the physical world we experience is not necessarily solid and real. This can be understood clearly through the example of a dream. When we are dreaming, we have subject, we have object, and we have the action between the subject and the object. This is the experience of the threefold situation. As long as we remain in the dream state, we experience these three things as solid and existing.

But these three exist only in the dream state—if you look back at your dream after waking up, they do not exist. And if you look back at yesterday's experience of life, it does not exist either. Neither your dream of last night nor your experience of yesterday is solid, as far as today is concerned. There's no sound basis for saying that yesterday's events were more solid than last night's dream. There's no logical reason, except that we cling to our dreamlike experience of yesterday more than to our experience of last night's dream.

Therefore, in the Mahayana path, our whole experience of the body and the physical world is seen as simply a projection of our mind. It is a production of our karmic mind and will remain as long as we remain in this dream of samsara.

Maintaining the discipline of seeing the dreamlike nature of our body is mindfulness of body in the Mahayana path. But in order to really practice this mindfulness of body, we must begin with the Theravadan approach of simply being there in the physical sense, experiencing the presence of our body. Then, going further into the experience of body, we see the illusory, dreamlike nature of our body as a reflection of our mind. Finally, going into the depth of that experience, we see body as emptiness.

That is the complete practice of mindfulness of body. Practices such as sitting or walking meditation are situations where we can have strong experiences of this mindfulness. In contrast, we usually go about our regular existence in the world mindlessly, and we do not really experience our own presence on the physical level.

THE SECOND FOUNDATION: MINDFULNESS OF FEELING

The practice of the second foundation, mindfulness of feeling, is relating to our basic existence as samsaric beings. In the general Buddhist approach, "feeling" refers to working with our basic fear, which is the fear of suffering, or the fear of fear. Actually, fear itself is not suffering, but the fear of fear is the most troubling presence in the realm of our feeling.

Therefore, mindfulness of feeling relates with the three objects of our existence in the samsaric world: the pleasant object, the unpleasant object, and the neutral object. In relation to these three objects, we experience three different states or aspects of fear. Towards the pleasant object, we feel a fear of attachment, a fear of desire. Towards the unpleasant object, we feel a fear of hatred or aggression. And towards the neutral object, we feel a fear of neutral feeling, of numbness or stupidity. Every day we experience these three aspects of feeling in surviving our existence in the samsaric world.

To relate with these three feelings, the Buddha taught that we have to relate properly to the three objects—to understand them and work with their nature. He said that when we examine the nature of these three feelings and their three objects, we discover that the fundamental nature of all of them is suffering. The pleasant object, the unpleasant object, and the neutral object all have the same nature of suffering, regardless of whether we're relating to attachment, aggression, or ignorance. Consequently, practicing mindfulness of suffering is the mindfulness of feeling, and relating with the three objects is the way to relate with the three levels of suffering.

The Three Levels of Suffering

The practice here is to meditate on the three expressions of suffering and to experience their nature. The Buddha said there is one word that can describe the meaning of suffering, and that is fear. Fear is what suffering means. But what is this fear? It is the fear of losing something that is pleasant, something that is very dear and beloved, something to which you have become attached. It is also the fear of gaining something that is unpleasant and that you don't want. Overall, you always get what you don't want, and you don't get what you really want. Therefore, we have three levels of suffering, which we call the suffering of suffering, the suffering of change, and all-pervasive suffering.

All-pervasive suffering is the fundamental fear that exists whether we're feeling happy or down. All of our feelings are pervaded by this fundamental fear, which is why it is called all-pervasive suffering. It's compared in traditional Buddhist literature to developing a fatal disease that has not fully ripened. You haven't really experienced it yet, but its presence is there all of the time, growing every minute. That kind of fundamental situation is known as all-pervasive suffering, which grows into the suffering of change.

The traditional metaphor for the suffering of change is a very delicious cookie baked with poison. When you eat that cookie, it's very pleasurable—but it is deadly poisonous. In order to show that more dramatically, Shantideva, in the *Bodhicharyavatara*, said the suffering of change is like honey on a razor blade. When we lick this honey, it's very sweet, and because of our desire and attachment, we want more and more all the time. With our poverty mentality, we lick the honey harder each time we experience its sweetness, and the harder we lick the honey, the deeper we cut our tongue on the razor blade. So the suffering of change is experienced initially as a pleasurable, pleasing feeling, but it leads us to suffering.

The suffering of change leads us to the suffering of suffering, which is the most obvious level of suffering. This simply means that, in addition to our fundamental fear, we accumulate further sufferings, one on top of the other. For example, after experiencing the delicious honey, we notice that we have cut off our tongue. When we notice that our tongue is gone, not only do we feel the pain of our wound, we also realize we won't be able to taste the sweetness of honey again in this lifetime.

As we work with and examine the three levels of experience—pleasant, unpleasant, and neutral—we can see they are related with the three sufferings. Pleasurable feelings are connected to the suffering of change, unpleasant feelings connected to the suffering of suffering, and the neutral state of mind is connected to fundamental suffering, all-pervasive suffering. So mindfulness of feeling is being totally watchful and present with every level of our fear. This is the mindfulness of feeling from the perspective of the general Buddhist approach.

Mahayana Approach: Fearlessness and Selflessness

In the Mahayana tradition, mindfulness of feeling means seeing the selfless nature of suffering, which is seeing the true nature of fear as not being fear. On the most fundamental level, our suffering is fear of being in the state of fear. Relating to this fundamental fear without fear is the way to practice Mahayana mindfulness of feeling.

What we are doing here is simply looking at our fear. We experience our suffering—our so-called suffering—nakedly, without any filters of fear. That's how the Mahayana mindfulness works. Looking at it directly, face-to-face, we transcend our fear and become a fearless warrior on the Mahayana path. Without working with the mindfulness of feeling, which deals directly with our fear, it is very difficult to follow the path of Mahayana. Without it, there's no way to become a fearless warrior.

THE THIRD FOUNDATION: MINDFULNESS OF MIND

The third stage of mindfulness is working directly with our basic state of mind, which is our consciousness or awareness. We're not speaking of one giant, all-pervasive mind, which does not exist in any case. In the general Buddhist approach, the mind refers here to a detailed classification of mind, and our practice is working with every single experience of our consciousness. We have a very detailed explanation of mind, and our practice is being mindful of every individual movement of our mind, every momentary experience of thought, perception, and memory.

In the Mahayana tradition, mindfulness of mind is closely connected to the meditative experience, beginning with our practice of shamatha and vipashyana and continuing all the way up to tantra. The Vajrayana practices are closely connected to this mindfulness of mind.

In this practice, we develop the discipline of watching our mind—guarding the mind and bringing it down to some experience of groundedness. Right now, our mind is up in the air. It's totally in the state of dreaming, in the state of nonreality, in the state of nonexistence. This mindfulness brings the mind down to the fundamental state of nowness—nowness of this reality, of this moment. That is the mindfulness of mind in the Mahayana.

Dwelling in the Past and Anticipating the Future

Because of the dream state that is our basic experience of mind, we have never, ever lived. We have never, ever lived in all of these years. We think we are living. We believe we are living. We dream we are living. But although we imagine we are living, we have never actually lived.

We are either in the state of "having lived" or "will be living"— that's how our mind functions in the samsaric world. Often, our mind is dwelling in and dreaming about the past. Experiences of the past are always occurring in our mind, and we are always "sort of living" in the state of past memories. Our mind has never been free to live in the present: it's always under the dictatorship of our memories of the past or dreams of the future. We have a long list of plans for how we will live in the future—how we will practice, how we will achieve this and that—and we invest our energy, time, and effort in these dreams. As a result, we may actually achieve a certain number of our dreams, but when the future becomes the present, we don't have the time or prajna to experience it. We don't have the space, the freedom, to enjoy the dreams that have come true in the present.

We have totally, totally, gone out of control. We have lost our freedom and our dreams, along with our basic beliefs in those dreams. Our idea of living has altogether disappeared, slipped out of our hands, like the present moment. Therefore, this practice of mindfulness teaches us to bring our mind to a greater state of freedom. It teaches us to free our mind from the imprisonment of dwelling in the past or future. In that freedom, we are able to experience the actual sense of living, the simplicity of being completely present with our living state of mind.

The Present Moment

When we look at it, the present state of our mind is a very tiny spot. It's a very tiny and slippery spot, so tiny and slippery that we always miss it. It's so tiny that it's an infinite spot.

The whole purpose of mindfulness of mind is to bring us back to this tiny spot of the present, the momentary nature of our mind, and to experience the infinite space and freedom within that speck of existence. In order to do that, we must experience the lively nature of our mind, which is so present, so momentary, and so fresh. Every individual moment, every individual fragment of that mind, is completely pure and fresh in its own state.

The whole point is to experience this freshness and genuineness—the honest face of that tiny spot—without coloring it with our memories, concepts, philosophies, or expectations. Experiencing it without all these is what we call simply being there. That can't happen if we don't let go of our memories of our understanding, our memories of our expectations. We have to see the nature of our thoughts directly, and genuinely be there, rather than living in our memories of understanding, our memories of meditation, or our memories of our expectations of our meditation. If we are living in the memory of thoughts, then we are still not being there. We are still not experiencing that fundamental, tiny, infinite spot.

Imprisonment

To the extent that we live in the memory of thoughts, we are not experiencing the freedom of space. To the extent that we live in the memory of understanding, even though we may have good memories or a good understanding, it's like we are decorating our prison. Our prison may look a little better and more refreshing, but we still are living within a limited space. We haven't freed ourselves from the prison of dwelling in the past and anticipating the future. Mindfulness of mind is being there in that tiny spot, that infinite space, and that only comes through totally letting go of our expectations. When we totally let go of our thoughts, we totally free our thoughts.

In a way, our thoughts are imprisoning us. On the other hand, we are imprisoning them. We imprison our thoughts in the same way they imprison us. We're not letting thought be thought. We're not letting these thoughts be thoughts in their own state. We are coloring them. We are clothing them. We're painting the face of our thoughts. We're putting hats and boots on them.

That's very uncomfortable for the thoughts. We may not recognize it, but if you really look at the thoughts themselves, it's very uncomfortable for them to be what we want them to be. It's like dressing up a monkey in the circus. The monkey is all dressed up in a beautiful tuxedo and bow tie, with a dignified hat and beautiful shiny boots. But you can imagine the discomfort the monkey feels at that point. No matter how beautiful he may look, no matter how dignified this monkey may appear to be, from the point of view of the monkey's basic instinct, it's uncomfortable to put up with all the expectations of your human boss.

Freeing Our Thoughts and Ourselves

Mindfulness of mind is freeing our thoughts and coming back to the basic spot. How do we practice this? In our meditation and post-meditation, we have to recognize the arising of our thoughts and emotions. We have to acknowledge them at the first stage of their arising. For example, if strong anger arises in our mind, the first thing to do is simply recognize it. However, we have to recognize it again and again, because it only exists in this tiny spot. Every moment, every fragment, is a new anger. One anger may have hundreds of moments, and we have to distinguish these moments as many times as they appear.

Then, when we identify a moment of anger, we just let the anger be anger. We give some freedom to the anger. As much as we want freedom from our anger, our anger is striving for freedom from us. Therefore, at this stage of recognition, we must let it go, allow it to be in its own state. There is a great need for us to practice this, because recognition is the first stage in working with our thoughts. It is the first stage of freeing our thoughts and freeing ourselves.

Recognition: The Speed Bump

Recognition is like a speed bump. What does a speed bump do? It slows us down; it slows down the speed of our car. The purpose of the speed bump is not to stop the car, and the purpose of recognizing our anger is not to stop it. Recognition slows down the speed of our klesha mind. Whether it's anger, passion, or jealousy we're feeling, it slows down the speed of that klesha mind. In the process of slowing down, we are creating more space, and in the space created by the simple moment of recognition is the space of wisdom, of compassion, of love, and of mindfulness.

This space will help us handle this car we are driving. That gives a greater sense of safety not only to us as the driver but also to the pedestrians who are walking on the street. We're not creating more space just for ourselves; it's for others, too. We're creating some space between ourselves and our anger, between ourselves and our klesha mind. The space we experience because of the speed bump is this tiny spot, which is the beginning of experiencing our infinite space.

Three Stages of Recognition

There are three stages of recognition. The first stage is recognizing the very tip of the arising of thought. This is the very first moment of the movement of thought or emotion. This is the foremost way of recognizing thought, which happens only after we have some *shin-jang*, some development of suppleness in our practice.

The second stage of recognition is recognizing thought when it has arisen. At this stage, our thoughts are a little bit grown-up. It's like diagnosing a disease at a later stage of development. Because it has already developed, its treatment requires a little more work. It's a little bit late, but still manageable.

The third stage of recognition is recognizing thought after everything has happened. We don't recognize thought until after it has arisen and grown to the full-blown stage. This is like recognizing our monkey in the zoo. We recognize our monkey wearing the full tuxedo, but it's a little late, because we have totally imprisoned him at that stage. We have totally imprisoned our emotions, our thoughts and ourselves. This is the stage where our disease is fully grown, and there's nothing much we can do except to take painkillers and wait.

These are the three stages of recognition; the Mahayana path very much emphasizes the first stage. Through the development of our courage, skill, and compassion, we increase our power to recognize thought at its very beginning. As soon as any thoughts or emotions arise, at the very first trace of their arising, we must try to maintain our mindfulness. In this process, we're letting emotions be emotions and mind be mind—we simply observe the movement of mind and work with it. When we experience that tiny spot of the nowness, we are experiencing the infinite space of our mind, the infinite space of our thoughts and the infinite space of our emotions. We are freeing our thoughts and emotions, and we are freeing ourselves at that very moment.

In a way, it's a very simple process, although it takes many words to describe it. In the practice of meditation, we repeatedly bring our mind back to its present state of nowness, to the present momentary fragment of our mind. That's why we use all these different techniques—to come back to that very tiny spot and experience its infinite space. That is the whole purpose of our meditation.

THE FOURTH FOUNDATION: MINDFULNESS OF PHENOMENA

The fourth mindfulness is called the mindfulness of phenomena, or the mindfulness of dharmas. After working with the mindfulness of mind, this mindfulness brings us to the next stage, which is panoramic awareness of the phenomenal world.

The phenomenal world is not only within our mind. The phenomenal world is also the object of our mind. It is the world we experience with our body, speech, and mind. Relating with these surrounding phenomena in a mindful way is what we call the mindfulness of phenomena.

In the general Buddhist approach, this mindfulness means recognizing the interdependent relationship between our mind and the phenomenal world. This means having a 360-degree awareness of the phenomenal world existing around us. The mindfulness of phenomena is having the prajna to relate directly and precisely with the world outside, without any fear and without any conceptions. Without any philosophical conceptions, we relate to the most fundamental state of phenomena.

What we are working with here are the six objects of our sensory perceptions. We work with form, sound, smell, taste, touch, and *dharmas*. The sixth sensory object, dharmas, is also called the mind perception. Working with these six objects in a precise way leads to a full understanding of the true nature of *pratityasamutpada*, the interdependent origination of the phenomenal world. That begins with understanding the twelve links of interdependent origination, known as the twelve *nidanas*.

Mahayana Interdependence

Beginning with the twelve nidanas, the Mahayana understanding of interdependent origination is that everything arises from emptiness and dissolves into emptiness. There is no separation between appearance and emptiness. Emptiness arises from appearance, and appearance arises from emptiness. Basically, we are talking about the inseparability of the two truths. There is no absolute truth without the relative truth, and there's no relative truth without the absolute truth. They depend on each other.

Therefore, in the Mahayana, mindfulness of phenomena means understanding the emptiness of phenomena, the egolessness of phenomena. That realization is developed through the cultivation of the three prajnas of hearing, contemplating, and meditating. By going through this three-stage process of analyzing the phenomenal world from the Mahayana perspective, we can realize the nonexistence, or selflessness, of these outer phenomena, which we had previously believed to be solid and real.

Analytical Meditation: The Gong

We practice this mindfulness by taking the objects of our sensory perceptions as the objects of our meditation, and analyzing them by being present with each object in the tiny spot of its existence. Through the analytical meditation process, this state of nowness—the state of the present—clicks us into the experience of infinite space.

Take the ringing of a gong. The actual beauty of the sound is produced by our effort. First, we pick up the striker with our hand, then we move our hand and the striker to ring the gong. From that the sound is produced, the beautiful humming sound, which is beyond our hand, our effort, the striker, and the bell itself. It is beyond all of this, beyond the combination. It is beyond all this existence.

As beginners, we get attached to the beauty of that sound. As soon as we hear it, we become totally passionate about it, so we unskillfully grasp the gong. We want to hug the gong and make it our own and say, "I got it!" In that process, we have already frozen this beautiful humming sound. As soon as we say, "I got it," it's gone miles away.

At a certain point, when we reach the peak of holding on to the gong, we can totally let go. We can let go of the thought of hugging the gong, of touching it and making it ours. Only then can we live in the presence of this beautiful sound of humming.

It is through analytical meditation that this beautiful humming sound of the experience of selflessness, the shunyata experience, is produced. The analytical process is equivalent to the ringing of the gong, and our effortless enjoyment of the beautiful humming sound that is produced corresponds to resting meditation. The resting meditation experience of egolessness is very difficult to attain without the analytical process of meditation. In order to let go of our attachment to the gong, we need to ring the bell again and again. It is the work we do in analytical meditation that leads us to the stage of resting meditation.

THE RESULT

On the basic Buddhist level, the result of these four mindfulnesses is the realization or actualization of the Four Noble Truths. Through the mindfulness of body and the mindfulness of feeling, we come to the realization of the truths of suffering and the causes of suffering. With the mindfulness of mind, we come to the realization of the truth of cessation, of completely being freed. And the fourth mindfulness, the mindfulness of phenomena, brings us to the realization of the path that leads to cessation. If we understand the interdependent nature of all phenomena, if we can relate with all phenomena as emptiness, then that is the path leading us to the result of nirvana, or cessation.

From the Mahayana point of view, the result of these four mindfulnesses is the realization of twofold egolessness—the egolessness of self and the egolessness of phenomena. That is essentially what mindfulness is all about.

Intimate Distances ⟫

Francisco J. Varela

The late Francisco J. Varela, a famed cognitive scientist and Buddhist practitioner, was one of the world's leading thinkers on what constitutes human consciousness and embodiment, on what creates our experience of self, other, boundary, and mind. How ironic, then, that he was forced to undergo a major organ transplant, perhaps the greatest violation of bodily integrity, the greatest intrusion of other into self. Francisco J. Varela died two years after his liver transplant. He left behind an important intellectual legacy, including this extraordinary meditation on the experience we call physical life.

The scene is viewed from the side. The patient is lying on his half-raised hospital bed. Tubes, sutures, and drains cover his body from nose to abdomen. On the other side of the bed, two masked men in surgical outfits look at the screen of a portable scanner. The senior doctor explains and demonstrates rapidly to his apprentice, the probe searching around the right side under the ribs and over the stomach, in sweeping motions. The intern listens raptly, nodding repeatedly. The screen is turned so that the patient can also see it. It is J+5.

Five days ago, I emerged from surgery with the liver of an un-known. My attention now shifts to the two men as they speak. I follow their conversation and wait expectantly for words directed to me. It is a crucial moment: if the veins and arteries have not taken to their new place, my whole adventure comes to a halt. The graft, from their point of view, represents hardly anything more than a successful fixture. I am short of breath as I pick up the doctor's over-heard telegraphic comments: Good portal circulation, no inflam-mation. . . . Abruptly he smiles at me and says, "Tout va bien!"

I am now my prostrate body. It feels broken up, in bits and pieces, aching from a visible incision that goes from right to left in an arching path, and suddenly bifurcates over the chest right to my sternum; it is almost immobile from the multiple intubations and perfusions. His reassuring statement oddly makes me feel my liver as a small sphere, as if I am carrying an infant (I remember the pictures of my last son's beating heart in his mother's belly); it is tinged with a light pain; it is definitely present.

In the background, the brokenness of my body beckons me with an infinite fatigue and a primordial desire to close my eyes and rest for eternity. Yet the screen is a few centimeters away and a simultane-ous curiosity perks up unflinchingly. I can see my new liver, inside me. I follow the details: the anastomoses of the cava and the porta veins, the two large hepatic arteries, the II and then the III lobule squished one into the other. I travel within, gliding inside and out of the liver capsule, like an animation. I listen with unabashed interest to the explanations to the intern ("Here, look at how best to catch the flow with the Doppler"; it goes swishhh, swishhh now, as his-tograms display the parameters in charts and line drawings. "Here is the best way not to miss the hepatic peduncle"; this time the object is lost to me in a sea of gray).

Multiple mirrors echo shifting centers, each of which I call "I," each one a subject that feels and suffers, that expects a word, that is redoubled in a scanner's image, a concrete fragment that seems to partake with me of a mixture of intimacy and foreignness.

CONTINGENCY, OBSOLESCENCE

Some two years ago I received the liver of another human being. An organ came tumbling down a complex social network from a recently dead body to land into my insides on that fateful evening of June 1. My sick liver was cut from its circulatory roots and the new one snugly fitted in, replacing the vital circulation by laborious suture of veins and arteries. I can thus pronounce a unique statement (with a few hundred people around the world): I have received someone else's organ!

Such an assertion has no echo in the past. Ten years ago I would have died rapidly from complications of Hepatitis C, transformed into cirrhosis, then rampantly turned into liver cancer. The surgical procedure is not what creates the novelty of a successful transplant. It is the multiple immunosuppressor drugs that prevent the inevitable rejection. (A code word for a phenomenon specious in itself; we will return to it.) Had it happened in ten more years it would have been a different procedure and my post-transplant life entirely different. I would surely have been another kind of survivor. In the thousands of years of human history, my experience is a speck, a small window of technical contingency in the privileged life of upper-class Europeans.

From this narrow window I must (we must) reflect on and consider an unprecedented event, one that no accumulated human reflection and wisdom has ventured into. I take tentative steps, consider everything as only a tentative understanding. I am a lost cartographer with no maps. Only fragments, no systematic analysis. We are left to invent a new way of being human where bodily parts go into each other's bodies, redesigning the landscape of the boundaries of what we are so definitively used to calling distinct bodies. Opening up the landscape where we can borrow a piece from another, and soon enough, order it to size from genetically modified animals. One day it will be said: I have a pig's heart. Or from stem cells they will graft a new liver or kidney and pre-select the cells that will colonize what was missing in us, in a sort of permanent completion that can be extrapolated beyond imagination, into the obscene. This is the challenge that is offered us to reflect on through and through, to give us the insight and the lucidity to enter fully into this historical shift.

My life in its contingency mirrors the history of techniques, the growing know-how about human bodies, which knows nothing about the lived-bodies that can and will come from it. Technology, as always, stands as the mediation that reveals the interrelatedness of our lives—contingencies of life that accumulate in the history of body-technologies, from antibiotics, to tailor-made drugs, to genetic engineering. All the more so now that the contingency of life, always at the doorstep of reflection on human destiny, acquires a speed that impinges even on our ability to conceive, to assimilate, to work through the ramifications. In ten years, these reflections will probably be obsolete, the entire reality of transplantation having changed the scenario from top to bottom; all the work I must do is for a little window of history before it snaps out of focus and we are to start anew.

REJECTION, TEMPORALITY

I've got a foreign liver inside me. But: Which me? Foreign to what? We change all the cells and molecules of a liver every few weeks. It is new again, but not foreign. The foreignness is the unsettledness of the belonging with other organs in the ongoing definition that is an organism. In that sense my old liver was already foreign; it was gradually becoming alien as it ceased to function, corroded by cirrhosis, with no other than a suspended irrigation of islands of cells, which are then left to decay and wither away. Years before the transplant, during a biopsy the surgeon came to see me: "I saw your liver, it looks very sick. You must do something about it." The statement made this silent organ suddenly un-me, threatening and already designated to be put at a distance in the economy of the body's self. Seeing from outside had penetrated me as a blade of otherness, altering my habitual body forever.

"Self" is just the word used by immunologists to designate the landscape of macromolecular profiles that sit on the cell surfaces and announce the specificity of a tissue during development. Each one of us has a particular signature, an ecology of somatic markers. Within that landscape, the lymphocytes, the active cells of the immune system, constantly touch and bind to each other and to the tissue markers, in a tight network of two-way interaction. This ongoing mutual definition between the immune network and the tissues is the nature of this bodily self and defines its borders: not the skin, a mere thin veil, but the self-defining network of molecular profiles. The boundaries of my body are invisible, a floating shield of self-production, unaware of space, concerned only with permanent bonding and unbonding.

The self is also an ongoing process every time new food is ingested, new air is breathed in, or the tissues change with growth and age. The boundaries of the self undulate, extend and contract, and reach sometimes far into the environment, into the presence of multiple others, sharing a self-defining boundary with bacteria and parasites. Such fluid boundaries are a constitutive habit we share with all forms of life: microorganisms exchange body parts so often and so fast that trying to establish body boundaries is not only absurd, but runs counter to the very phenomenon of that form of life.

Is a graft as foreign as the rigid boundaries of a skin-enclosed boundary suggest? Conversely, what is this me that is being intruded upon? The intrusion is always already happening—the constant intrusion and extrusion dancing at the edge of a tenuous, fragile identity (my self, then), with no boundary defined except as a fleeting pattern. But the boundary is reinforced and sharply marked nonetheless, and easily irritated when the alteration is imposed too fast, too soon, too much. As when a new microorganism penetrates the mucosa, and the organism mounts an intense reaction (inflammation, fever, allergy). It is too much change, too quickly.

"Rejection," they say. ("There's a rejection!" The intensive care doctor bursts into my room at J+7, just as I was recovering from the trial of massive surgery, patiently recovering a sense of this place-marker called my body. I am abruptly thrown off balance. Yet, I knew about the stages of the transplantation adventure: the recovery from traumatic surgery is almost always followed by rejection, where the true danger zone begins. But in the joy of feeling more recovered, those words opened an abyss into which no sensation pointed, which showed no signs or indices, silent and imaginary in the suddenness of its irruption.) My process-identity of making a somatic home I call "self" was being thrown out; new mechanisms acquired in the Ur-ancestry of my molecular cellular environment were awakened. A whole new organ is way too much, too quickly. The extrusion is initiated by massive tagging of the cells marked as foreign; the cells destroyed by T lymphocytes; the new organ slowly but surely dissolved into biochemical air.

The body-technologies to address rejection are absurdly simple: disable the ongoing process of identity, weaken the links between the components of the organism. Immunosuppression is, to date, the inescapable lot of transplantation. One starts by taking special suppressive drugs and massive doses of corticoid (leaving the mind disjointed, hallucinating, and with an obsessive compulsion to repeat certain inner discourses; nights spent in the corticoid desert are certainly a form of hell). As the rejection does not yield, the treatment mounts one step. I am treated with the "heavy" means, as the doctor says. As in napalm warfare, the entire repertoire of immune cells is massively eliminated by a slow injection. (As I felt the effect coming in a few minutes, my whole body was swept by uncontrollable shaking, like an alien possession that left the me [who?] in a limbo of nonexistence; looking steadily into my wife's face, the only reference point in a disappearing quagmire.)

Complete immunosupression does stop the rejection, but now simply being in the world is a potential intrusion, as the temporality, the finitude, of my somatic identity has been erased for a few days. A new lifestyle of masks, careful watching for the slightest sign of fever, and concern about opening windows makes the body into a life of withdrawal, its proud movement and agency shriveled down.

In time, the body is allowed to reconstitute; I recover my assurance of my daily embodiment, as the immunosuppression is milder. This becomes a life condition. Weakening the links that are the backbone of the temporality of the lived-body, this alteration is experienced as a newly acquired attention to symptoms, as a traveling to destinations of unknown hygiene. Immunosuppression is a walking stick; I feel the world as through an extension.

THE IMAGE, THE TOUCH

Modern medical imaging accomplishes what began in the eighteenth century as a desire and a search for illuminating every dark corner, especially for seeing the insides of the human body. Modern man has since been rendered somatically transparent, in gestures that extend into putting on full view not only the hidden but the ultimate microscopical—the DNA fingerprinting, the biochemical profiles, the immune cellular probes and markers.

Our times have renewed the visible and the explicit as a preeminent presence, compared with times when the rarefied world of pure ideas and Logos was supreme and the image mere appearance. Increasingly, we communicate with images of people, with virtual persons existing as bytes in optical fiber ready for multiple displays. The radiologist looks at his echography machine, not at me. The image becomes the inevitable mediator between my lived intimacy and the dispersed network of the expert medical team for which the images are destined. I am disseminated in image fragments that count more as the relevant interface than this presence (my lived body then, but again the question of which one?). The image holds the bond at just the right distance: sufficiently close so as to be a habitual part of my intimacy, sufficiently detachable so as to introduce a wide space wherein the intrusion of otherness arrives massively every time I go back to the stretcher and raise my shirt and the probe glides over my abdomen. (In these situations, habit has transformed them almost into a self-touching—a tribute to the force of the image: I can feel those black and white patterns on the screen.)

Occasionally, in one of the check-up visits the clinician asks me to lie down and he touches my liver region. I experience it as a relief, as return to an embodied presence. The touch reestablishes an older intimacy through his touching hand. Touching/being-touched is the paradigm of oneness, me-ness. These gestures are always considered supplementary: only the images and the charts speak the reliable truth, having captured the essence of the story. These body-techniques seem to stand for all that was tactile, tangible, and ready-at-hand, now transformed into weightless apparitions. The new body is constantly on the verge of losing its seemingly invincible spatial and temporal structure.

It would be idle to set up an opposition of correct/incorrect between these pervasive images and the contrasting sense of touch, anchored in the lived body. Even in touching, the otherness is constitutive; the image rides on this doubling as a thorough mediation. We witness a push and counter-pull between depth and imaginary surfaces that become a new identity in post-transplantation life.

INTIMATE DISTANCE

The encounter with the radical alteration of death approached closely over the years, and then finally made its irruption in all the brutality of a night when my chest and abdomen were laid open. It was done; I was not there, drowned in anesthetics (which "I"?; certainly there was presence, I suffered).

The descent was slow. First, waiting in a room; then getting undressed and covered with a hospital gown; then naked under a sheet so that the nurse could shave me entirely in a form of nudity that seemed to reach me under the skin. Then transferred to a wheeling stretcher, parked in the surgical room, shaking from cold and fear as nurses made conversation. The anesthesiologist comes, takes the perfusion tube, and perfunctorily injects the first wave of anesthetic. I have a minute or so to let anything that was left of me go as if in an involuntary flight. Never have I felt more acutely my fragile ontology, the impossibility of grasping onto anything, a living dot suspended in a space that goes so beyond anything representable. The utter loneliness for which there is no utterance. Deprived of any intimacy, nothing left but gaping gap for intrusion. Then they open me up, cut the circulation, replace it by machines, take the organ from an ice pack, and proceed to rebuild me again back into a normal body. Or that is what they say.

Awakening into my new state, I see that the night when death traveled through my open body is to remain indelibly. It is there each time somebody looks at my torso, and I see their eyes darting quickly down to check the trace that crosses from side to side and up the chest with suture point (with big stitches, like a sack of merchandise). It's death's trace, which never lets me slip by this memory that is not a memory, but rather a feeling of recognition of its presence, of an inevitable guest whose movements are way beyond anything within my reach. From then on the trace of death has set its own agenda, its own rhythm to my life. I have, in fact, become another, never entirely redone after being so meticulously undone.

Which Life?

The life retaken is taken differently, forever changed (but to whom shall we attribute this change?) by a triple movement: the one that led to being on the waiting list; the one that led to an organ to be transferred; and the one that leads me into my present condition. This is the living reality of transplantation—my entire identity grazed profoundly by the opening to death, sutured back and left to function in the world with a "new" life. Soon the traces of the last movement begin to enter my life as multiple foreignness.

There are first and foremost the drug treatments, which are prescribed in quantities and taken by grams per day, and that mark the temporality of the day, of travel always present in its medicine bags, bulky and obtrusive. Then the drugs themselves. The cortisone and immunosuppressors, which induce a diabetes that needs careful checking three or four times a day. The effect on the stomach, producing sometimes uncontrollable diarrhea that in all its undignified presence overtakes my life. And of course the repetitive medical controls: the enzyme levels to keep track of, the overload of the kidneys to verify. The Hepatitis C virus is, we all knew it, still with me, and we know it to be back in full action, the most mysterious of my foreignness, degrading the new liver. It must also be suppressed and controlled. It is an imaginary circle: I am back where I started from, intertwined with these amazing dots whose molecular structures I sometimes contemplate in awe of their twisted proteins and minute RNA. But the only known antiviral treatment is interferon, an immunitary stimulant, which produces a permanent feeling of fatigue as if one has a budding cold. In fact, for effectiveness it must be taken with ribavirine, which leads to anemia. Oddly, the immunosuppression to avoid rejection is exactly a countermove to interferon, so that the body is pushed on opposite sides at the same time. (A constant paradox: immunosuppressed to avoid rejection; immunostimulated to avoid the virus. A telling symbol of my condition.) There is also the return to the hospital for a sudden explosion of viral activity, for the accumulation of liquid around the liver that needs extensive examinations.

Changing symptoms emerge and subside: echographies, weight control, blood samples so often that my veins seem to expect the needles. Thus the foreignness of the grafted liver is less and less focused. The body itself has become a constant, ongoing source of foreignness, altering itself as in echo, touching every sphere of my waking life. This is the life that I have survived for, not a coming back to where I was (though I was already alienated by the disease for long years, and before seems distant and abstract). A life with its own temporality to put together and to live with the multiple manipulation that technology demands (once again the historical contingency of the body-technologies: in ten years more I would have been some other kind of survivor). Compensation to the decompensations that multiply in a hall of mirrors. The suffering varies from one person to the next in its extremes. The phenomenon rests: transplantation has made the body a fertile ground of opposed, coincidental intrusions.

INCONCLUSION

Transplantation produces an inflection in life that keeps an open reminder from the trace of the scar altering my settledness, bringing up death's trace. It is my horizon, an existential space where I adapt slowly, this time as the guest of that which I did not arrange, like a guest of nobody's creation. This time, the foreign has made me the guest, the alteration has given me back a belonging I did not remember. The transplant exposes me, exports me in a new totality. The expression of it all, I know, eludes me, makes me face a twilight language.

Perhaps we are all (the growing numbers who have entered into the sphere of this transference) "the beginning of a mutation," as Jean-Luc Nancy says. I can see it: all of us in a near future being described as the early stages of a mankind where otherness and intimacy have been expanded to the point of recursive interpenetration. Where the body altered technically will and can redesign the boundaries ever more rapidly, toward a human being which will "intrude into the world as well as into itself." We would do well to consider this.

It is this urgency that drives this examination of the ancient ethos of the human will to power re-expressed as transplantation, even if my own window on it is narrow in time and fragmented in understanding. Somewhere we need to give death back its rights.

Rucksack Poetry: How Haiku Found a Home in America))

Andrew Schelling

Seeking to describe the indescribable, to speak words about the nonconceptual, what better tool than allusion and metaphor— poetry. The Tibetans, the Chinese, and especially the Japanese have long traditions of expressing dharma through poetry. Poet Andrew Schelling explains the spare, down-to-earth Japanese form called haiku and why it has been so appealing to American poets.

> The old pond
> a frog jumps in—
> kerplunk!

Matsuo Basho's haiku about the frog and the old pond has become so deeply scored in the popular imagination that it seems to have distilled into pure image. The seventeenth-century poet Basho, dressed in mud-spattered robes, wandering rugged mountain land-scapes, or sequestered in a tiny hut in the rain on the outskirts of town, has become almost as vivid a figure of international folklore as of poetry. It was under his influence that haiku's reputation emerged as a poetry humble in subject, unfriendly to pretension, and devoted to Buddhist-inspired insights into the natural world—and the sphere of human nature.

As many are aware, Basho was the poet's pen name. He had previously published under the name Sobo, but took the epithet under which he is now known from a banana tree planted by students outside his hermit hut, his *basho-an*. He loved the tree for its uselessness: The basho's flowers are not much to look at, lacking the delicacy you'd want on an altar. Japan's northerly, sea-blown climate is too cold for the tree to bear edible fruit; and one could not make a decent piece of furniture of its fibrous wood. In the spirit of renunciation, Basho declared haiku equally useless: "a fireplace in summer, in winter a fan."

Basho and his contemporaries insisted on plain or commonly used language for haiku, distinguishing it from the classical poetry of the past, which was aristocratic in both tone and vocabulary, and carefully restricted in subject matter. The frugal, democratic idiom haiku assumed perhaps accounts for its particular appeal to Americans, who tend to fancy themselves lean in character, and sculpted by hard work if not by outright hardship. Jack Kerouac articulated the same ideals as Basho in his own lifestyle and writings, and Allen Ginsberg noted, "He's the only one in the United States who knows how to write haiku . . . [he] talks that way, thinks that way." In all his work Kerouac celebrated the down-home, the humble, the image so ordinary that a thousand people ignore it each day:

> The windmills of
>   Oklahoma look
> In every direction*

In Japan this aesthetic has been called *wabi-cha*: rough-hewn, rustic, without posture, solitary, even melancholy. As a lifestyle it means to appear poor on the outside, but inwardly to control enormous

---

*Jack Kerouac, *Book of Haikus* (New York: Penguin, 2003).

riches. To Kerouac, poetry mind and the mind of renunciation were not different. Looking back over a long heritage of wandering Buddhist poets, Kerouac wrote in his novel *The Dharma Bums,* "I see a vision of a great rucksack revolution, thousands or even millions of young Americans wandering around with their rucksacks, going up the mountains to pray, making children laugh and old men glad. . . . Zen lunatics who go about writing poems." Haiku writing was at the core of Kerouac's Zen poverty, and his own haiku capture the same qualities Basho settled on:

> In my medicine cabinet
>   the winter fly
> Has died of old age
>   —KEROUAC

>   A crow has settled
> on the withered branch—
>   autumn dusk
>   —BASHO

The term *haii*, which underpins the word *haiku*, means comic, lighthearted, sportive. It implies a sense of high-spirited innovation, some wise irreverence, and not a little reckless spontaneity. Even in melancholy it aims for an innovative use of popular language. Haiku itself developed out of the highly formalized, linked verse called *renga*, popular at gatherings among Japan's newly prosperous middle class during the seventeenth century. Each guest would contribute half a *tanka* (a traditional thirty-one-syllable poem), and a collaborative sequence would evolve, link by link. Invented on the spot, renga were subject to increasingly elaborate rules, which were outlined in books. Raucously democratic in tone, full of humor and put-downs, except in the hands of a few master poets, renga rarely resulted in inspired poetry. It was from these party-like occasions, though, that true haiku developed.

Guests would appear at the renga session, each with a satchel containing several opening verses, which were called *hokku*, hoping one of their own might receive the honor of being selected to initiate the sequence. At a gathering, of course only one hokku could be selected. It appears that poets began to accumulate such opening verses, the unused ones, and slowly these came to stand as poems in their own right. The term that eventually applied to them, *haiku*, may have been invented by Basho.

Haiku flourished in Japan during the Edo Period (1615–1868). The old base of power had shifted, away from an aristocratic minority secluded around the emperor in the ancient capital, Kyoto. With the rise of the Tokagawa shogunate, a system of military rule that established the shogun of the Tokugawa clan as chief of warlords, Japan's capital moved to Tokyo (then called Edo). The old social system began to open up, and a newly prosperous middle class emerged. Merchants in the cities and agrarian people in the towns began to receive education, and literacy became, if not universal, at least widespread. Haiku's popularity rose among the newly literate, a middle-class attempt to take part in traditional Japanese culture, appropriating the themes and elements of the artistic style that had once been the privilege of the aristocracy. Haiku in the hands of samurai and farmer, merchant and craftsman, however, introduced a riot of new possibilities to Japanese verse: vernacular words, colloquial phrasings, Chinese compounds, Buddhist terminology, and popular slogans. Cutting free from stodgy topics of the past, novel subject matter arose in the effort to break with outdated themes. "The old verse can be about willows," Basho told his students. He was gazing back across Japan's long tradition of elegant court poetry. "Haiku," however, "requires crows plucking snails in the rice paddy."

Yet in time—largely due to Basho's influence—haiku's jostling new language came to be imbued with profound silences and great open spaces for the mind as well. The irresistible effect of Basho's "old pond and frog" haiku seems to derive from a visceral feeling that the silence surrounding the pond has been made more palpable—deeper—by the sound of the frog-splash; as the sound dies away the scene takes on a more resonant silence.

There is a solidity to the best haiku images. The old crow or the fly in a medicine cabinet linger on in the mind's eye long after the words themselves have been examined from every angle and exhausted. This is why haiku holds the flavor of Zen: from one essential detail, a sudden direct apprehension of the great Void. Haiku is simply too short for explanation, indirection, bombast, descriptiveness, complicated figures of speech, or sermonizing. Its linguistic effect is close to magic or mantra. For the modern poet brought up on traditional Western poetry, what a relief to leave theology, mythologies, and big claims behind! As Kerouac saw, haiku is the "rucksack" form of poetry; its practice has come to seem nearly inseparable from a pilgrimage through natural and human landscapes, an outward journey that is vividly an inward journey too.

Traditional Japanese haiku—as even American schoolchildren know—occurs in seventeen syllables; the opening verse of the renga was written in this form, and haiku retained the pattern. Traditionally the poem has three parts (usually written in three lines in English) measured in a sequence of five, seven, and five syllables. Need to remember the sequence? Contemporary New York poet Ron Padgett gives this ready lesson—

First five syllables.
Second seven syllables.
Third five syllables.

American poets who take up haiku, however, often discard the seventeen-syllable structure as irrelevant to American speech or writing. Japanese and American English are substantially different; a rigid structure that worked for several hundred years in feudal Japan transported to this continent may simply hamper spontaneity—an element that has become almost an ethos in the past fifty years. In haiku, spontaneity may not be the single most important aspect (it surprises many to discover how much revision Basho could put into a single verse, sometimes keeping at it for six months), but haiku that don't carry a good whiff of freedom, innovation, or the unpredictable fall pretty flat. Basho charged us: "Don't follow in the footsteps of the old poets; seek what they sought." Three centuries later, Kerouac provided an American definition of the form: "POP-American (non-Japanese) Haikus, short three-line poems, or 'pomes,' rhyming or nonrhyming, delineating 'little Samadhis' if possible, usually of a Buddhist connotation, aiming towards enlightenment." Basho, who wore patchwork monk robes, might have remained silent on the enlightenment target.

The other requirement for traditional haiku was that each poem conjure a particular season, and most of the celebrated anthologies in Japanese, English, and other languages fall into seasonal chapters. Close attention to nature, and from that an awareness of the impermanence of life: In this lies the moon-in-a-dewdrop reflection of Buddhist teachings, Kerouac's "little Samadhis"—nondual states of consciousness. The Japanese poets and early diarists, under the impress of such teachings, referred to life as the "the floating world," sometimes "this floating bridge of dreams." But what lies behind the dream? Buddhism has in its view of existence no creator figure, no higher power, no heaven. There is no "meaning" behind existence to try to discern, not in nature, not in the poem.

If haiku, then, points to no higher meaning, what makes a good one seem so vast? so rounded by silence? so full of emotion and insight that we can't explain? "It's there," says Kerouac, "and nothing you can say or do about it, except look in dismay at the power of looking." This actual moment! That bedraggled crow! This moonlit evening, that cold rain on your skull! There you stand, inhabiting your body with animal clarity, wide-open senses, and no preconception or abstract idea can touch the experience itself. Buddhists call this *tattva*, thusness. "No ideas but in things," William Carlos Williams famously wrote, setting ten thousand poems free from abstraction. He could have been reading Basho: "To know the pine, go to the pine. To know the bamboo, go to the bamboo."

For sixty years, English-speaking Americans have been tending an exotic plant in their gardens, observing what makes it grow best and debating the essence of haiku. Curiously, had poets of the western United States peeked over their back fences in the decades before

World War II, they could have found haiku in a neighboring garden, growing in profusion—though not in English.

In 1915 the Japanese poet Ippekiro Nakatsuka (1887–1946), living in Tokyo, helped found a circle of freestyle, modernist haiku writers. Japan had not produced much notable haiku for decades, and some of the more innovative poets felt the form needed airing out. They noted that even Basho had continually reevaluated what made good haiku, changing his style to keep poetry fresh, even breaking the strict seventeen-syllable count when a higher truth required it. In this spirit, Nakatsuka decided poetry should not be restricted by arbitrary rules—the strict syllable count or the use of seasonal words. A flowering quince with crimson blossoms grew around the inn where he lived, and he named a newly founded haiku journal *Kaiko*, "crimson sea," after the flower. *Kaiko* became the term for the freestyle haiku Nakatsuka advocated. A number of young Japanese with literary interests emigrated to California during this time and took with them an enthusiasm for kaiko haiku.

The same year *Kaiko* appeared in Tokyo, one of these emigrants, Nieji Ozawa, founded a freestyle haiku society in San Francisco. Moving to Stockton, California, he founded the Delta Haiku Society in 1918. He later settled in Fresno, where most of the agricultural workers were of Japanese ancestry, and in 1928 convened the first meeting of the Valley Ginsha Haiku Kai (*kai* means "club") at his house. Violet Kazue de Crostoforo, a member of the Fresno group, described its members: "grape growers, onion farmers, teachers, housewives, bankers, pharmacists, and others." The members of the early California haiku societies probably looked not too different from Basho's crew of pupils three hundred years earlier, which included rich samurai, shrewd merchants, hardscrabble radish farmers, a beggar, and a thief.

From their inception in 1915, for nearly thirty years the unassuming but free-spirited California haiku clubs met, usually once a month. The members arrived with poems to exchange and to offer up for critique. With the bombing of Pearl Harbor, however, and the subsequent signing of Executive Order 9066 by President Franklin

D. Roosevelt in February 1942, all persons of Japanese ancestry on the West Coast were removed from their homes and placed in detention centers. Both American citizens and resident aliens were permitted to bring with them only the barest belongings. In their hasty, uncertain departures, most destroyed any Japanese writing—including haiku—for fear they might incite hostility. In the climate of uncertainty, anger, and unrest, would arresting officers or paranoid neighbors be able to discern a Buddhist sutra from a military dispatch? haiku from a coded communiqué?

The detention centers were located far from the strategic coast, in northeastern California, Wyoming, the Utah desert, Arkansas, North Dakota, and Colorado, and were notoriously overcrowded and unsanitary. The Japanese Americans arrived in high-security trains and under armed guard. Inside the camps the detainees tried to resume lives that felt as normal as possible, under very primitive conditions. Compared with the fertile Central Valley of California, the new landscapes seemed hostile and frighteningly desolate, but the resilience of haiku, tempered by its Zen equanimity perhaps, made a home with astonishing bravery.

The war detainees' haiku reflect the landscape of their experience. There had been the abrupt, unexplained removal, by law enforcement officers, of intellectuals and Buddhist monks from West Coast communities. Then the coordinated dispersal of thousands to the various detention camps deep inland. The locomotive clank of their deportation, hard screech of brakes under the desert moon, primitive barracks, barbed wire, armed sentries, guard towers. The haiku societies gradually reconstituted themselves inside the camps, and published their work in camp newsletters, most of which have not survived. Haiku from some found their way to the Japanese-language newspaper of Salt Lake City, the *Utah Nippo*, and these poems survived destruction when their authors were transferred to other far-off camps, ordered to carry only "necessary items."

From poets of the Fresno and Stockton haiku clubs a few handfuls of notable verse survive. By "notable," I mean they capture with unsentimental precision the texture of an American experience that until recent years has been routinely dismissed or ignored. Remember that these poets are American citizens charged with no crime. Some were grandmothers, or children.

> Misty moon
> as it was
> on my wedding night.
> —KAZUE MATSUDA

> Rain shower from mountain
> quietly soaking
> barbed wire fence
> —HEKISAMEI MATSUDA

> Even the croaking of frogs
> comes from outside the barbed wire fence
> this is our life
> —SHIZUKU UYEMARUKO*

The San Francisco poet Itaru Ina ended up in the high-security facility at Fort Lincoln, Bismarck, North Dakota. Angered at the treatment he and his fellow detainees were receiving at Topaz, Utah's center, he renounced his American citizenship. He was shortly arrested as an enemy alien, separated from his family, and sent to Fort Lincoln.

> Having my fingerprints taken—
> the new-leaf trees
> come and rustle at the window.

> Over the fence
> we touch hands—
>   autumn farewell.

May Sky: There Is Always Tomorrow, An Anthology of Japanese American Concentration Camp Kaiko Haiku, compiled by Violet Kazue de Cristoforo (Los Angeles: Sun & Moon Press, 1997).

The iron door is closed,
the guards have all gone—
Moths dance around the light.
        —ITARU INA*

Until the end of World War II, there were few books in English
that could provide an accurate sense of haiku or its history. It was
the writings of the scholar R. H. Blyth that finally brought haiku
to English-speaking citizens of the United States. His *History of
Haiku*—four volumes published between 1949 and 1952—gave a
richly illustrated account of the form, along with its Zen Buddhist
underpinnings, to Gary Snyder, Philip Whalen, and other poets,
who were largely responsible for bringing haiku into the American
mainstream.

Blyth was a British citizen who had been studying Zen and
Japanese literature in Japan prior to World War II. Along with other
foreigners, he was detained by the Japanese military and eventually
placed in a loosely guarded camp in the hills above Kobe. This was
where he encountered Robert Aitken, and was the first to introduce
the now-celebrated Zen teacher to Buddhism. Aitken, a civilian in-
ternee from Guam, had also been transferred to Kobe by the Japanese authorities. In his essay "Remembering Blyth Sensei," in the
Spring 1998 *Tricycle*, he recalls a drunk Japanese guard handing him
a copy of Blyth's *Zen and English Literature*, then learning that the
book's author was being housed nearby. He gives a level portrait of
Blyth the scholar:

> He had his bed in the tokonoma, the alcove usually reserved
> for scroll and flower arrangement in Japanese homes and
> offices. . . . All day long he sat on his bed, sometimes cross-
> legged and sometimes with his feet on the floor, writing on
> a lectern placed on a bedside table, with his reference books

---

Snow Country Prison, translated by Leza Lowitz and Hisako Ifshin (Grand Forks:
North Dakota Museum of Art brochure, 2003).

and notebooks among the bedcovers. . . . I recall that he wrote rapidly, with his words connected, using two sets of pens, black for his text and red for his quotations.

Shortly after the war ended, Blyth's books appeared in bookstores and libraries around the United States. Gary Snyder recalls finding them in San Francisco, "and they have been with me ever since." Zen and the literatures of Japan quickly drew the interest of large numbers of American intellectuals and poets who were skeptical not only of Western ideology and military prowess, but of the sorts of poetry that celebrated Western civilization and expansionism. Asia had come close to North America, and the next step was to embrace its most portable art: haiku.

Meanwhile, also in the aftermath of the war, and alongside American military occupation forces, a lively expatriate community developed in Japan. The dollar was strong, Japan was rebuilding and modernizing, and English teachers were needed. Influential poets Gary Snyder, Joanne Kyger, Cid Corman, and Philip Whalen lived in Kyoto for years, along with an ongoing stream of American scholars, travelers, artists, and writers. Zen and Zen-inspired arts attracted each of the poets, and they began to experiment with haiku, linking it to the poetry that was being written in postwar America. Snyder composed "Hitch Haiku" based on hobo trips he'd made up and down the West Coast looking for seasonal work:

> They didn't hire him
> > so he ate his lunch alone:
> the noon whistle

> A great freight truck
> > lit like a town
> through the dark stony desert*

---

*Gary Snyder, *The Back Country* (New York: New Directions, 1968).

Haiku's simplicity of spirit is what so quickly allies it to Zen Buddhism. I like to think the current popularity of Zen in America is due in part to a tenacious belief that we remain a no-nonsense people, a people who talk straight and try to keep life simple—this and a mounting restlessness with our overabundance of things. How do we go into the mountains? or into the street? Clad in high-cost, high-tech gear? or in boots, blue jeans, and an old hat? Basho seems the prototype of simplicity—he wore sandals and carried a rucksack on a six-month haiku journey by foot into the rough, mountainous rural districts of northern Japan. On that famous journey late in life he slept in a horse stall; one haiku has the horse pissing on his pillow.

This Thoreau-like hunger for unadorned living, and the belief that the richest insights can only be acquired through close-to-the-bone experience, carries on in the spirit of modern poets. It is nowhere more evident than in the embrace of the haiku ethic. Remember Basho's admonition that haiku is useless as a ragged old banana tree? Deep within the contemporary poem lies a similar ethos—skeptical of the rush to utility in our technologically driven, warfare-mad world. Sometimes the haiku ethos comes in three lines, sometimes the form sculpts itself differently: "in place of haiku." The spirit remains—that old urge toward vernacular language, and that quick precision that marked haiku from its start.

> I have to go water
>   the lettuce
> then I have to go listen to Zen tonight
> —JOANNE KYGER*

---

*Joanne Kyger, *Again: Poems, 1989–2000* (Albuquerque: La Alameda Press, 2001).

Have a Cup of Tea ꩜

John Daido Loori

Life is an art. Art is a way of life. When each is at its best, life and art inform and pervade the other, each flowing from the same awakened mind. In traditional Japanese culture, saturated as it is with Buddhism and other spiritual traditions, art is a teaching on life, and activities we treat as mundane, like designing a garden, eating a meal, or drinking a cup of tea, can be beautiful spiritual and artistic exercises. The Zen teacher John Daido Loori talks about the way of tea, and the way of life it implies.

Tea is to East Asian Buddhism what wine is to the Judeo-Christian traditions. It holds a sacred place. *Chado,* the way of tea, has been called the expression of Buddhism's spiritual, philosophical, moral, artistic, and social aspects. It embodies the spirit of the artless arts of Zen and contains all the essential characteristics that define the Zen aesthetic. Many of the other Zen arts—calligraphy, poetry, flower arrangement, and gardening—are also prominently featured in the context of the tea ceremony.

Although I've experienced the formal tea ceremony, many times and in a variety of circumstances, my first encounter with it in a traditional teahouse at a small temple in Japan was a memorable occasion.

The path to the teahouse was a winding trail of stepping-stones that guided us through the tea garden. The slow approach made my companion and me appreciate the mountain setting and gently disconnected us from the urban turmoil we were leaving behind. The garden was simple, yet beautiful. Little clusters of moss on stone and a meandering stream that disappeared behind the teahouse embodied serenity and a timeless beauty.

The teahouse itself was surprising in its simplicity, contrasting with the more elaborate buildings of the temple compound. It was a small hut, like a hermitage or for a single person. It had a thatch roof and was constructed of rustic materials. The natural tones matched its setting. We approached a low stone basin into which water flowed through a bamboo pipe. We stopped to rinse our hands and mouths in a symbolic act of purification—a preparation for the ceremony.

The entryway to the hut was a four-foot-high sliding door. In order to come in, we had to lower ourselves nearly to the ground. Once inside, the first thing we encountered was the tokonoma, a small alcove that held a single scroll of calligraphy with a poem that was appropriate to the season. There was also a modest flower arrangement, the blossoms reflecting the spring months. The light, filtering through shoji screens, was subdued. The room had a glow to it, and the walls were bathed in gentle, warm colors. As my tea partner and I took our places, settling ourselves comfortably on the tatami mats, we could hear the sound of boiling water in a cast iron kettle and birdsong outside.

Usually, conversation in a teahouse avoids business matters or controversial subjects such as politics. It focuses rather on nature and the unfolding season, or relaxed silence is maintained. In this case we chose to simply remain silent and absorb the atmosphere.

The tea master appeared. Kneeling, he placed his fan in front of him and lowered his head to the ground, welcoming us. We returned his bow. He exited the room and began to bring in the implements for the ceremony. Holding one corner of a silk cloth in his left hand, he ran his right hand down the cloth and smoothly folded the cloth into three parts. Reaching the end of the cloth, he joined the corners together, folding the cloth again in three parts. He then used this piece of silk to symbolically clean each of the ceremonial objects—symbolically, because the tea implements were already meticulously clean. He ritualistically rinsed the bowls with hot water taken from the kettle as we watched. He dipped a bamboo whisk in the water, examined it, and placed it to one side. He poured the hot water into the tea bowl, and then wiped the bowl with a damp cloth.

The master gestured to us, inviting us to enjoy the sweets that he had placed before us. While we ate, he proceeded to prepare the tea. With deft movements he opened the tea caddy and with a bent bamboo spoon measured jade-green powdered tea into the bowl. He dipped a long-handled dipper into the kettle and poured hot water into the tea. Then, with bamboo whisk, he whisked the tea into a froth. He turned and set a bowl in front of me, with the most striking side of the bowl deliberately facing toward me. I lifted the bowl and brought it closer. I bowed to my tea partner. I lifted the bowl into the palm of my hand and turned it two short turns so its "front" faced away from me. I bowed to the tea and drank it in a few sips, slurping the last bit, which is considered in good taste in Japan.

Finishing the tea, I rotated the bowl to its original position and placed it on the floor in front of me. I bowed. The tea master retrieved the bowl and washed it with hot water. Meanwhile, my companion enjoyed his tea. After he was finished and the master had cleaned his bowl, the master returned the bowls to us so we could examine them and appreciate their uniqueness.

Historically, many of the most sought-after bowls for tea ceremony in Japan were dull colored and roughly finished, not elegant or refined in their craftsmanship. A few of the favored tea bowls were originally inexpensive but wonderful Korean rice bowls intended for everyday use. They were accidental masterpieces of form and design—asymmetrical, cracked, occasionally wobbly, with a thick coating of glaze and an unglazed foot.

The appreciation of the utensils and bowls we used was an important part of the ceremony. Each of them was picked especially for us, brought out for the occasion by our host. We leisurely examined the bowls and the utensils, appreciating their finer qualities, and then returned them to the tea master. He put them away in a little alcove and returned to kneel in front of us. The ceremony concluded the way it began. He placed his fan on the ground in front of him and lowered his head to the floor. We all returned the bow, and he retired to the alcove. We left the way we came, down the winding path through the garden, back into the fray of our lives, yet somehow more buoyant, more fulfilled than when we had entered the tea house.

I realized that the tea ceremony was a manifestation of the merging of host and guest, the apparent differences that are spoken of in the teachings of Zen, as well as a beautiful reflection of the liturgy I had experienced in Zen monasteries.

A well-performed tea ceremony will provide the participants with the taste of certain qualities of the artless arts. To the eye of an experienced tea master, the tea bowls display *wabi* and *sabi,* qualities that have become synonymous with the Zen aesthetic. *Wabi* is a feeling of loneliness or solitude, reflecting a sense of nonattachment and appreciation for the spontaneous unfolding of circumstances. It is like the quiet that comes from a winter snowfall, where all the sounds are hushed and stillness envelops everything. *Sabi* is the suchness of ordinary objects, the basic, unmistakable uniqueness of a thing in and of itself.

Two other qualities used to describe the feelings that Zen art evokes are *aware* and *yugen.* *Aware* is a feeling of nostalgia, a longing for the past, for something old and worn. It's an acute awareness of the fleeting nature of life, its impermanence. *Yugen* is the mystery, the hidden, indescribable, or ineffable dimensions of reality. These qualities are expressed by the bowls, the hut, the master's movements. They are in the atmosphere itself. This is the classic expression of the Zen aesthetic, which can be found not only in the arts of Zen, but throughout Japanese culture as well.

There is also the overarching theme of poverty in chado—not the poverty of down and out, but of bare-bones simplicity, the simplicity of not clinging to anything.

Ryokan, a Zen master and poet, lived in a simple thatched hut.

He was born around 1758 and ordained at the age of eighteen. Shortly after receiving dharma transmission, Ryokan's teacher died. The poet went to live in a hermitage on Mount Kugami, where he spent his time sitting zazen, talking to visitors, and writing poetry. Many stories of Ryokan's simplicity and his love for children have come down to us, as well as of his indifference to worldly honor. In fact, Ryokan called himself Daigo (Great Fool).

One evening, when Ryokan returned from his hut, he surprised a thief who was naively trying to rob the hermit. There was nothing to steal in the hut. Yet Ryokan, feeling sorry for him, gave him his clothes, and the thief, shocked, ran away as fast as he could. Ryokan, shivering as he sat naked by the window, wrote the following haiku:

> The burglar
> neglected to take
> the window's moon.

To be simple means to make a choice about what's important, and to let go of all the rest. When we are able to do this, our vision expands, our heads clear, and we can better see the details of our lives in all their incredible wonder and beauty.

Simplicity does not come easily to us in the West. In general, we don't like to give anything up. We tend to accumulate things, thinking that if something is good, we should have more of it. We go through life hoarding objects, people, credentials, ignoring the fact that the more things we have to take care of, the more burdensome our lives become. Our challenge is to find ways to simplify our lives.

Rikyu, the founder of the tea ceremony, was a serious student of Zen. He spent many years in rigorous training in the monasteries of Japan. After perfecting the ritual aspects of the tea ceremony, he became widely known and respected. Rikyu's close friend, the shogun, regularly frequented Rikyu's teahouse. The shogun, Toyotomi Hideyoshi, though known to be a despot, was also a great patron of the tea ceremony. In praise of Rikyu he recited the following poem at one of his tea parties:

When tea is made with water drawn from the depths of Mind
We really have what is called chado.

One summer, Rikyu managed to acquire blue morning glory
seeds, virtually unknown in Japan at the time. He planted them in
the garden around his tea hut. This was discussed widely, and eventually word of the morning glories reached the shogun. He sent his
messenger to tell the tea master that he would come for tea in order
to see the new flowers. A couple of days later, the shogun appeared at
Rikyu's place, but when he strolled into the garden, he couldn't find
a single morning glory.

"Where are those beautiful new flowers I've been hearing so
much about?" asked the shogun.

"I had them removed," answered Rikyu.

"Removed!" said the shogun, surprised and not a little per-
turbed. "Why?"

"Come," said Rikyu, leading the shogun to the teahouse. The
shogun angrily removed his swords and shoes and then bowed down
to enter through the low door of the tea room. In the tokonoma, resting in a slim bronze vase, lay a single, freshly cut morning glory still
wet with the morning dew. At that instant, without any distractions
standing in the way, the shogun saw that flower, singular in its beauty,
completely filling his universe.

The quality of simplicity that is present in traditional Zen
monasteries also exists in Zen gardens. A Zen garden features a few
carefully placed rocks, raked sand, and trees trimmed to expose the
hills in the distance. Each rock is chosen because of its characteristic
shape and form. In the West, by contrast, our gardens tend to over-
flow with beauty, so much of it that we miss the beauty.

Our culture of excess is growing, infiltrating even our most
basic activities. Overeating and obesity are epidemic in the United
States. The size of servings at restaurants has doubled in the past
twenty years. In Japanese restaurants a small steak comes on a very
large plate with a little cluster of potatoes, a few spears of vegetables, and a sprig of parsley. The portion is reasonable in size and

appealing in its presentation, with the same dynamic of form and space seen in a Zen garden. We are nourished by the presentation as we are nourished by the food. And we walk away a little hungry. My dharma grandfather Yasutani Roshi used to say, "You should always stop eating before you feel completely full." That's one of the themes in *oryoki,* the ceremonial meal taken at Zen monasteries during long meditation intensives.

In developing the tea ceremony Rikyu was influenced by oryoki or *juhatsu,* the liturgy of eating practiced respectively in the Soto and Linji schools of Zen. *Oryoki* roughly means "that which contains just enough," and it also refers to the Buddha bowl monks receive at their ordination. Oryoki, like the tea ceremony, is a very detailed ritual. Each movement is attended to with care and painstaking detail. Everyone begins and finishes together. Starting with the five bowls that are lined up over a folded cloth, to the serving and receiving of the food, to the cleaning and wrapping of the bowls, each movement in oryoki is precise and deliberate. Chants accompany the ceremony which emphasizes that what is taking place is not only the ordinary act of eating, but a sacred activity.

In Zen monasteries, the beginning and end of each activity is punctuated with appropriate liturgy. This ranges from a simple gesture of placing both hands together palm-to-palm in *gassho* and bowing before entering a room, to an elaborate, two-hour-long funeral service. This mindful engagement of an activity is designed to help us awaken to what we are about to do. Formal ceremonies, work and study, the practical functions of eating and washing, are carried out with a mind that is alert, attentive, and completely present. When the mind is in that state, every single thing we encounter is as complete and simple as Rikyu's morning glory.

It is easy to imagine that the formality of the tea ceremony or oryoki is confining, or that the spirit of simplicity calls for everything to be stripped away, leaving only a bare form. Nothing could be further from the truth. When completely embodied, the true spirit of simplicity is freedom in action. Within the specific form we become free of that form.

Once Soen Roshi and a group of students were meeting some-one at Kennedy Airport in New York City. One of the students ar-rived late. When he appeared, Soen said to him, "You missed the tea ceremony."

"A tea ceremony at Kennedy Airport?" said my friend, looking around him incredulously. "Where?"

"Ah," mused Soen. "Maybe you're not too late. Come with me." Soen dragged him into a nearby doorway. Two women rushed by pulling huge suitcases behind them, while a man waved frantically at someone in the distance. They didn't notice a strange Japanese man in flowing robes, with his arm around his bewildered companion.

Soen reached into his sleeve and pulled out a little porcelain container with powdered green tea and a small bamboo spoon. He took a spoonful of tea and said "Open your mouth." My friend obeyed and Soen plopped the tea in his mouth, lifted his chin so his jaw was closed and said, "Now, make water."

The elaborate ritual of the classic tea ceremony, which can take over an hour, was reduced to its essence in this simple act. All that was left was the taste of tea.

The fact that both of these manifestations of tea ceremony—Soen's improvisational form and the traditional and elaborate rit-ual—can exist side by side is a testimony to the true spirit of freedom implicit in the teachings and practice of the Zen arts.

Ultimately, oryoki, like the tea ceremony, is a state of mind. It has nothing to do with a set of bowls or being in a meditation hall. It has everything to do with being completely present, and doing what we're doing—whether we're at a Burger King, an airport, or a monastery. If our mind is cluttered with thoughts or worries, we're not doing oryoki. We're not being simply present. The way we use our mind is the way we live our lives. If we understand these princi-ples and take them up as practice, we will liberate ourselves.

The Zen arts in their bare-bone simplicity and sobriety may sometimes appear archaic, but they are surprisingly modern, both in appearance and function. The lines of a classic Japanese teahouse, a rock garden, or a simple ceramic pot are invariably clean and elegant. By avoiding overstatement, the Zen artist conveys the impression of disciplined restraint, of having held something in reserve. And in the art's empty spaces we sense a hidden plenitude. The result is a feeling of implied strength, a suspicion that we have only glimpsed the power and full potential of the artist.

In a society that assures us that more is better, it's not always easy to trust that we have enough, that we *are* enough. We have to cut through the illusion that abundance is security, and trust that we don't have to buffer ourselves against reality. If we have learned to trust abundance, we can learn to trust simplicity. We can practice simplicity.

Zen, and by extension the Zen aesthetic, shows us that all things are perfect and complete, just as they are. Nothing is lacking. In trying to realize our true nature, we rub against the paradox: We don't know that we already are what we are trying to become. In Zen, we say that each one of us is already a Buddha, a thoroughly enlightened being. It's the same with art. Each one of us is already an artist, whether we realize it or not. In fact, it doesn't matter whether we realize it—this truth of perfection is still there. Engaging the creative process is a way of getting in touch with this truth, and to let it function in all areas of our lives.

If I were asked to get rid of the Zen aesthetic and just keep one quality necessary to create art, I would say it's trust. When you learn to trust yourself implicitly, you no longer need to prove something through your art. You simply allow it to come out, to be as it is. This is when creating art becomes effortless. It happens just as you grow hair. It grows.

Danger on Peaks

Gary Snyder

Gary Snyder would be a national treasure of the United States, if only we had that marvelous form of recognition. Prickly, durable, tender, and astute, at the age of seventy-five he is the last of the great Beat poets, and still a powerful force for poetry, the environment, and dharma. To me, he embodies much of the best of what it means to be American. Here are some poems from his new collection.

Almost Okay Now

She had been in an accident: almost okay now,
but inside still recovering,
bones slow-healing—she was anxious
still fearful of cars and of men.
As I sped up the winding hill road
she shuddered—eyes beseeching me—
I slowed the car down.
Out on a high meadow under the moon,
With delicate guidance she showed me
how to make love without hurting her
and then napped awhile in my arms,

smell of sweet grass
warm night breeze

For Philip Zenshin Whalen
d. 26 June 2002

(and for 33 pine trees)

Load of logs on
chains cinched down and doublechecked
the truck heads slowly up the hill

I bow namaste and farewell
these ponderosa pine
whose air and rain and sun we shared

for thirty years,
struck by beetles   needles
turning rusty brown,
and moving on.

—decking, shelving,   siding,
stringers, studs, and joists,

I will think of you   pines from this mountain
as you shelter people in the Valley
years to come

For Carole

I first saw her in the zendo
at meal time   unwrapping bowls
head forward folding back the cloth
        as server I was kneeling
to fill three sets of bowls each time
up the line

                Her lithe leg
                proud, skeptical,
                passionate, trained
                by the
                heights   by the
                danger on peaks

Steady, They Say

Clambering up the rocks of a dry wash gully,
warped sandstone, by the San Juan River,

look north to stony mountains
shifting clouds and sun

—despair at how the human world goes down

Consult my old advisors

"steady" they say

"today"

> *(At Slickhorn Gulch on*
> *the San Juan River 1999)*

Experiments
in Consciousness

Sam Harris

Sam Harris's best-seller The End of Faith *was celebrated and condemned as a frontal assault on literalist religion. Less recognized was the alternative he offered. Harris argued that human happiness, reason, and ethics are all served well by a spiritual path that looks very much like Buddhism (well, actually, it is Buddhism).*

At the core of every religion lies an undeniable claim about the human condition: it is possible to have one's experience of the world radically transformed. Although we generally live within the limits imposed by our ordinary uses of attention—we wake, we work, we eat, we watch television, we converse with others, we sleep, we dream—most of us know, however dimly, that extraordinary experiences are possible.

The problem with religion is that is blends this truth so thoroughly with the venom of unreason. Take Christianity as an example: it is not enough that Jesus was a man who transformed himself to such a degree that the Sermon on the Mount could be his heart's confession. He also had to be the Son of God, born of a virgin, and destined to return to earth trailing clouds of glory. The effect of such dogma is to place the example of Jesus forever out of reach. His teaching ceases to be a set of empirical claims about the linkage between ethics and spiritual insight and instead becomes a gratuitous, and rather gruesome, fairy tale. According to the dogma of Christianity, becoming just like Jesus is impossible. One can only enumerate one's sins, believe the unbelievable, and await the end of the world.

But a more profound response to existence is possible for us, and the testimony of Jesus, as well as that of countless other men and women over the ages, attests to this. The challenge for us is to begin talking about this possibility in rational terms.

The Search for Happiness

Though the lilies of the field are admirably clothed, you and I were driven from the womb naked and squalling. What do we need to be happy? Almost everything we do can be viewed as a reply to this question. We need food, shelter, and clothing. We need the company of others. Then we need to learn countless things to make the most of this company. We need to find work that we enjoy, and we need time for leisure. We need so many things, and there seems no alternative but to seek and maintain them, one after the next, hour after hour.

But are such things sufficient for happiness? Is a person guaranteed to be happy merely by virtue of having health, wealth, and good company? Apparently not. Are such things even necessary for happiness? If so, what can we make of those Indian yogis who renounce all material and familial attachments only to spend decades alone in caves practicing meditation? It seems that such people can be happy as well. Indeed, some of them claim to be perfectly so.

It is difficult to find a word for that human enterprise which aims at happiness directly—a happiness of a sort that can survive the frustration of all conventional desires. The term "spirituality" seems unavoidable here, but it has many connotations that are, frankly, embarrassing. "Mysticism" has more gravitas, perhaps, but it has unfortunate associations of its own. Neither word captures the reasonableness and profundity of the possibility that we must now consider: that there is a form of well-being that supersedes all others, indeed, that transcends the vagaries of experience itself. I will use both "spirituality" and "mysticism" interchangeably here, because there are no alternatives, but the reader should remember that I am using them in a restricted sense. While a visit to any New Age bookstore will reveal that modern man has embraced a daunting range of "spiritual" preoccupations—ranging from the healing power of crystals and colonic irrigation to the ardors of alien abduction—discussion will focus on a specific insight that seems to have special relevance to our pursuit of happiness.

Most spiritual teachings agree that there is more to happiness than becoming a productive member of society, a cheerful consumer of every licit pleasure, and an enthusiastic bearer of children disposed to do the same. Indeed, many suggest that it is our search for happiness—our craving for knowledge and new experience, our desire for recognition, our efforts to find the right romantic partner, even our yearning for spiritual experience itself—that causes us to overlook a form of well-being that is intrinsic to consciousness in every present moment. Some version of this insight seems to lie at the core of many of our religions, and yet it is by no means always easy to discern among the articles of faith.

While many of us go for decades without experiencing a full day of solitude, we live every moment in the solitude of our own minds. However close we may be to others, our pleasures and pains are ours alone. Spiritual practice is often recommended as the most rational response to this situation. The underlying claim here is that we can realize something about the nature of consciousness in this moment that will improve our lives. The experience of countless contemplatives suggests that consciousness—being merely the condition in which thought, emotion, and even our sense of self arises—is never actually changed by what it knows. That which is aware of joy does not become joyful; that which is aware of sadness does not become sad. From the point of view of consciousness, we are merely aware of sights, sounds, sensations, moods, and thoughts. Many spiritual teachings allege that if we can recognize our identity as consciousness itself, as the mere witness of appearances, we will realize that we stand perpetually free of the vicissitudes of experience.

This is not to deny that suffering has a physical dimension. The fact that a drug like Prozac can relieve many of the symptoms of depression suggests that mental suffering can be no more ethereal than a little green pill. But the arrow of influence clearly flies both ways. We know that ideas themselves have the power to utterly define a person's experience of the world. Even the significance of intense physical pain is open to subjective interpretation. Consider the pain of labor: How many women come away from the experience traumatized? The occasion itself is generally a happy one, assuming all goes well with the birth. Imagine how different it would be for a woman to be tortured by having the sensations of a normal labor inflicted upon her by a mad scientist. The sensations might be identical, and yet this would certainly be among the worst experiences of her life. There is clearly more to suffering even physical pain than painful sensation alone.

Our spiritual traditions suggest that we have considerable room here to change our relationship to the contents of consciousness, and thereby to transform our experience of the world. Indeed, a vast literature on human spirituality attests to this. It is also clear that nothing need be believed on insufficient evidence for us to look into this possibility with an open mind.

CONSCIOUSNESS

Like Descartes, most of us begin these inquiries as thinkers, condemned by the terms of our subjectivity to maneuver in a world that appears to be other than what we are. Descartes accentuated this dichotomy by declaring that two substances were to be found in God's universe: matter and spirit. For most of us, a dualism of this sort is more or less a matter of common sense (though the term "spirit" seems rather majestic, given how our minds generally comport themselves). As science has turned its reifying light upon the mysteries of the human mind, however, Descartes's dualism (along with our own "folk psychology") has come in for some rough treatment. Bolstered by the undeniable successes of three centuries of purely physical research, many philosophers and scientists now reject Descartes's separation of mind and body, spirit and matter, as the concession to Christian piety that it surely was, and imagine that they have thereby erased the conceptual gulf between consciousness and the physical world.

Our beliefs about consciousness are intimately linked to our ethics. They also happen to have a direct bearing upon our view of death. Most scientists consider themselves physicalists; this means, among other things, that they believe that our mental and spiritual lives are wholly dependent upon the workings of our brains. By this account, when the brain dies, the stream of our being must come to an end. Once the lamps of neural activity have been extinguished, there will be nothing left to survive. Indeed, many scientists purvey this conviction as though it were itself a special sacrament, conferring intellectual integrity upon any man, woman, or child who is man enough to swallow it.

But the truth is that we simply do not know what happens after death. While there is much to be said against a naive conception of a soul that is independent of the brain, the place of consciousness in the natural world is very much an open question. The idea that brains produce consciousness is little more than an article of faith among scientists at present, and there are many reasons to believe that the methods of science will be insufficient to either prove or disprove it.

Inevitably, scientists treat consciousness as a mere attribute of certain large-brained animals. The problem, however, is that nothing about a brain, when surveyed as a physical system, declares it to be a bearer of that peculiar interior dimension that each of us experiences as consciousness in his own case. Every paradigm that attempts to shed light upon the frontier between consciousness and unconsciousness, searching for the physical difference that makes the phenomenal one, relies upon subjective reports to signal that an experimental stimulus has been observed. The operational definition of consciousness, therefore, is reportability. But consciousness and reportability are not the same. Is a starfish conscious? No science that conflates consciousness with reportability will deliver an answer to this question. To look for consciousness in the world on the basis of its outward signs is the only thing that we can do. To define consciousness in terms of its outward signs, however, is a fallacy. Computers of the future, sufficiently advanced to pass the Turing test, will offer up a wealth of self-report—but will they be conscious? If we don't already know, their eloquence on the matter will not decide the issue. Consciousness may be a far more rudimentary phenomenon than are living creatures and their brains. And there appears to be no obvious way of ruling out such a thesis experimentally.

And so, while we know many things about ourselves in anatomical, physiological, and evolutionary terms, we currently have no idea why it is "like something" to be what we are. The fact that the universe is illuminated where you stand, the fact that your thoughts and moods and sensations have a qualitative character, is an absolute mystery—rivaled only by the mystery, famously articulated by the philosopher Schelling, that there should be anything at all in this universe rather than nothing. The problem is that our experience of brains, as objects in the world, leaves us perfectly insensible to the reality of consciousness, while our experience as brains grants us knowledge of nothing else. Given this situation, it is reasonable to conclude that the domain of our subjectivity constitutes a proper (and essential) sphere of investigation into the nature of the universe, as some facts will be discovered only in consciousness, in first-person terms, or not discovered at all.

Investigating the nature of consciousness directly, through sustained introspection, is simply another name for spiritual practice. It should be clear that whatever transformations of your experience are possible—after forty days and forty nights in the desert, after twenty years in a cave, or after some new serotonin agonist has been delivered to your synapses—these will be a matter of changes occurring in the contents of your consciousness. Whatever Jesus experienced, he experienced as a consciousness. If he loved his neighbor as himself, this is a description of what it felt like to be Jesus while in the presence of other human beings. The history of human spirituality is the history of our attempts to explore and modify the deliverances of consciousness through methods like fasting, chanting, sensory deprivation, prayer, meditation, and the use of psychotropic plants. There is no question that experiments of this sort can be conducted in a rational manner. Indeed, they are some of our only means of determining to what extent the human condition can be deliberately transformed. Such an enterprise become irrational only when people begin making claims about the world that cannot be supported by empirical evidence.

What Are We Calling "I"?

Our spiritual possibilities will largely depend on what we are as selves. In physical terms, each of us is a system, locked in an uninterrupted exchange of matter and energy with the larger system of the earth. The life of your very cells is built upon a network of barter and exchange over which you can exercise only the crudest conscious influence—in the form of deciding whether to hold your breath or take another slice of pizza out of the fridge. As a physical system, you are no more independent of nature at this moment than your liver is of the rest of your body. As a collection of self-regulation and continually dividing cells, you are also continuous with your genetic precursors: your parents, their parents, and backward through tens of millions of generations—at which point your ancestors begin looking less like men and women with bad teeth and more like pond scum. It is true enough to say that, in physical terms, you are little more than an eddy in a great river of life.

But, of course, your body is itself an environment teeming with creatures, in relation to which you are sovereign in name alone. To examine the body of a person, its organs and tissues, cells and intestinal flora (sometimes fauna, alas), is to be confronted by a world that bears no more evidence of an overriding conscious intelligence than does the world at large. Is there any reason to suspect, when observing the function of mitochondria within a cell, or the twitching of muscle fibers in the hand, that there is a mind, above and beyond such processes, thinking, "L'état c'est moi"? Indeed, any privilege we might be tempted to accord the boundary of the skin in our search for the physical self seems profoundly arbitrary.

The frontiers of the mental self are no easier to discern: memos, taboos, norms of decorum, linguistic conventions, prejudices, ideals, aesthetic biases, commercial jingles—the phenomena that populate the landscape of our minds are immigrants from the world at large. Is your desire to be physically fit—or your taste in clothing, your sense of community, your expectation of reciprocal kindness, your shyness, your affability, your sexual quirks, etc.—something that originates with you? Is it something best thought of as residing in you? These phenomena are the direct result of your embeddedness in a world of social relationships and culture (as well as a product of your genes). Many of them seem to be no more "you," ultimately, than the rules of English grammar are.

And yet, this feeling of being a self persists. If the term "I" refers to anything at all, it does not refer simply to the body. After all, most of us feel individuated as a self within the body. I speak of "my" body more or less as I speak of "my" car, for the simple reason that every act of perception of cognition conveys the tacit sense that the knower is something other than the thing known. Just as my awareness of my car demonstrates that I, as a subject, am something other than it, as an object, I can be aware of my hand, or an emotion, and experience the same cleavage between subject and object. For this reason, the self cannot simply be equated with the totality of a person's mental life or with his personality as a whole. Rather, it is the point of view around which the changing states of his mind and body appear to be constellated. Whatever the relationship between consciousness and the body actually is, in experiential terms the body is something to which the conscious self, if such there be, stands in relation. Exactly when, in evolutionary or developmental terms, this point of view emerges is not known, but one thing is clear: at some point in the first years of life most human beings are christened as "I," the perennial subject, for whom all appearances, inside and out, become objects of a kind, waiting to be known. And it is as "I" that every scientist begins his inquiry into the nature of the world and every pious man folds his hands in prayer.

The sense of self seems to be the product of the brain's representing its own acts of representation; its seeing of the world begets an image of a one who sees. It is important to realize that this feeling—the sense that each of us has of appropriating, rather than merely being, a sphere of experience—is not a necessary feature of consciousness. It is, after all, conceivable that a creature could form a representation of the world without forming a representation of itself in the world. And, indeed, many spiritual practitioners claim to experience the world in just this way, perfectly shorn of self.

A basic finding of neurophysiology lends credence to such claims. It is not so much what they are but what they do that makes neurons see, hear, smell, taste, touch, think, and feel. Like any other function that emerges from the activity of the brain, the feeling of self is best thought of as a process. It is not very surprising, therefore, that we can lose this feeling, because processes, by their very nature, can be interrupted. While the experience of selflessness does not indicate anything about the relationship between consciousness and the physical world (and is thus mute on the question of what happens after death), it has broad implications for the sciences of mind, for our approach to spirituality, and for our conception of human happiness.

As a mental phenomenon, loss of self is not as rare as our scholarly neglect of it suggests. This experience is characterized by a sudden loss of subject/object perception: the continuum of experience remains, but one no longer feels that there is a knower standing apart from the known. Thoughts may arise, but the feeling that one is the thinker of these thoughts has vanished. Something has definitely changed at the level of one's moment-to-moment experience, and this change—the disappearance of anything to which the pronoun "I" can be faithfully attached—signals that there had been a conscious experience of selfhood all the while, however difficult it may be to characterize.

Look at this book as a physical object. You are aware of it as an appearance in consciousness. You may feel that your consciousness is one thing—it is whatever illuminates your world from some point behind your eyes, perhaps—and the book is another. This is the kind of dualistic (subject/object) perception that characterizes our normal experience of life. It is possible, however, to look for your self in such a way as to put this subject/object dichotomy in doubt—and even to banish it altogether.

The contents of consciousness—sights, sound, sensations, thoughts, moods, etc.—whatever they are at the level of the brain, are merely expressions of consciousness at the level of our experience. Unrecognized as such, many of these appearances seem to impinge upon consciousness from without, and the sense of self emerges, and grows entrenched, as the feeling that that which knows is circumscribed, modified, and often oppressed by that which is known. Indeed, it is likely that our parents found us in our cribs long before we found ourselves there, and that we were merely led by their gaze, and their pointing fingers, to coalesce around an implied center of cognition that does not, in fact, exist. Thereafter, every maternal caress, every satisfaction of hunger or thirst, as well as the diverse form of approval and rebuke that came in reply to the actions of our embodied minds, seemed to confirm a self-sense that we, by example, finally learned to call "I"— and thus we became the narrow locus around which all things and events, pleasant and unpleasant, continue to swirl.

In subjective terms, the search for the self seems to entail a paradox: we are, after all, looking for the very thing that is doing the looking. Thousands of years of human experience suggest, however, that the paradox here is only apparent: it is not merely that the component of our experience that we call "I" cannot be found; it is that it actually disappears when looked for in a rigorous way.

The foregoing is just a gloss on the phenomenology here, but it should be sufficient to get us started. The basic (and, I think, uncontestable) fact is that almost every human being experiences the duality of subject and object in some measure, and most of us feel it powerfully nearly every moment of our lives. It is scarcely an exaggeration to say that the feeling that we call "I" is one of the most pervasive and salient features of human life, and that its effects upon the world, as six billion "selves" pursue diverse and often incompatible ends, rival those that can be ascribed to almost any other phenomenon in nature. Clearly, there is nothing optimal—or even necessarily viable—about our present form of subjectivity. Almost every problem we have can be ascribed to the fact that human beings are utterly beguiled by their feelings of separateness. It would seem that a spirituality that undermined such dualism, through the mere contemplation of consciousness, could not help but improve our situation. Whether or not great numbers of human beings will ever be in a position to explore this terrain depends on how our discourse on religion proceeds. There is clearly no greater obstacle to a truly empirical approach to spiritual experience than our current beliefs about God.

The Wisdom of the East

Inevitably, the foregoing will strike certain readers as a confusing eruption of speculative philosophy. This is unfortunate, for none of it has been speculative or even particularly philosophical—at least not in the sense that this term has acquired in the West. Thousands of years have passed since any Western philosopher imagined that a person should be made happy, peaceful, or even wise, in the ordinary sense, by his search for truth. Personal transformation, or indeed liberation from the illusion of the self, seems to have been thought too much to ask; or rather, not thought of at all. Consequently, many of us in the West are conceptually unequipped to understand empirical claims of the sort adduced above.

In fact, the spiritual differences between the East and the West are every bit as shocking as the material differences between the

North and the South. Jared Diamond's fascinating thesis, to sum
it up in a line, is that advanced civilization did not arise in sub-
Saharan Africa, because one can't saddle a rhinoceros and ride it into
battle. If there is an equally arresting image that accounts for why
nondualistic, empirical mysticism seems to have arisen only in Asia,
I have yet to find it. But I suspect that the culprit has been the Christian, Jewish, and Muslim emphasis on faith itself. Faith is rather like
a rhinoceros, in fact: it won't do much in the way of real work for
you, and yet at close quarters it will make spectacular claims upon
your attention.

This is not to say that spiritual realization has been a common
attainment east of Bosporus. Clearly, it has not. It must also be con-
ceded that Asia has always had its fair share of false prophets and
charlatan saints, while the West has not been entirely bereft of wisdom. Nevertheless, when the great philosopher mystics of the East
are weighed against the patriarchs of the Western philosophical
and theological traditions, the difference is unmistakable: Buddha,
Shankara, Padmasambhava, Nagarjuna, Longchenpa, and countless
others down to the present have no equivalents in the West. In spiritual terms, we in the West appear to have been standing on the
shoulders of dwarfs. It is little wonder, therefore, that many Western
scholars have found the view within rather unremarkable.

While this is not a treatise on Eastern spirituality, it does not
seem out of place to briefly examine the differences between the
Eastern and Western canons, for they are genuinely startling. To illustrate this point, I have selected a passage at random from a shelf of
Buddhist literature. The following text was found with closed eyes,
on the first attempt, from among scores of books. I invite the reader
to find anything even remotely like this in the Bible or the Koran.

> In the present moment, when (your mind) remains in its
>   own condition without constructing anything,
> Awareness at that moment in itself is quite ordinary.
> And when you look into yourself in this way nakedly (without
>   any discursive thoughts),

Since there is only this pure observing, there will be found
   a lucid clarity without anyone being there who is the
   observer;
Only a naked manifest awareness is present.
(This awareness) is empty and immaculately pure, not being
   created by anything whatsoever.
It is authentic and unadulterated, without any duality of clarity
   and emptiness.
It is not permanent and yet it is not created by anything.
However, it is not a mere nothingness or something annihi-
   lated because it is lucid and present.
It does not exist as a single entity because it is present and clear
   in terms of being many.
(On the other hand) it is not created as a multiplicity of things
   because it is inseparable and of a single flavor.
This inherent self-awareness does not derive from anything
   outside itself.
This is the real introduction to the actual condition of things.
   —PADMASAMBHAVA*

One could live an eon as a Christian, a Muslim, or a Jew and
never encounter any teachings like this about the nature of consciousness. The comparison with Islam is especially invidious, because Padmasambhava was virtually Mohammed's contemporary.
While the meaning of the above passage might not be perfectly
apparent to all readers—it is just a section of a longer teaching on
the nature of mind and contains a fair amount of Buddhist jargon
("clarity," "emptiness," "single flavor," etc.)—it is a rigorously empirical document, not a statement of metaphysics. Even the contemporary literature on consciousness, which spans philosophy, cognitive
science, psychology, and neuroscience, cannot match the kind of
precise, phenomenological studies that can be found throughout the

---

*Padmasambhava, *Self-Liberation through Seeing with Naked Awareness*, translated by J. M. Reynolds (New York: Station Hill Press, 1989).

Buddhist canon. Although we have no reason to be dogmatically attached to any one tradition of spiritual instruction, we should not imagine that they are all equally wise or equally sophisticated. They are not. Mysticism, to be viable, requires explicit instructions, which need suffer no more ambiguity or artifice in their exposition than we find in a manual for operating a lawn mower. Some traditions realized this millennia ago. Others did not.

Mysticism is a rational enterprise. Religion is not. The mystic has recognized something about the nature of consciousness prior to thought, and this recognition is susceptible to rational discussion. The mystic has reasons for what he believes, and these reasons are empirical. The roiling mystery of the world can be analyzed with concepts (this is science), or it can be experienced free of concepts (this is mysticism). Religion is nothing more than bad concepts held in place of good ones for all time. It is the denial—at once full of hope and full of fear—of the vastitude of human ignorance.

A kernel of truth lurks at the heart of religion, because spiritual experience, ethical behavior, and strong communities are essential for human happiness. And yet our religious traditions are intellectually defunct and politically ruinous. While spiritual experience is clearly a natural propensity of the human mind, we need not believe anything on insufficient evidence to actualize it. Clearly, it must be possible to bring reason, spirituality, and ethics together in our thinking about the world. This would be the beginning of a rational approach to our deepest personal concerns. It would also be the end of faith.

The Politics of Interdependence ☁

Peter Coyote

Here's a pithy statement by the multitalented Peter Coyote—actor, prize-winning writer, Zen practitioner—outlining his principles for a Buddhist view of politics. It's a holistic and subtle understanding that's realistic about the limits of what can be achieved politically.

Normally the word *politics* means "competition between competing interest groups or individuals for power and leadership." This is actually the fourth of eight definitions for the word listed in *Webster's Third New International Dictionary*. The first definition, which I find more useful, defines politics as "the art of adjusting and ordering relationships between individuals and groups in a political community." The words "adjusting" and "ordering" stress relationship and interdependence, whereas "competition" implies domination and hierarchy.

Relationship and interdependence are "mutually dependent arising"—the core of the Buddha's understanding. This core insight implies some procedures and goals for the practice of politics that might beneficially alter the way it is presently construed. At the very least it affords an opportunity to consider the practice of politics from the perspective of Buddha.

The first principle might be expressed as: Political acts and solutions should afford all beings maximal opportunity to fulfill their evolutionary destinies. (In this context, "beings" should be understood to include insects, plants, animals, and the soil itself.) Practically, this requires considering the needs of all beings when evaluating political goals and strategies. To say, "There can be no more factories in such and such a place," is a flat denial that creates conflict, because there may be people who need the work and others who need the products. An alternative set of statements such as, "We may need factories or power plants, but they should be constructed in a way that does no harm. Furthermore, they should be located where the interests of plants, animals, and humans are not negatively affected, and their products should sell at a cost that does not oppress those who require them for survival," is inclusive. It invites higher degrees of complexity and problem-solving, which in turn invites increased participation.

The second principle might be: If there is no self, there is no other. Our "opponent," however disagreeable, is highlighting an aspect of mind we may have difficulty owning, an aspect that must be understood and addressed if we hope to make progress. It can only be accessed by intimacy. Resistance builds strength (as it does in a gym) and hardens the position of one's opponent. Careful evaluation of the first principle will gradually unpack and expose the conflicting "interests" and desires of the proponent. These interests must be pursued to their roots in one's own psyche until they can be faced without the wrath and judgment that diminish one's opponent. Doing so will, at the least, win the respect of those with whom you struggle. This respect increases intimacy and a sense of relationship—the deep goal of all political work.

The third principle might be: Procedures or solutions that compromise the dignity ("intrinsic worth") of one's opponent imply domination and hierarchy, not relationship. Consequently, they should be excluded from political discourse.

It is hard to imagine too much harm arising from a diligent practice of these three principles. Nothing will work in every situation, and a corollary of all political work must be, "No one always wins." Since outcomes are beyond our control, what we can control are our intentions and personal behavior. By adhering to these three principles, we model the world we hope to establish through politics. This can never be understood as a defeat.

Three Means to Peace))

Joseph Goldstein

All the problems in society and among nations are ultimately a form of warfare—of self against other, either collective or individual—and that conflict is precisely what Buddhism addresses. Here, vipassana teacher Joseph Goldstein offers three Buddhist techniques we can use to make the world a more peaceful place.

A central question confronting spiritual life today is how we can best respond to the tremendous conflicts and uncertainties of these times. The war on terror, the seemingly intractable violence of the Middle East, poverty and disease, racism, the degradation of the environment, and the problems in our own personal lives, all call us to ask: What is the source of this great mass of suffering? What are the forces in the world that drive intolerance, violence, and injustice? Are there forces that hold the promise of peace? Do we really understand the nature of fear and hatred, envy and greed? Do we know how to cultivate love and kindness, energy and wisdom?

The great discovery of the meditative journey is that all the forces for good and for harm playing out in the world are also right here in our own minds. If we want to understand the world, we need to understand ourselves. Can we do this?

I believe something helpful has emerged from the interaction of various Buddhist traditions in the West over the last thirty years. I call what has arisen from this sometimes confusing, and other times illuminating, interaction of traditions the "One Dharma of Western Buddhism." This term does not refer to some hodgepodge of teachings mixed together in a watered-down, confused mix of methods and metaphysics. Rather, its defining characteristic is the very Western quality of pragmatism. It is allegiance to a simple question: "What works?" What works to free the mind from suffering? What works to engender the heart of compassion? What works to help us awaken from ignorance?

This pragmatism not only serves our individual practices, but it also illuminates a question that has plagued religious (and other) traditions for thousands of years: is it possible to hold differences of view in a larger context of unity rather than in conflict and hostility?

Rather than take religious views and teachings to be ultimate statements of absolute truth, they might be better understood as skillful means to liberate the mind. Instead of pitting one view against another, we might let go of rigid attachment to any view, and ask the very pragmatic question, "Is this teaching leading my heart and mind to greater wisdom and peace, to greater kindness and compassion? Or does it lead to more divisiveness, to more selfishness, to more violence?"

This approach to religion is of vital importance now, as we explore methods for understanding the various forces at work in the mind. Whatever particular spiritual path we follow, we can draw on elements from different traditions, harmonizing methods of mindfulness, the motivation of compassion and the liberating wisdom of non-clinging. These three qualities—mindfulness, compassion, and wisdom—are not Burmese or Tibetan, Thai or Japanese, Eastern or Western. They do not belong to any religion but are qualities in our own minds and hearts, and many different practices enhance their growth.

Mindfulness is the key to the present moment. Without it we simply stay lost in the wanderings of our minds. Tulku Urgyen, the great Dzogchen master of the last century, said, "There is one thing we always need and that is the watchman named mindfulness—the guard who is always on the lookout for when we get carried away by mindlessness."

Mindfulness is the quality and power of mind that is aware of what's happening—without judgment and without interference. It is like a mirror that simply reflects whatever comes before it. It serves us in the humblest ways, keeping us connected to brushing our teeth or having a cup of tea. It keeps us connected to the people around us, so that we're not simply rushing by them in the busyness of our lives. The Dalai Lama is an example of someone who beautifully embodies this quality of caring attention: after one conference in Arizona, His Holiness requested that all the employees of the hotel gather in the lobby so that he could greet each one of them before he left for his next engagement.

The Buddha also spoke of mindfulness as being the path to enlightenment: "This is the direct path for the purification of beings, for the overcoming of sorrow and lamentation, for the disappearing of pain and grief, for the attainment of the Way, for the realization of nirvana."

We can start the practice of mindfulness meditation with the simple observation and feeling of each breath. Breathing in, we know we're breathing in; breathing out, we know we're breathing out. It's very simple, although not easy. After just a few breaths, we hop on trains of association, getting lost in plans, memories, judgments, and fantasies. This habit of wandering mind is very strong, even though our reveries are often not pleasant and sometimes not even true. As Mark Twain so aptly put it, "Some of the worst things in my life never happened." So we need to train our minds, coming back again and again to the breath, simply beginning again.

Slowly, though, our minds steady and we begin to experience some space of inner calm and peace. This environment of inner stillness makes possible a deeper investigation of our thoughts and emotions. What is a thought—that strange, ephemeral phenomenon that can so dominate our lives? When we look directly at a thought, we see that it is little more than nothing. Yet when it is unnoticed, it wields tremendous power. Notice the difference between being lost in a thought and being mindful that we're thinking. Becoming aware of the thought is like waking up from a dream or coming out of a movie theater after being absorbed in the story. Through mindfulness, we gradually awaken from the movies of our minds.

What, too, is the nature of emotions—those powerful energies that sweep over our bodies and minds like great breaking waves? In a surprising way, mindfulness and the investigation of emotions begin to deepen our understanding of selflessness; we see that the emotions themselves arise out of conditions and pass away as the conditions change, like clouds forming and dissolving in the clear, open sky. As the Buddha said to his son, Rahula, "You should consider all phenomena with proper wisdom: 'This is not mine, this is not I, this is not myself.'"

On the subtlest level, we learn not to identify with consciousness itself, cutting though any sense of this knowing faculty as being "I" or "mine." As a way of cultivating this radical transformation of understanding, I have found it useful to reframe meditation experience in the passive voice; for example, the breath being known, sensations being known, thoughts being known. This language construction takes the "I" out of the picture and opens us to the question, "Known by what?" And rather than jumping in with a conceptual response, we can use this question to experience directly the unfolding mystery of awareness, moment after moment.

The wisdom of understanding selflessness finds expression in compassion. We might say that compassion is the activity of emptiness. Compassion arises both on the personal level of our individual relationships and on the global level of great cultures and civilizations interacting with one another. The integration of the understanding of our own minds with what is happening in the world today has enormous implications.

Six weeks after 9/11, I was teaching loving-kindness meditation (*metta*, in Pali) at a retreat for lawyers. In this practice, we start sending loving wishes to ourselves, and then send those loving wishes to various categories of beings, including benefactors, friends, neutral persons, enemies and, finally, all beings. At the retreat, I suggested the possibility of including in our metta even those involved in acts of violence and aggression. One of the participants from New York commented that he couldn't possibly send loving-kindness to al-Qaeda, nor would he ever want to.

For me, that simple and honest statement raised a lot of interesting questions. What is our response to violence and injustice? How do we understand the practices of loving-kindness and compassion? What are our bedrock aspirations for the world and ourselves?

In doing the meditation on loving-kindness, we repeat certain phrases; for example, "May you be happy, may you be free of mental and physical suffering, may you live with ease." However, when we get to people who have done us harm, either individually or collectively, often we don't want to include them in our loving wishes. We don't want to wish them happiness. In fact, we may well want to see them suffer for the great harm they have done. These are not unusual feelings to have.

But right there, in that situation, is the critical juncture of contemplative practice and our life of action in the world. If we want to enhance the possibilities for more compassion and peace in the world—and in ourselves—we need to look beneath our usual and, perhaps, instinctive emotional responses. In situations of suffering, whether small interpersonal conflicts or huge disasters of violence and destruction, there is one question that holds the key to compassionate response: in this situation of suffering, whatever it may be, what is our most fundamental wish?

In the current Middle East situation, with so much violence on both sides, I find my metta practice including all in the wish, "May you be free of hatred, may you be free of enmity." If our aspiration is peace in the world, is there anyone we would exclude from this wish, whether they are terrorists, suicide bombers, soldiers lost in violence or government policy-makers? "May everyone be free of hatred, free of enmity." These are the mind states that drive harmful acts. If our own response is enmity or hatred or ill will, whether we acknowledge it or not, we are part of the problem.

This message is not new, but the challenging question remains of what to do with these feelings when they do arise, because for almost all of us, in different situations, they will. How do we find compassion in the middle of storms of anger, hatred, ill will, or fear?

Most important, we need to acknowledge that these feelings are arising. In this regard, it is mindfulness that can bring the gift of compassion, both for ourselves and others. Mindfulness sees the whole parade of feelings, however intense, without getting lost or drowning in them, and without judging ourselves for feeling them.

One of the transforming moments of my meditation practice happened when I was lost for several days in recurring feelings of intense fear. I tried being aware of them as they arose, noting "fear, fear," but I still felt caught in the intensity of the emotion. Then, at a certain point, something shifted in my mind and I said to myself, "If this fear is here for the rest of my life, it's O.K." That was the first moment of genuine acceptance, and it entirely changed my relationship to fear. Although it would still arise, I was no longer locking it in with my resistance. Genuine mindful acceptance allowed the fear to just wash through.

Through mindfulness, our hearts become spacious enough to hold the painful emotions, to feel the suffering of them, and to let them go. But it takes practice—and perhaps several different practices—to open to the difficult emotions that we're aware of and to illuminate those that are hidden.

There are some particular difficulties and challenges in being with difficult emotions. We often live in denial. It's not always easy to open to our shadow side. And even when we are aware, we can get caught in justifying these feelings to ourselves: "I should hate these people—look at what they did." From justifying these feelings of hatred and enmity (which is quite different from being mindful of them), there can come a strong feeling of self-righteousness. We forget that the feelings and emotions we have are all conditioned responses, arising out of the particular conditions of our lives. Other people in the same situation might feel very different things. Although at times it may be hard to believe, our feelings are not necessarily the reflection of some ultimate truth. As Bankei, the great seventeenth-century Zen master, reminded us: "Don't side with yourself."

Self-righteousness about our feelings and view is the shadow side of commitment. We sometimes confuse this self-justification with the feeling of passionate dedication. But great exemplars of compassion and social justice, people like Martin Luther King, Jr., Gandhi, Aung San Suu Kyi, and others, illuminate the difference.

It is not a question of whether unwholesome mind states will arise in us—or in the world around us. Feelings of hatred, enmity, fear, self-righteousness, greed, envy, and jealousy all do arise at different times. Our challenge is to see them all with mindfulness, understanding that these states themselves are the cause of suffering and that no action we take based on them will lead to our desired result—peace in ourselves and peace in the world.

The method is mindfulness, the expression is compassion, and the essence is wisdom. Wisdom sees the impermanent, ephemeral nature of experience and the basic unreliability of these changing phenomena. Wisdom opens our minds to the experience of selflessness, the great liberating jewel of the Buddha's enlightenment. This understanding, in turn, engenders a compassionate engagement with the world. Dilgo Khyentse Rinpoche, a great Tibetan master, taught: "When you recognize the empty nature, the energy to bring about the good of others dawns, uncontrived and effortless." And wisdom reveals that non-clinging is the essential unifying experience of freedom. We see that non-clinging is both a practice to cultivate and the nature of the awakened mind itself.

T. S. Eliot expressed this well in a few lines from "The Four Quartets":

A condition of complete simplicity
(Costing not less than everything)
And all shall be well and
All manner of thing shall be well.*

---

*T. S. Eliot, *Four Quartets,* "Little Gidding V" (New York: Harvest Books, 1968).

Contributors

FAITH ADIELE, the daughter of a Nordic-American single mother and an absent Nigerian father, was raised as the sole black girl in a small farming community in Washington State and attended Harvard on scholarship. *Meeting Faith*, her account of ordaining as the first black Buddhist nun in Thailand, was published in 2004. The same year, PBS aired *My Journey Home*, a documentary based on Adiele's memoir-in-progress about growing up Nigerian-Nordic-American and then traveling to Nigeria to find her father and siblings. A graduate of Harvard College and the Iowa Writers' Workshop, she has worked as a community activist and diversity trainer, and currently is assistant professor of English at the University of Pittsburgh.

GEOFFREY SHUGEN ARNOLD, Sensei is a dharma heir of the outstanding American Zen teacher, John Daido Loori, Roshi. He received his M.A. in music from the State University of New York and did graduate work in mathematics. He completed his formal training in the Mountains and Rivers Order and received dharma transmission from Loori Roshi in 1997. He is currently the director of training and operations at Zen Mountain Monastery and manages the National Buddhist Prison Sangha.

RICK BASS is the author of twenty-one books, including nonfiction, a collection of short stories, and a novel, *Where the Sea Used to Be*. His newest book is *The Diezmo: A Novel*. He lives with his family in northwest Montana's Yaak Valley, one of the wildest and most biologically diverse areas of the northern Rockies. For the last eighteen years, he has been working to get the last roadless areas in the valley's national forest designated as wilderness, and he is a board member of the Yaak Valley Forest Council. He writes frequently on nature and the environment and has won the Pushcart Prize and the O. Henry Award.

EDWARD ESPE BROWN is a Zen teacher, the editor of a book of lectures by Shunryu Suzuki entitled *Not Always So*, and the author of a series of celebrated cookbooks, including the classic *The Tassajara Bread Book*. Brown was the first head cook at the famed Tassajara Zen Mountain Center and was ordained as a Zen priest by Suzuki Roshi in 1971. Since 1985 he has been teaching vegetarian cooking classes throughout the United States and in recent years he has been leading workshops on Liberation through Handwriting and Mindfulness Touch.

MICHAEL CARROLL is the founding director of Awake at Work Associates, a consulting group that works with individuals and organizations to rediscover balance and well-being in the workplace. He worked for more than twenty years as a human resources professional and is an authorized teacher in the Shambhala Buddhist lineage of Chögyam Trungpa Rinpoche. He has taught mindfulness meditation at the New York Open Center, the Omega Institute, OM Yoga, and the Wharton School of Business.

PETER COYOTE is an actor, writer, and Zen practitioner. He became a professional actor during his early twenties at San Francisco's renowned Actor's Workshop, and then an actor, writer, and director at the San Francisco Mime Troupe. His fascinating memoir of life in the late 1960s, *Sleeping Where I Fall*, won a Pushcart Prize for excellence in nonfiction. As an actor, Coyote has been sought out for his strong characterizations by some of the world's most famous directors, including Steven Spielberg, Pedro Almodóvar, and Roman Polanski. He does stage, television, and voice-over work, and recently created a television show called *The Active Opposition*, an in-depth look at political topics.

The fourteenth DALAI LAMA, Tenzin Gyatso, is the spiritual and temporal leader of the Tibetan people and a winner of the Nobel Peace Prize. Unique in the world today, he is a statesman, national leader, spiritual teacher, and deeply learned theologian. He advocates a universal "religion of human kindness" that transcends sectarian differences.

SCOTT DARNELL is serving a natural life sentence at the Menard Correctional Center in Menard, Illinois. He has written a number of articles on prison life and Buddhist practice.

GRETEL EHRLICH is a poet, novelist, essayist, outdoorswoman, and adventure traveler. She began reading the Zen writer D. T. Suzuki at age fourteen and eventually became a student of the Tibetan teacher Chögyam Trungpa Rinpoche. An accomplished rider and dog-sledder, she divides her time between California and Wyoming, and travels frequently in Greenland and the Canadian Arctic. Her writing has won many awards; its combination of elegant thought, poetic sensibility, and courage in the face of hardship places it in the great tradition of travel and exploration writing.

GAYLON FERGUSON grew up on a farm in segregated East Texas. After graduating from Phillips Exeter Academy, he studied philosophy and psychology at Yale University. After hearing D. T. Suzuki say that "it's not possible to learn Buddhist meditation entirely from a book," he dropped his studies and worked on a fruit farm in Michigan with a group of radical Catholics. After meeting Chögyam Trungpa Rinpoche, he moved in 1973 to Tail of the Tiger (now Karmê-Chöling) in Barnet, Vermont. Ferguson returned to Yale in 1987 to get his degree in African Studies and in 1994 completed his doctorate in cultural anthropology at Stanford. Ferguson is an Acharya (senior teacher) in the Shambhala Buddhist tradition.

NORMAN FISCHER is a father, a poet, a Zen priest, and one of Western Buddhism's most inquiring thinkers. For many years he has taught at the San Francisco Zen Center, where he served as co-abbot from 1995 to 2000. He is currently a senior teacher there, as well as the founder and spiritual director of the Everyday Zen Foundation, an organization dedicated to adapting Zen Buddhist teachings to Western culture. His interests include the adaptation of Zen meditation and understanding to the worlds of business, interreligious dialogue and practice, care of the dying, and mentoring youth. His written works reflect his great range as a thinker and writer, including collections of poetry, frequent essays in Buddhist publications, a Zen-inspired translation of the Psalms, a memoir about Buddhism and Judaism, and a book on the nature of maturity.

GEHLEK RIMPOCHE is a traditional Tibetan teacher who has immersed himself in modern society, which is one of the great strengths of his teaching. A high incarnate lama of Tibet's most conservative school of Buddhism, he gave up the monastic life at the age of twenty-five and worked for All India Radio as the head of its Tibetan Service department and as an editor for the Library of Tibetan Works and Archives in Delhi. In the late 1970s, he was directed by his own teachers, Ling Rinpoche and Trijang Rinpoche, to begin teaching Western students. In 1985 he founded Jewel Heart, which now has chapters throughout the United States as well as in Singapore, Malaysia, and the Netherlands. Gehlek Rimpoche's contemporary style and passionate presentation of the dharma has attracted an eclectic and talented group of students, including such artist-practitioners as Philip Glass and the late Allen Ginsberg. He is the author of *Good Life, Good Death: Tibetan Wisdom on Reincarnation.*

NATALIE GOLDBERG is the author of many books, including *Long Quiet Highway, Thunder and Lightning,* and *Top of My Lungs.* Her classic book, *Writing Down the Bones,* introduced thousands of people to writing as a spiritual practice. Her most recent book is *The*

Great Failure: My Unexpected Path to the Truth, excerpted here. Goldberg has practiced Zen for more than thirty years and is ordained in Dainin Katagiri Roshi's lineage. She lives in New Mexico and teaches workshops and retreats at the Mabel Dodge Luhan House in Taos.

JOSEPH GOLDSTEIN has played a key role in the establishment of the vipassana tradition in North America. He is one of the co-founders of the Insight Meditation Society in Barre, Massachusetts, one of the most important practice centers in American Buddhism, and in 1999 he helped envision and design the Forest Refuge, a new center for long-term meditation practice. After graduating from Columbia, he did a stint teaching English as a Peace Corps volunteer in Thailand, where he first became interested in Buddhist meditation. He spent most of the next seven years in India, studying and practicing with Anagarika Munindra, S. N. Goenka, and Dipa Ma, three renowned teachers of vipassana meditation. Since 1974 he has been teaching and leading meditation retreats around the world, including an annual three-month retreat. Since 1984 he has been a student of Sayadaw U Pandita, and has also meditated under the guidance of Tulku Urgyen Rinpoche and Nyoshul Khen Rinpoche, two eminent Tibetan masters. He is a resident guiding teacher at the Insight Meditation Society and is the author of several books, including the influential *One Dharma: The Emerging Western Buddhism.*

JEFF GREENWALD has traveled extensively through five continents, working as a writer, artist, and photographer. He now divides his time between California and Asia, publishing stories and essays in a variety of publications, including the *New York Times Magazine, National Geographic Adventure,* and *Outside. The Size of the World,* a chronicle of his 29,172-mile overland journey around the world, was a national bestseller and won the 1995 Lowell Thomas Silver Award. He is executive director of Ethical Traveler, a global community dedicated to exploring the ambassadorial potential of world travel.

THICH NHAT HANH is, along with His Holiness the Dalai Lama, the leading proponent of a Buddhist approach to politics and social action. He is a Zen teacher, poet, and founder of the Engaged Buddhist movement. A well-known antiwar activist in his native Vietnam, he was nominated for the Nobel Peace Prize by Martin Luther King, Jr. The author of more than forty books, he resides at Buddhist practice centers in France and Vermont. In 2005 he returned to Vietnam for the first time since his exile in 1966.

ERIK HANSEN is a writer who studied Zen meditation with the late Dr. Edward Wortz, who integrated a distinguished scientific background with a deep study of Buddhism. Through Dr. Wortz's group, Hansen met his wife, the artist Shannon Landis Hansen, and says he gives thanks every day for a life touched by two such remarkable people.

SAM HARRIS is the author of the controversial bestseller *The End of Faith: Religion, Terror, and the Future of Reason*. While Harris's principal interests are meditation and understanding how the brain creates the sense of self, the events of September 11 persuaded him that the most important challenge facing the world is finding a rational alternative to literalist religious belief. Now completing his doctorate in neuroscience, he is a graduate in philosophy from Stanford University. He spent many years practicing vipassana meditation and later studied Dzogchen under Tulku Urgyen Rinpoche and Nyoshul Khen Rinpoche.

TRALEG KYABGON RINPOCHE was enthroned at the age of two as the supreme head of Tra'gu monastery in Eastern Tibet. Two years later, following the Chinese invasion of Tibet, he was taken to safety in India, where he continued the rigorous training of a tülku, or incarnate teacher, under the direction of His Holiness the sixteenth Karmapa, the head of the Kagyü lineage. Moving to Australia in 1980, he established the Kagyü E-Vam Buddhist Institute in Melbourne, and has recently founded the Evam Buddhist Institute, a retreat and conference facility in New York's Hudson Valley.

Another of the outstanding young Tibetan teachers who combine traditional training and modern sensibility, he is the author of *The Essence of Buddhism: An Introduction to Its Philosophy and Practice* and *Mind at Ease: Self-Liberation through Mahamudra Meditation*, excerpted here.

JOHN DAIDO LOORI, Roshi is one of America's leading Zen teachers, a builder of institutions and a protector of tradition, yet also a creator of modern forms. He is abbot of Zen Mountain Monastery in Mount Tremper, New York. He received transmission in both the Rinzai and Soto lines of Zen and is a dharma heir of the late Taizan Maezumi Roshi. Loori Roshi lives at the monastery year round and is very active in its day-to-day activities. Devoted to maintaining authentic Zen training, he has developed a distinctive approach called the Eight Gates of Zen, a program of study for both monastic and lay practitioners that embraces every aspect of daily life. He is a prolific author as well as an accomplished photographer.

CHOKYI NYIMA RINPOCHE is the eldest son of the late Tulku Urgyen Rinpoche, who was considered one of the greatest Dzogchen teachers of the twentieth century. Fluent in English, with a style that is both clear and profound, he has been instructing Western students since 1977. In 1976, at the age of twenty-five, he was named abbot of Ka-Nying Shedrub Ling monastery in Kathmandu, and in 1981 he founded the Rangyung Yeshe Institute, where international students could study Buddhism in Nepal. He later established Rangjung Yeshe Publications, an outstanding small publisher that makes profound Dzogchen teachings and translations available in English.

JOAN DUNCAN OLIVER drew on twenty-five years of Buddhist practice and thirty years' experience with the Twelve Steps for her short memoir, "Drink and a Man." A contributing editor at *Tricycle: The Buddhist Review* and a regular contributor to *O, the Oprah Magazine*, she is the author of *Contemplative Living* (Dell, 2000) and *Happiness: How to Find It and Keep It*. Formerly an editor at the *New*

York Times Magazine and editor-in-chief of *New Age Journal*, she has written on international affairs, women's issues, spirituality, psychology, and self-help for numerous publications.

THE DZOGCHEN PONLOP RINPOCHE is one of a group of impressive young Tibetan teachers born and trained in the Tibetan diaspora. Highly learned, fluent in English, and familiar with the ways of the modern world, these teachers are a bridge between the ancient traditions of Tibet and the needs of contemporary students. An accomplished meditation master, scholar, and artist, Ponlop Rinpoche has founded several institutions that are already proving important in the development of the Tibetan tradition in the West. He is founder and president of Nalandabodhi and Nitartha International, head teacher of the Nitartha Institute, and publisher of *Bodhi* magazine. Nalanda West, recently established in Seattle, is the primary seat of his educational and spiritual activities in North America. The Dzogchen Ponlop Rinpoche's most recent book is *Wild Awakening: The Heart of Mahamudra and Dzogchen*.

BARBARA RHODES (Zen Master Soeng Hyang) is the School Zen Master of the international Kwan Um School of Zen. She is a leading figure in one of the largest communities of Western Buddhists, and at the same time a woman of warmth and heart. She was one of the first students of the Korean Zen master Seung Sahn when he came to the West in 1972, and received dharma transmission from him in 1992. She helped found the Providence Zen Center, headquarters of the Kwan Um School of Zen, and lived there for seventeen years. A registered nurse since 1969, she works for Hospice Care of Rhode Island. She has a daughter and lives in Providence.

LEWIS RICHMOND is an ordained disciple of Zen teacher Shunryu Suzuki Roshi and a lineage holder in his tradition. He is the author of three books: the national bestseller *Work as a Spiritual Practice*, *Healing Lazarus: A Buddhist's Journey from Near Death to New Life*, and, most recently, *A Whole Life's Work: Living Passionately, Growing Spiritually*. He leads the Vimala Sangha, a Zen meditation group in Mill Valley, California. An accomplished musician as well as the founder of his own software company, Richmond has released a number of piano solo albums featuring his own compositions. In keeping with his background as businessperson and musician, the emphasis in his community is on the path of householder Zen.

ELEANOR ROSCH is a leading figure in the field of cognitive science. She was a young psychology student doing research on the color and form categories of a Stone Age people in Indonesian New Guinea when she realized that psychological concepts and categories didn't have the arbitrary logics, defining features, and clearcut boundaries assumed by classical philosophy. She went on to pioneer the field of concepts and categories, and has also been a leader in the dialogue between Buddhism and Western mind science. A student of the late Chögyam Trungpa Rinpoche, she participated in the first Mind and Life Conference with the Dalai Lama, and collaborated with Francisco Varela and Evan Thompson on the seminal book *The Embodied Mind: Cognitive Science and Human Experience*. She is Professor of Psychology at the University of California, where in addition to her other teaching she has developed courses in Eastern psychologies and their clinical usefulness. For two years, she has also participated in the colloquia of the "Awake: Art, Buddhism, and Dimensions of Consciousness" project.

ANDREW SCHELLING first practiced zazen with Kobun Chino Roshi in Santa Cruz, then studied at the Berkeley Zen Center. In 1990 Schelling joined the faculty of Naropa University. He has published several collections of poetry and essays, and five books of translations of ancient Indian poetry, including songs of Mirabai, poems of the early Buddhist orders, and secular poems of the classical Sanskrit poets. He is the editor of *The Wisdom Anthology of North American Buddhist Poetry* and teaches poetry and Sanskrit at Naropa University.

DAVID R. SHLIM, M.D., was the medical director of the CIWEC Clinic Travel Medicine Center in Kathmandu, Nepal, from 1983 to 1998. In addition to providing health care for travelers and expatriates, he offered free medical care to Tibetan refugees and the Tibetan monastic community in Kathmandu. He was also the lead singer and rhythm guitarist for Fear of Heights, the most popular rock and roll band in Nepal at that time. He helped create two courses on medicine and compassion taught to Western doctors and nurses by Chokyi Nyima Rinpoche, which led to the book *Medicine and Compassion: A Tibetan Lama's Guidance for Caregivers*, excerpted here. Shlim now lives Jackson Hole, Wyoming, with his wife and two children. He practices travel medicine and works to promote compassion in medicine.

GARY SNYDER is a longtime practitioner of Zen Buddhism, a key member of the Beat generation, a powerful voice in defense of the environment, and one of America's greatest living poets. He was born in San Francisco and raised in the Pacific Northwest, and his earliest experiences there in the natural and wild worlds imprint his work and thought to this day. He graduated from Reed College with a degree in literature and anthropology, and he was instrumental, with Allen Ginsberg and Jack Kerouac, in the Beat Generation/San Francisco movements of the late 1950s. For most of the 1960s he lived in Japan and studied formally in a Zen monastery. In 1970 he returned to the United States to live with his wife and two young sons in the Sierra Nevada foothills of northern California. Reflecting his literary, ecological, and public policy interests, in 1997 he was awarded both the Bollingen Prize for Poetry and the John Hay Award for Nature Writing. He is a member of the Ring of Bone Zendo, and in 1998 he was the first American literary figure to receive the prestigious Buddhism Transmission Award from the Buddhist Awareness Foundation of Japan. It honored his contributions in linking Zen thought and respect for the natural world in a lifelong body of poetry and prose. Since 1985 he has taught at the University of California, Davis.

JOHN TARRANT was born in Australia and worked in copper mines while writing poetry in his spare time. Later he was a fisherman on the Great Barrier Reef and a lobbyist for Aboriginal land rights before graduating from the Australian National University. An original thinker who draws on insights from Buddhism, the arts, and psychology, he has a Ph.D. in koan Zen and practiced Jungian psychotherapy for twenty years. He now directs the Pacific Zen Institute, a venture in transforming consciousness through meditation, inquiry, and the arts. He also teaches culture change in organizations. He is author of *The Light inside the Dark* and *Bring Me the Rhinoceros*, excerpted here.

THANISSARO BHIKKHU (Geoffrey DeGraff) graduated from Oberlin College in 1971 and received a fellowship to teach at Chieng Mai University in northern Thailand. In 1974 he began practicing meditation with his teacher, Ajaan Fuang Jotiko, a member of the Thai forest tradition. In 1976 he was ordained as a Buddhist monk (*bhikkhu*). In 1991 Ajaan Suwat Suvaco, another teacher of the Forest tradition, invited him to southern California to help set up Metta Forest Monastery. He was made abbot of the monastery in 1993 and was appointed as a preceptor by the Dhammayut Order in Thailand in 1995. He also teaches regularly at the Barre Center for Buddhist Studies in Barre, Massachusetts, and at the Sati Center for Buddhist Studies in Palo Alto. Ajaan Geoff, as he is known by his students, is a prolific and provocative writer, commenting on both traditional and contemporary themes, and he has translated a four-volume anthology of Pali suttas, *Handful of Leaves*. Many of his writings and teachings are available at www.accesstoinsight.org.

CLAUDE ANSHIN THOMAS began his Zen practice in 1961 through his study of martial arts. He joined the U.S. Army after high school and served as a helicopter crew chief in Vietnam, where he was wounded, was shot down five times, and received numerous decorations. After his discharge, he completed his education, pursued a musical career, and worked to address the social and psychological problems suffered by many Vietnam veterans, including himself. As told in the excerpt here from his book, *At Hell's Gate*, his life turned around when he met the Vietnamese Zen teacher Thich Nhat Hanh. In 1995 he was ordained as a Zen priest by Roshi Bernie Glassman. He has undertaken long pilgrimages for peace and is founder of the Zaltho Foundation, a nonprofit organization promoting peace and nonviolence.

FRANCISCO J. VARELA (1946–2001) was an innovative thinker and researcher in the field of cognitive science and a pioneer in the dialogue between science and Buddhism. He studied biology at the University of Santiago de Chile and at Harvard, and held a series of important academic positions in the United States, Chile, and Europe. At the time of his death he was the director of research at the Centre Nationale de Recherche Scientifique in Paris. Varela's work has had a profound impact on philosophy, cognitive science, and organizational theory. With his mentor, Humberto Maturana, he sought to develop a characterization of living beings that did not separate them from their environment. They created a structure called autopoiesis (self-organizing systems), in which the environment, the organism, and even the mind of the scientist are seen as interdependent systems. Varela also argued that first-person experience, including the experience of Buddhist meditation, can be a legitimate contributor to science. He was a founder of the ongoing dialogue between Buddhism and the mind sciences. and an outcome of his conversations with the Dalai Lama was the establishment of the Mind and Life Institute, which today is the leading catalyst of East-West dialogue on the nature of mind. Among his many publications were the influential books, *Autopoiesis and Cognition: The Realization of the Living*, with Humberto Maturana, and *The Embodied Mind: Cognitive Science and Human Experience*, with Eleanor Rosch and Evan Thompson.

Credits

Thich Nhat Hanh, "Touching the Earth": From *Touching the Earth: Intimate Conversations with the Buddha* by Thich Nhat Hanh. Copyright © 2004 by Unified Buddhist Church. With permission from Parallax Press. www.parallax.org.

Erik Hansen, "Sunset Boulevard": From the Spring 2004 issue of *Tricycle: The Buddhist Review*. Copyright © 2004 by Erik Hansen.

Sam Harris, "Experiments in Consciousness": From *The End of Faith* by Sam Harris, edited by AVL. Copyright © 2004 by Sam Harris. Used by permission of W. W. Norton & Company, Inc.

Traleg Kyabgon Rinpoche, "The Path of Mahamudra": From *Mind at Ease* by Traleg Kyabgon. Copyright © 2004 by Traleg Kyabgon. Reprinted by arrangement with Shambhala Publications, Inc., Boston. www.shambhala.com.

John Daido Loori, "Have a Cup of Tea": From *The Zen of Creativity: Cultivating Your Artistic Life* by John Daido Loori. Copyright © 2004 by Dharma Communications. Used by permission of Ballantine Books, a division of Random House, Inc.

Chökyi Nyima Rinpoche with David R. Shlim, M.D., "Recognizing Our Natural State": From *Medicine and Compassion: A Tibetan Lama's Guidance for Caregivers* by Chökyi Nyima Rinpoche with David R. Shlim, M.D. Copyright © 2004 by Chökyi Nyima Rinpoche and David R. Shlim, M.D. Reprinted with permission of Wisdom Publications.

Joan Duncan Oliver, "Drink and a Man": From the Summer 2004 issue of *Tricycle: The Buddhist Review*. Copyright © 2004 by Joan Duncan Oliver.

The Dzogchen Ponlop Rinpoche, "The Infinite Dot Called Mind": From the Nalanda West Inauguration special issue of *Bodhi: The*

About the Editor

MELVIN MCLEOD is editor-in-chief of the award-winning *Shambhala Sun*, North America's oldest and most widely read Buddhist magazine. The *Shambhala Sun* offers accessible, authentic Buddhist teachings and examines all aspects of modern life from a contemplative perspective. He is also editor-in-chief of *Buddhadharma: The Practitioner's Quarterly*, an in-depth, practice-oriented journal for Buddhists of all traditions. A former correspondent for the Canadian Broadcasting Corporation, he is a student of the late Chögyam Trungpa Rinpoche and Khenpo Tsultrim Gyamtso Rinpoche.